Y0-BRH-118

WITHDRAWN

THE THIRD KING

Books by FLETCHER PRATT

THE HEROIC YEARS

ORDEAL BY FIRE

HAIL, CAESAR!

NIGHT WORK

THE NAVY: A HISTORY

SECRET AND URGENT

THE NAVY'S WAR

SHORT HISTORY OF THE ARMY AND NAVY

THE MARINES' WAR

ELEVEN GENERALS

ROAD TO EMPIRE

EMPIRE AND THE SEA

THE EMPIRE AND THE GLORY

FLETCHER PRATT

The Third King

Maps by Rafael Palacios

WILLIAM SLOANE ASSOCIATES, INC.
Publishers   *New York*

Carl A. Rudisill Library
LENOIR RHYNE COLLEGE

948.9
P88t

Copyright, 1950, *by*
FLETCHER PRATT

First Printing

Typography and format designed by
LEONARD W. BLIZARD

Manufactured in the United States of America
by H. Wolff Book Manufacturing Co.

Published simultaneously in Canada
by George J. McLeod, Ltd., Toronto

27402
Sept'51

To my favorite Scandinavian
—the one in the front room behind the drawing board

CONTENTS

Note on Orthography and Money   9

Note on History   11

Cast of Principal Characters in the order of their appearance   15

Stage Set (1340)   19

1. Midsummer Night's Dream (1340)   35

2. Dolorosia Dania (1157; 1219; 1340)   39

3. The Sense of Form (1157; 1319-1332)   50

4. Interlude—The Laws of King Valdemar   65

5. Cambell and Triamond (1340; 1157-1159)   74

6. Failure (1341)   89

7. Hermitage in Jutland (1341; 1170; 1342)   99

8. First Revolution (1342-1344)   114

9. Ruffle of Drums; Enter the Villain (1180-1181; 1344-1345)   126

10. Brief History of Esthonia (1346-1347; 1204-1218)   140

11. The Saint and the Sodomist (1347-1349; 1181-1204)   152

Contents

12. The End of the World (1332-1350) 167

13. International (1349-1350; 1197-1215) 176

14. Interlude—Carking Castle (1351) 189

15. Second Revolution (1351-1356) 192

16. Trumpet Blown, Distantly (1354-1356; 1214) 201

17. Jutland; the Old Ways (1356-1358) 214

18. Signature of a Contract (1214-1218; 1358-1360) 226

19. The Fisheries of Skaane (1360-1361) 238

20. Come to Judgment (1361-1363) 250

21. "And Those Who Fall Will Die for Naught" (1231-1252; 1364-1368) 260

22. Revenge (1368-1370) 270

23. Home from the Hill (1371-1375; 1223-1227) 284

24. Postlude—Seven Securities 295

The Inscription on Valdemar's Tomb 303

Index 305

Maps

The Provinces of Fourteenth Century Denmark 34

The Partition of Denmark as it was in 1340 49

The Castles of Denmark as they were toward the end of Valdemar IV's reign, 1340-1375 178

The Fisheries of Skaane 239

Note on Orthography and Money

The Danes have the engaging characteristic of not knowing how to spell their own language and not caring very much. Until quite recently there were two different ways of spelling the Danish name of Copenhagen, both official. The one you used depended upon what political party you belonged to. Sometimes one will find a word beginning with "dje-" in text; the dictionary is quite as likely to have it as "djæ-" or even "de-," which must make things complicated for Danish librarians. I have even seen an old book in which King Valdemar's name appears as "Vollmer." Moreover there is no consistency in the methods by which the (for Danes) almost identically pronounced words are rendered into letters. The spellings used in this book all came from some authority, and it is at least as good as any authority that can be quoted for another version. The rule has been followed of spelling German names in the German fashion, Danish names in Danish, except for one or two, like *Copenhagen,* where it would be pedantic.

The reason for Danish spelling confusion lies in the pronunciation of the language. For an English-speaking person, it is one of the easiest of all languages to learn, almost identical in grammatical structure with our own. But it is full of slurred and swallowed letters, and the "rules" of how a given printed word shall be rendered into sound are so complex that in my Danish grammar they occupy seventy pages. I shall not attempt to cover all that ground here, but some few indications are necessary, if only for the reader's inner ear, which often plays so important a part in comprehending the spirit of what is being said.

To begin with, Danish has two letters we lack—æ and ø, which as initial letters appear after z in the dictionaries. Ø is simply the German ö; we do not have the sound in English. Æ is not far from the "ai" in "fairy," but all one sound, not a diphthong. Y has the sound of German ü, which we do not have; if a Dane wants the sound we indicate by y, he uses i or j. Aa is rather like "aw."

To continue, v and g are almost always swallowed, shading down to a mere catch in the voice, a modification of the preceding vowel, except at the beginning of words. D is seldom pronounced after a consonant, with an exception in favor of proper names. The spelling of Valdemar as "Vollmer" shows there was probably a time when the exception did not exist. After a vowel, d tends to take the sound of "th"; the name of the Danish (and English) king which appears in our histories as Canute is spelled Knud and pronounced something like "K'nuth." Sj is "sh."

. . . Now about money. The standard coin, in the period covered here, was the silver mark. There was naturally some fluctuation in value, but if you want to get a fair idea of the purchasing power of any sum named here in 1949 dollars, multiply the number of marks by 120 and stick a dollar sign in front of the result.

Note on History

Why should anyone bother with Danish pronunciations, or with the story of three kings who, among them, occupy hardly seven pages in the seven fat volumes of the *Cambridge Medieval History?*

One reason is that if we are to know our destiny, or even fully to understand the life about us, it is fairly important to have some acquaintance with our origins. This is, of course, the reason for concerning ourselves with history of any kind— aside from the pretty pictures. The story of the three kings Valdemar is a somewhat special case within this domain. There are very few passages in the story of the relations of men which so convincingly make the point that the game is worth the candle; that by patience and dedication and firmness, even mountains may be moved. I think this is something of which we need to be reminded many times, especially today. It is conceded that there are some sequences of events which appear to demonstrate the opposite point, but they do not really demonstrate anything, except that people are far too ready to announce that there is no solution, or none but fortitude and/or selfishness—the Existentialists, for example.

The tale of the Valdemars is also worth hearing for another reason. The tendency of modern historical thought is to speak as though the western world began with Francis Bacon, perhaps tossing a backward glance in the direction of Magna Charta; to look at *Dark Ages* and *Middle Ages* as though they were synonymous terms; to regard nothing that happened in either Dark Ages or Middle Ages as very important; and to regard everything that has happened since 1453 as the result of the enlightenment that spread from Italy. This is a very convenient view, since it spares people the trouble of finding out what the Italian Renaissance really was and enables them to discover that democracy in the form we have it is the only possible solution to the problem of obtaining both a square deal for the individual and strength for the state.

I think it can be demonstrated that other methods have been used to solve this problem, and still others will be. But the important point is the ideal that sees it as a problem, the demand that the problem shall be solved. The common view, referred to above, is that this ideal was forward-passed up to us from ancient Greece by the Renaissance Italians.

As a general truth, this is at least debatable. The Italian Renaissance furnished some valuable instruments for thinking, devices that can be applied to any type of intellectual task. But it had almost nothing to do with politics and nothing whatever to do with religion. Machiavelli, yes; but his politic represented no new ideals—and the Catholic Revival, yes; but when it came around the Renaissance was over.

The idea that politics and religion were as important as the turn of a sonnet or the structure of a syllogism had another origin, at least as that idea exists in our world. In fact, the idea of the importance of human relations has probably affected our daily lives more than anything we got through Italy. Certainly, it produced an atmosphere in which the Italian kind of renaissance could be more fruitful than that of Hellenistic Alexandria or that of the Ming dynasty. It can be maintained that these movements were at least as important as the Italian one, but that they came to a bad end because their seed fell on stony soil.

It is not claimed here that the origins, the sequences are fully set forth in this book. But it is claimed that there are lines along which not much thinking has been done. It is, I believe, the business of history to investigate new areas and to pronounce judgments on the basis of its findings, but not lump-sum judgments. Otherwise we get into Toynbee, the circular argument, and the parts distorted to fit a structural whole that never really existed.

History itself is essentially disorderly, composed of the interplay of human elements which decline to adapt themselves to pattern, however the humans themselves seek pattern in everything around them. It is precisely because the Marxists deny the individual element, because they reduce human beings to typed groups of reacting mechanisms, that they write history so badly and come out of it with such absurd conclusions. The attempt at pattern in history always fails as it does when historical people attempt to repeat a pattern, because the man who tries is not the same as the one who drew the original design, nor is he drawing it on the same canvas. In making the attempt, one succeeds only in producing the infinite variety which is the fascination of history.

That fascination, the views along that stream, are the concern of the reader of history. The writer can only be a barker in the bow of the barge, indicating that here the batteries stood on the day of test and there the hero fell. The integration, the completion of the picture by reference to other things seen or apprehended, will necessarily belong to the reader, who will remember heroes before Achilles and the sites of other great guns. Out of these he will form a new relation with what the barker has given him. No writer of history can hope to comprehend more than a small part of the view in what he says, he must suggest the rest. But he will fail in his task if he does not make the suggestions, point out the resemblances. For then he will be narrowing history down to chronicle. The fact that the sources are mainly chronicles is one of the specific difficulties in dealing with the history of the Middle Ages.

Judged by the standards of the school of history that came in with Mommsen, these chronicles are pretty hot stuff. They are calm, normally pretty objective, and they state physical facts that can usually be checked—"King Erik died on the third Tuesday in Lent of a bloody flux." But if you ask what day the third Tuesday in Lent fell on that year, or what a bloody flux is, or what brought it on in King Erik's case, or (most important) what kind of man King Erik was, you will have to ask somebody beside the chronicler. The questions are of no interest to him; or rather, if they did interest him, he felt he would be unworthy of his high duty as a historian to be concerned with something that belonged in Walter Winchell's column.

Apology is therefore made for the inadequate human portraiture in this book, the lack of Winchell. The source material was produced by the academic historians of their own day, or let us say, the professors of history. It is not their fault that they got that way, any more than it is the fault of their modern representatives that they get into the same frame of mind. They hold office by reason of virtues other than literary. It is merely unfortunate that writing has come to be regarded as a necessary subsidiary activity of professors of history, one that will frequently earn them a certain amount of promotion in the profession. The Middle Ages understood a few things better than we do today, and one of them was that chroniclers teach and write works of reference, but if you want history, you had better go to a saga-teller.

This does not contain an implication that the dividing line is fact. Indeed there is record (in *Burnt Njals Saga*) of a man who got his head cut off for dealing loosely with narrated fact, which is more than anyone would do today. It did mean that the collection of records and the writing of history were recognized as different things. The danger lies in mixing up the two, and saying that it is history when a painstaking monograph is produced on the secret societies of the Civil War, with four footnotes per page, and that it is not history when Catherine Drinker Bowen (on extremely good evidence) tells what was in the mind of Mr. Justice Holmes.

Cast of Principal Characters in the order of their appearance

---

VALDEMAR DOSMER, Duke of Slesvig, who owes homage for his duchy to the King of Denmark, and who was himself once King, but not man enough to keep the crown.

NIELS EBBESSEN, a man of family, dispossessed of his lands in the troubles that came on Denmark.

FRIEDRICH VON LOCHEN, a wise German professional soldier, who took service with a landless prince because he could find no higher master.

VALDEMAR IV ATTERDAG, last of the three kings Valdemar.

VALDEMAR I THE GREAT, first of the three kings Valdemar.

LUDWIG, Markgraf of Brandenburg, as stupid a man as there is in the world, who will cause trouble if it is not remembered that he has a father named Ludwig, Kaiser of Germany, and a brother also named Ludwig.

VALDEMAR II THE VICTORIOUS, second of the three kings Valdemar.

JOHANN THE MILD, Graf of Holstein-Stormarn, who believes less in battle than in intrigue; by which means he has acquired nearly a third of Denmark as the story opens.

GERHARD THE GREAT, Graf of Holstein-Rendsborg, a kinsman of the foregoing; a clever man with some claim to the crown of Denmark through his wife; as the story begins over a third of the country is in his personal power.

KRISTOFFER II, King of Denmark, father to Valdemar IV Atterdag, who is adequately described later.

Cast of Principal Characters

ABSALON, Bishop of Roskilde and eventually Archbishop of Denmark, friend and close counsellor of Valdemar I.

KNUD V LAVARD, co-king of Denmark, and father to Valdemar I.

SVEYN IV PEDER, sometimes called Sveyn Grade, from the place where they cut off his head; King of Denmark and rival to Valdemar I.

HEINRICH, Graf of Holstein-Rendsborg, son to Gerhard the Great above, who calls himself "Heinrich the Iron-hard" without realizing that the title applies more closely to his head than to his body.

NICHOLAS, younger brother to the foregoing, also a Graf in Holstein-Rendsborg, made out of the same material as his brother, only not quite so much of it.

HELVIG, sister to Valdemar Dosmer, Duke of Slesvig.

ERICH, Duke of Saxe-Lauenburg, about whom we know only his capacity for friendship, but about whom we would willingly know more.

MAGNUS SMEK, King of Sweden, Norway and Skaane; as the story begins nearly a third of Denmark has been made over to him in perpetuity.

STIG ANDERSSEN, a soldier who came from the island of Bornholm, but who has married into Jutland and become a great man there.

BO FALK, a knight who behaves as though he really believes in the laws of chivalry.

KLAUS LIMBEK, a soldier who came from Holstein, but who married into Jutland and became a great man there.

TOVE, a little girl.

HENNING PODBUSK, brother to the foregoing.

JUNKER KRISTOFFER, son to King Valdemar Atterdag.

BLANCHE OF NAMUR, Queen of Sweden, whose ambition is to relieve her husband of every care.

ST. BIRGITTE of Sweden, a bluestocking, whose ambition is to relieve everyone of every responsibility.

Cast of Principal Characters

ARCHBISHOP VALDEMAR, a kinsman of Valdemar II; the man who would be king.

NIELS BUGGE, lord of Hald in Jutland, called "King Bugge" for his magnificence; head of the great families.

ALBRECHT, Lord and later Duke of Mecklenburg, a clever Slavonian.

OTTO THE WELFING, Kaiser of Germany, but one of the less effective sort.

MARGRETE, daughter to Valdemar Atterdag, who is not much in this story, but has left a considerable name outside it.

ERIK VI, King of Denmark, son to Valdemar II, a weak man.

ABEL, King of Denmark, son to Valdemar II, a bad man.

HEINRICH, Graf of Schwerin, who becomes angry and so alters history.

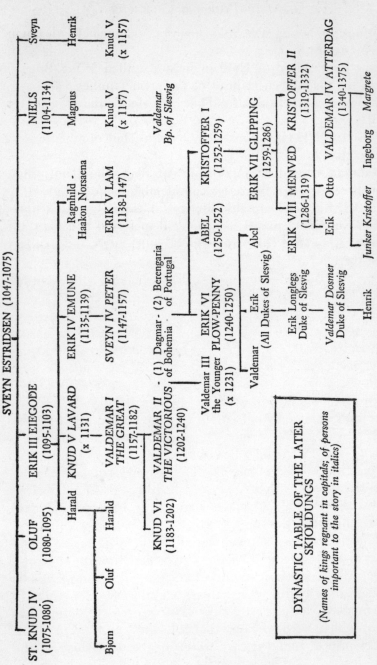

For the sake of clarity this table has been much abbreviated, and marriages are not noted except where they play an important part in events.

DYNASTIC TABLE OF THE LATER
SKJOLDUNGS

(Names of kings regnant in capitals; of persons
important to the story in italics)

SVEYN ESTRIDSEN (1047-1075)

ST. KNUD IV (1075-1080)

OLUF (1080-1095)

ERIK III EIEGODE (1095-1103)

NIELS (1104-1134)

Sveyn

Bjorn

Oluf

Harald

Harald

KNUD V LAVARD (x 1131)

VALDEMAR I THE GREAT (1157-1182)

KNUD VI (1183-1202)

VALDEMAR II THE VICTORIOUS (1202-1240)

ERIK IV EMUNE (1135-1139)

SVEYN IV PETER (1147-1157)

Ragnhild - Haakon Norsaena

ERIK V LAM (1138-1147)

Magnus

Knud V (x 1157)

Henrik

Knud V (x 1157)

Valdemar Bp. of Slesvig

VALDEMAR II - (1) Dagmar - (2) Berengaria of Bohemia   of Portugal

Valdemar III the Younger (x 1231)

ERIK VI PLOW-PENNY (1240-1250)

ABEL (1250-1252)

KRISTOFFER I (1252-1259)

Valdemar

Erik

Abel

Erik (All Dukes of Slesvig)

Erik Longlegs Duke of Slesvig

Valdemar Dosmer Duke of Slesvig

ERIK VII GLIPPING (1259-1286)

ERIK VIII MENVED (1286-1319)

KRISTOFFER II (1319-1332)

Erik

Otto

VALDEMAR IV ATTERDAG (1340-1375)

Henrik

Junker Kristoffer   Ingeborg   Margrete

Stage Set (1340)

Most of the key actions of history are the result of efforts to relieve despairs; and these are sometimes so thoroughly resolved that worlds shake into a new pattern.

For example, it is little thought of now, but far away and long ago, in Denmark looking on the Baltic, there were forged tools with which much of the modern world was built and a new age had its beginning because an old one had miserably died. The agony of that death was called the Time of Uproar; in 1340 there had been no king or regent or government in Denmark for eight years on end, and the neighboring chronicler put it that "The crown fell from the head of the Danes and they became the laughing-stock of all nations."

Now a Time of Uproar is not to be thought of as an isolated event in the history of medieval states, most of which were rather generally uproarious throughout the Middle Ages, with special intervals when things seemed to get completely out of hand—as in the times of bad King John in England or during the collapse of the Carolingians in France. Not infrequently the states themselves perished in their tumult before they could crystallize out as nations, as Flanders did, and Leon, and later, Burgundy.

The reason for this readiness of medieval states to disappear without leaving anything but a name and a romantic memory was inherent in their structure, which must not be thought of as bearing the slightest resemblance to anything in the modern world. Partly this was a matter of communications, which were so poor that all kings' arms were short. Lesser princes found it easy to set up statelets which, if the

line that headed them were a strong one, took on the linea-
ments of permanence, like Castile. Partly it was because no
European country, with such isolated exceptions as Iceland
and Navarre, yet possessed a unified economic system or culture, or even a language exclusively its own. All the integration was political, through the head of the state; and the usual
pattern was that this integration had been imposed from
without upon what might have struck the man from Mars as
an exceedingly unstable mixture of races—as in England and
Sicily.

Denmark had a more logical racial and economic background than either of these last two, but by 1340 it was a wonder that she had survived so long, for though the Time of
Uproar had technically lasted for eight years, it had actually
endured almost a century. There were observers, not from
Mars, who thought the disappearance of the kingdom inevitable. The last ruler of Denmark had held nothing but his
title; after he disappeared the whole heritage was split up and
was now held in direct right—was owned by, we should call it
—various princelings. If a new king were chosen he would
have over these actual rulers only a suzerainty as shadowy as
that held by the German Emperor over the Italian cities. The
lords and the land would be under no obligation to use the
royal law-courts, they would not owe him a minute of military
service, or a copper penny in taxes.

The internal political history of feudalisms was concerned
with the struggles of crown and nobles to the exclusion of
practically every other theme, so the only unusual feature here
might be stated as the complete triumph of the latter. But
there were two features that rendered the Danish case peculiar
and of special interest.

One was that the nobles who held most of Denmark were
foreigners, chiefly Germans from Holstein and Mecklenburg,
whose feudal obligations were to the Kaiser of the Holy Roman Empire. Since Denmark was not part of that body, this

made the German grafs independent sovereigns while they were on her soil.

The second unusual, and indeed, unique feature was that there had never been a struggle between crown and lords in Denmark until the appearance of these southern intruders. The country was without feudal holdings. There were great men and great landowners, but not in any chain of allegiance leading up to the crown. Under the king men were theoretically equal unless they belonged to the churchly estate. This is not to say that the relations between the crown and its more exalted subjects were always harmonious—far from it. But when contests developed, they were on a personal basis— not over the question of where the limits lay between kingly and baronial authority, but over which individual should exercise powers quite clearly defined in written law, and limited by it.

The new foreign landholders did not understand this system and, as has been remarked, were responsible to no one for its observance. The idea of a law standing between the executive and his subjects was one which they would have found incredible and intolerable; and during the Time of Uproar they had so consistently violated the laws that the whole structure was breaking down under what was, effectively, conquest. At least that was how it struck the man on the ground.

II

Let us start with that man on the ground, the Danish yeoman or *bonder*. In normal times he occupies a farm which is fairly close to a self-contained living-machine. It is assembled with other steads of the same kind in a ring, facing inward to the village church and market place, running outward like the spokes of a wheel to where the pines and beeches stand close, to covert of wolf and fallow-deer. All the realm of Denmark is so heavily wooded that the farm villages have the character of islands. Across the Sound, and beyond Halland, Blekinge and Skaane, the trees close in darker and darker until they become the true troll-haunted forest of legend, almost impenetrable except for narrow ways, shutting off these three provinces from the rest of the Swedish peninsula and giving them to Denmark, whose they have always been.

Among the islands, in Jutland and in the three provinces themselves, the woods are somewhat friendlier, furnishing the mast on which the famous fat pigs of Denmark feed, as well as one of the main export crops—timber. Bornholm island, which six centuries later was almost naked of trees, now gives 3,000 cartloads of logs every year, and Bornholm is one of the lesser timber centers. Where the trees have been cleared back, the ground is very rich, providing the yeoman bonder with more than he can use of fine Danish corn. This he takes to town on market day and barters it for articles not produced by the living-machine—fish for Lent, manufactures of crockery and metal, luxuries. These market days are very important, not only occasions of commerce, but of great jollification, the spread of news, the production of the period's literature in saga and song, and above all, the meeting of the law-courts.

The diet is barley-bread and pork mainly, dried herring on fast days, with beer to wet the whistle. The meat is occasionally supplemented by game taken with snares or javelin in the dark forest. Honey is the only sweet; it usually appears at table as a sauce for meat. Vegetables the yeoman bonder has none except an occasional turnip, recognized as starvation diet. Fruits are eaten only in play, when one persuades a girl to come among the trees in springtime. There is no light at night; we rise and sleep with the sun. An illness is God's visitation, to be cured by prayers from the village priest, the recitation of Psalm XVI, or by drinking a draft with a church bell for a cup. The old amusements of horse-fighting, the ball game and longbow archery have disappeared from the countryside and mead is no longer made in any quantity, but on feast-days there is arbalest-shooting at a target with the weapons kept in the village church against an emergency, and of a winter men play tric-trac in the chimney corner.

We wear woolen "hose," one-piece tights that come up to the waist, with a tunic or frock outside, the two garments held together by a multitude of laces, which take nearly half an hour to tie. If the bonder is well off, there will be an undershirt beneath the tunic. In any case the lower edge of the tunic flares out around the hips and it is held together down the front by more laces. Its sleeves are as wide as one can afford to have them—the greater the width, the greater the quality of the wearer—and serve the office of pockets. Outside all, the yeoman and his wife both wear cloaks with hoods that can be brought up to cover the face, or will lie back on the neck, garments much alike save for the coquettish touch of embroidery on hers.

Her dress is long and full at the hips, but in accordance with the latest dictates of fashion (which changes more slowly but otherwise operates as fashion in a later age) is cut low in front and has begun to leave the shoulders. Beneath her dress she wears hose, probably cross-gaitered; a snood on her hair. At night nobody wears anything unless they belong to the noble orders, in which case they take the insignia of rank to bed with them, thus making "Uneasy lies the head that wears a crown" not a figure of speech but a statement of fact. There are midwives, but soap has not been invented. The baths are in little houses to which steam is admitted.

It would not be too hard a life if the Holsteiners and Mecklenburgers, come in with the Time of Uproar, had not upset the natural order of things established by God from the beginning of time. These people say now that there is a new law that the land and all that grows on it belongs of right to the lord, and that no man may leave the place where he was born except to carry baggage in one of the lord's innumerable private wars. Out of every twelve measures of corn these Germans demand five, and come to collect it with a parade of sour-faced men-at-arms, riding under a bit of dirty wool that flutters from a lance head.

Of course the effect of this imposition was to eat up the barterable surplus and to drive the bonder into the ground through the destruction of his equipment (which he could not now replace) by the ordinary erosions and accidents of daily life. Nor is this all; the yeoman's sons show a tendency to run away and join the outlaw bands that live in the woods and render travel insecure. The roads are become so dangerous that only strongly-armed bands are safe on them, and it is no longer easy for the bonder to drive his cart of corn to market. Not that commerce has altogether ceased; it has merely been made so difficult that all the men of a village must go together, which risks that some German lord will levy a special imposition on the accumulated goods.

To many bonders the market journey is not worth the trouble and danger entailed. They stay home these days, allowing their cases at law to go by default, or instead of seeking redress from the assembly of the *herred*, district, try to obtain the support of some powerful man who has a train of sour-faced men-at-arms. In many parts the old Thing courts have not been held for years, and where they are held, it is frequently the foreign lord who pronounces judgment—according to his own lights, not Denmark's law.

For articles not produced by the living-machine, the bonder has become largely dependent upon the chapmen's caravans, conducted by merchants from cities of the Hanseatic League. These merchants would much prefer to set up booths at one of the market-fairs, since peddling caravans have a fundamental illegality in this departmented system of life, and those caught in the business are subject to heavy fines. In view of this danger and that from robbers, the prices of the peripatetic merchants are extremely high, operating still further to drain off the resources of the realm. Every man lives notably less well than his fathers and can see no prospect but that his sons will live less well still.

III

It was thus a society going downward, one in which a movement had failed, a civilization was being destroyed. The important point to be recognized is what movement, what society, what civilization.

Not the Teutonic. One of the main reasons for the disintegration was that the life of Denmark differed as widely from the polity which the Teutonic states were building on the fringes of the old Roman Empire as the Germanic civilization itself differed from the old Mediterranean system. That medieval Germanic culture was a very peculiar business, from some of whose effects we are not exempt even today. It is perhaps worth examining it at point of origin and looking into the question of why it had so disruptive an effect beyond its own frontiers.

The matter goes back to the barbarian invasions of the Roman Empire. It is a mistake to regard this movement as a massive surge of armed hordes engaged in conquest and loot. Save for a few cases, usually failures, like the drive that led the Cimbri to extermination in the time of Caius Marius, the inflow was a gradual seepage, a colonization. The root objective was not so much plunder as arable land, as it had been with the Helvetians and Ariovistus when Julius Caesar was in Gaul. Large tracts of land had fallen fallow in the general economic collapse that followed the Antonine emperors; still larger ones were in grazing under absentee landlords and the barbarians thought these plots could be better used. A typical frontier war of the later Empire was a guerilla operation, preceded by a request from some tribe for soil.

The Teutons colonized then, giving themselves superior social status to the native populations, but plowing and seeding like the English settlers in America. Like those settlers also, they brought with them their own form of social organization. It was a system excellently adapted to a semi-patriarchal life of clans, centered in small villages. Part of the basic prejudice generated by this system in the men who lived under it, part of their mental equipment, was a rooted unwillingness to recognize any authority not visibly and physically present. There was nothing in Teutonic experience which allowed them to understand how a magistrate from Africa, with no support but a set of insignia and a piece of parchment, could settle a dispute between two farmers at Lyon. In the world of the invaders such a dispute would be adjudicated by a village chieftain, advised by the elders as to what the clan tradition was in similar cases. The Teutons had no written law and no concept of that Ciceronian universal law on which both the Roman state and the Christian Church were founded.

Not enough attention is paid to such underlying thought-patterns. To be sure, it was possible for the Middle Ages to draw the analogy, "One God in heaven, one king on earth," but they did so on an exalted level of intellectualism which affected no one beyond the cloister and the palace. Even the universal Church came to the Teutonic village as a parish priest. Continuity was the chief means the Church possessed of making a wider impression, and continuity operates very slowly.

Placing the Holy Roman Empire atop the primitive structure of Germanic villages and calling it a universal state was a good deal like clapping a plug hat on a native of the Congo and referring to him as Sir N'goum M'goum, Privy Councillor. To the Teutons, Charlemagne was a grand captain, a successful conqueror; a Holy Roman Emperor was the head of a clan whose units were themselves clans. In the legends of the Paladins, which are accurate enough as a picture of thought-pattern, the great Emperor is forever umpiring the rows of individuals who, as family heads, control whole provinces. The men of that way of thinking were unable to conceive of large loyalties in the political field. The medieval Empire was an alliance under a president, whose most extensive efforts were usually spent in providing for his family. Of course, so much of this was true everywhere under feudalism that, except for the fact that the Kaiser was elective, it amounts to a description of the system. The special characteristic of feudalism in Germany was the intensity with which it was applied, and the absence of any background tradition of a universal and pacifying Empire, with its administrative methods and its law, everywhere the same. The Germans of Central Europe had only the name of empire. They were split from those of the west by lack of contact with an indigenous Romanized population. In Italy, Spain, France and even England considerable elements of the Latin law entered the new structure at once, and in all the Roman method eventually became dominant through consistency and operative efficiency.

The crucial point was that Roman law was invariable over a wide area and flowed from the highest authority in that area. For instance, a French seigneur was limited in his actions by the fact that he was in a Roman law country. When freemen, especially those of noble birth, were involved, the seigneur had to deal with the royal courts, operating under a law that ran for the whole country. Those courts had original jurisdiction in many cases and appellate authority in nearly all. There was a great deal of lawlessness in the Middle Ages, but it was accompanied by an almost passionate legalism, and the very existence of those royal courts was a brake on naked will.

But Roman law had never run east of the Rhine. The liberty of the graf to do as he pleased when not actually engaged in the service of his overlord was theoretical as well as practical. There were no royal courts outside Bohemia; the duke, graf, or even freiherr was himself a sovereign and the highest magistrate in his territory. The imperial courts, such as they were, concerned themselves solely with the question of who held the powers of justice in a given area, never with the nature of those powers or the manner in which they were exercised. The Emperor's court was called upon to decide such questions as whether a murder case should be tried before the Vogt of the Abbot of Prüm or before the Graf Jülich; it was uninterested in whether the accused received justice or what his punishment was if found guilty. That is, all laws were local in Germany, and since there was no appeal, the law and the political administration which was its expression into action, depended very much upon the will of the ruler. That will was tempered by custom and *Gemütlichkeit*, but in the pinch it was supreme.

By degrees, in various localities and through the juridical adoption of Latin legal principles to cover areas where German precedents were lacking, there took place the phenomenon known as "The Reception of the Roman Law," under which the laws of the Roman Empire were recognized as those of the Holy Roman Empire, on the theory that the one was heir to the other. But the process was extremely slow (the *Reichskammergericht*, high imperial court, did not admit a pleading in Roman law until 1495), and it was hampered by the very character of the legal system into which Latin precedents were being received.

There was, in fact, no real system at all in the period we are concerned with. No body of German law held good for more than a small area. The man who had spent his life learning the law of Halberstadt might be unable to plead a case in Anhalt, only a few miles away. The Teutonic law was also mostly unwritten and particularist in a lateral as well as a geographical sense. When in the course of the Reception, it became the practice to adopt Roman or Roman Canon precedent for cases where nothing in local custom-law applied, it was found that the gaps were not the same in all jurisdictions. The Roman law was thus adopted piecemeal and itself became non-consistent, Germanized. Roman administrative methods suffered a similar fate. Yet such as it was, this body of enriched tribal custom offered considerable restrainers to the naked will of the grafs—until they came to Denmark.

Upon that unhappy land the impact of the German system was that of an autocracy which was also anarchic. The grafs and knights who came in from the south were unrestrained by their home customs and, as has been noted, had not even the thin authority of the imperial allegiance to reckon with. In the conquered land they found laws and customs indeed, but of a nature so different from their own that they could not possibly have understood them, even if they had been so disposed. They were not so disposed, and the result was the Time of Uproar.

IV

The racial kinship of Dane and German should not be allowed to conceal the fact that the former was the child of quite a different system of life and course of national development. When the second and greatest wave of Germanic peoples, the wave headed by the big confederacies of Franks and Alemanni, irretrievably shattered the Roman Empire in the latter part of the third century, they broke apart from the branches of the race which became Scandinavians. For 700 years, longer than it took Greece to rise and decay, the two groups remained back to back; even their language separated into two parts, West and East Teutonic, wanderers and stay-at-homes.

While the invaders of the west were taking over what they could understand of Roman civilization and imitating what they could not understand, the Nordics who stayed in the north were developing a culture of their own, free from all but the most incidental influences, not only of the classical peoples, but also of the West Teutons. That culture has been called a barbarism,* which is a distinct understatement for a way of life which produced one of the great world literatures, lifted women to a position they were not to know elsewhere for a thousand years, practised rotation of crops,

* By Toynbee, among others.

invented its own system of writing and the sea-going ship, and discovered America. But the essential point is that it was different, autochthonous.

Even feudalism, on which Latin and Teutonic peoples agreed, reached Denmark late and in a form so aberrant that it was not feudalism at all. In Denmark there was no provision at law for serfdom, no nobility, and lifetime service to a given lord was unknown. The king was the only overlord; military service was owed to him not by the man but by the district, and the unit of service was not the "spear," or knight and his supporting retinue, but the "skipæn," or shipload of armed men. The last, in fact, is the sign-manual of a difference more profound than that which the long dissociation of cultures itself produced, a difference from which all the rest grew.

While they were still barbarians, the West Teutons pioneered into inland forest country, where communications except by the rivers were very poor, and even along the rivers by no means good, since the men who lived there lacked the physical techniques necessary to use the streams. A Frank or Alemann who travelled went in a cart or on horseback, with animals supplying the power. It is easy to exaggerate the isolation of the communities that resulted when the Germans settled down, but the tendency was clearly in favor of localism, and that localism found expression both in German law and in the politics of the medieval Empire.

Not so in Denmark. No Dane could go more than thirty miles in any direction without finding navigable water, its shores lined with forests of ship-timber. That water was beset by islands and fjords which made navigation safe and easy, even for primitive craft. In the very heart of Denmark the sea provided one of the richest and most desirable food sources of Europe—the famous runs of herring. When history first glimpses the Danes they are afloat and in close association with each other, discovering the necessities of common enterprise and of laws that would have more than local application.

The consequence was that while the fainéant Merovingians were still fragmenting the ruins of the Western Roman Empire along evanescent and uncertain lines—while Germany was still a seething mass of half-civilized tribal states—while England was a kaleidoscope of petty monarchies, Denmark was already a united nation, with a body of common tradition and experience. There is no date at which one hears of local rulers or any other ruler than the King of all Denmark till we come to the Time of Uproar and the Holsteiners. Now in the blackest of that night, in the midst of that tumult, the bishops and people of the Danes are seen preparing to resolve their despairs by raising up a new King.

THE THIRD KING

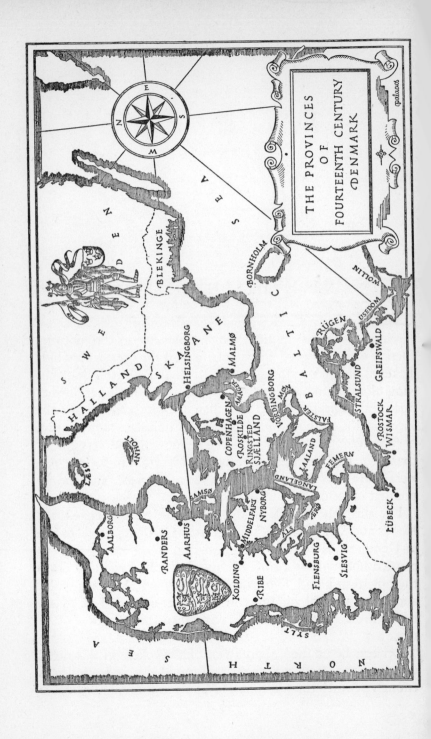

THE PROVINCES
OF
FOURTEENTH CENTURY
DENMARK

1
Midsummer Night's Dream (1340)

THERE WERE BONFIRES UNDER THE BEECH TREES, RING around the sacred hill. Midsummer Eve, St. John's Eve —or Freya's, when maids may learn of future lovers at witching midnight, by rites worth a penance in the morning. Clerkly men and good Christians tended the fires, whose light flickered on sleepy storks, sacred to Baldur, shifting foot and wing along thatched rooftops or the edges of the unfinished cathedral. The fires were less than half for warmth on this spring night, with all the bright leaves bursting; more to hold back among the shadows all the shades that lurked around that hill. If there were ever power in evil things that once were gods, this was surely the night, the place, and the appointed occasion.

For this was the Ve-hjærg, hill of the Skjoldungs—Eriks, Knuds and Valdemars descended from the demon-gods to rule in Denmark. Here once the priest-king stood among the suspended horses' heads, smote home the stone knife and drank the hot fresh blood. Hill of the gods beyond Odin, where jarl and carle brought offerings in the rover-days; hill of magic, beneath whose crest there lies entombed the mightiest of his race.

Let fear be no more than a word half-spoken on this night, with croziers lifted in firelight and torchlight, and priesthood enough beneath the hill to rout Appolyon himself—bishops of

Lund and Borglum, aged men and saintly; bishop of Aarhus, with his stern, sharp visage, armed in steel; young Roskilde; clerkly Odensee—with trains of deacons and prebends to out-number all the temporalities there present. Of the latter there were few indeed; among the great lords of the realm only a pop-eyed, slack-mouthed young man whose title draws more respect than his person, the Duke of Slesvig; among the lesser, a self-made peasant captain, Niels Ebbessen, a grizzled German knight named von Lochen, a handful of mercenary bill-men looking for something to drink. All the rest were local peasants with faces full of pudding-like wonder, who had come so that they could talk all their lives after about how they saw a coronation.

For this was the reason of the gathering; Denmark would have a new king, elected according to a form older than history in the sacred wood, crowned for luck and good guidance (with Holy Church permitting) over a half-god's grave on Ve's sacred hill. Holy Church would take luck or guidance from any source for this new king; there had been too many luckless lords in Denmark these late years, with and without the coronal, but all coming to the same bad end. Set them up; pull them down. One, two, three, four, five had come and gone in the eight-year Time of Uproar since the shameful death of the last unques-tioned monarch—or if one counted princes who did not claim the full heritage, the total runs to ten, more than one a year. Here was another; here the dead ceremonies were invoked to make a king of the last of the Skjoldung line—a king to be the toy of bishops, as the others had been of this interest or that, one more brawling little lad.

"One would gladly have seen a single king in Denmark if only for peace's sake, that no one found by land or sea," wrote the banker-chronicler of Lübeck. Had other bankers of the merchant cities a hand in bringing this new king to Denmark? He came to the hill from Lübeck, but voices among the fires could not be sure; the young man was there as the bishops' pawn—and double-damned for it. Bad was the churchmen's choice when they elected that last King, and badly they stewarded the realm in his name; or perhaps they could do no better, the whole Skjoldung line was run out into bishops' pawns, this one was even less than his father, who died a shameful death beneath the lash.

Last and youngest son of that last King, he came to coronation; more than half a foreigner, brought up from boyhood among the dubious splendors of the Wittelsbach court. He brought no money, no men-at-arms, no foreign aid, nothing but his thin claim to rule in Denmark; no proof that he was better than his two brothers gone down before him, only a little less shamefully than their father. *Geme, plange, moesto more, dolorosia Dania,* sang the clerks back in the shadows.

"Still!" The billmen cleared a space and formed a ragged line. Up through the fires and drifting bands of smoke came the king-to-be, beardless and slender, sour of aspect, dressed in German clothes, preceded by white-haired old Lund, attended by von Lochen, Ebbessen and the cipher-duke of Slesvig, till at the crest he turned with the others behind him, and Lund's chamberlain stepped forward to ask, according to the form:

"People of the Jutes and Danes, will you have this man for your king?"

There was a mild clashing of weapons, a cry of "Yo-o-o-o," long-drawn and notably unenthusiastic.

From somewhere a kite-shaped ceremonial shield was produced, on which the new king stood to be lifted up, balancing uncertainly as the strong Bishop of Aarhus, the Slesvig Duke and an embedsmand from Randers held him aloft. A trumpet was blown; as the man most near a king's marshal, the German knight brandished a sword to the north, where Knud the Mighty ended the Viking Age at the battle of Stiklestad; to the west, where this king's fathers won the islands of the Atlantic in the age of glory; to the south, where Denmark's blood battered the Saracens in Sicily; to the east, where Valdemar the Victorious rolled back a thousand pagan midnights to save all northern Europe. Old Lund lifted a crown of gilded brass, all the harried kingdom could afford, and lowered it to the brow of the young man as some magic of this pagan rite invoked by Christian bishops, some essence of Midsummer Eve among the fires and sweet green trees, touched the small assembled throng to realize that this was a third King Valdemar, son of Valdemar the Great and Valdemar Sejr. In a sudden burst of emotion they forgot the young man's cold face and German airs, shouting from full throats:

"King Valdemar!"

(Not he, but the name.) The dour face moved no line; he stood there impassive as horses were led through the circle. A few words for the bishops; the brass-crowned king mounted, and with only von Lochen and one or two behind him, rode down the hill, out of the circle of St. John's fires and away.

In the morning there would be another day.

2
Dolorosia Dania
(1157; 1219; 1340)

BEHIND VALDEMAR'S CORONATION AND NIGHT RIDE TO
Randers lay a sense of form; an invocation of magic,
if it had not been done by churchmen; at least an evo-
cation of the dim heroic past, only to be understood by such
men as Lund and Odensec. Here on Viborg Hill repeat we
the auspices of another summer night, two hundred years
gone, when in another time of distress another young King
Valdemar, the hope of Denmark, lifted his sword above the
Vikings' howe and rode down to win the name of Great—
God grant an equal issue. Five generations lie between this
new king and that earlier Valdemar; five generations and
many shadow-kings. The line is running out.

Ah, when the bonders first clashed their weapons for a
King Valdemar in that distant day, he stood before them with
a ghastly wound in his thigh and bloody murder hard on his
heels, a hunted man who came by flight through a ruined
countryside, where all the houses were gable ends only. But
he came as the best man of his stem, already the victorious
warrior and proved justiciar, around whom might rally every
heart that held belief in a brighter world.

This last of the shield-king line has known no sieges or
battles, brings nothing to his enterprise but what education
he could gather from the chit-chat of Italian schoolmen, and
the cadging, buffeted background of a minor medieval pre-

tender in exile. A background of big words and little deeds, surrounded by companions as questionable as himself, at a court as lack-lustre as either.

The court was that of the contested Kaiser, Ludwig of Bavaria, who all his life long must struggle down the corridors of Germany, not for his family, but for self and very crown against Hapsburgs, Luxemburgs and the implacable enmity of Popes, who set up one after another from the rival houses as Pfaffen-Kaisers or "priests' Emperors"; a dull do-little lord. The entourage of Prince Valdemar at that court would be equally divided among three groups—adventurers with nothing to lose, like the old knight von Lochen, impossible idealists like the Bishop of Aarhus, and businessmen from Baltic cities with a taste for gambling, willing to risk a few rosenobles on the chance that there would one day be some worth in the charters of privilege gravely signed by the landless prince as "Junker and rightful heir of Denmark."

A background unedifying and unpromising; one more little pretender who, at that court where all men dealt in futures, gained himself the special name of "Prince Tomorrow"— Valdemar Atterdag—out of his habit of receiving all news favorable or the reverse with the same stereotype *I Morgen er det atter Dag*—"In the morning will be another day." The court found it unpromising and ridiculous and laughed at him for it—once too often, for out of such a burst of laughter grew the beginning of these transactions, some years before the night on Viborg Hill.

There was a man named—what? the chroniclers do not tell us, except that he was a graf—who did a boy an evil turn among the Wittelsbachs, and laughed publicly when "I Morgen er det atter Dag" was flung at him. There was a young prince who on his eighteenth birthday (which was majority by medieval standards, the earliest day a man could do such a thing) called the insulter to the lists. They clashed; down went the German and cried an appeal through the bars of his helmet. "Atterdag," quoth Valdemar, and stabbed him through the brain.

Gunnar of Lithend's end, and how Queen Sigrid the Haughty dealt with the suitor who put her to shame would be unknown to Kaiser Ludwig, who found such manners a trifle too grim for his gracious court; nor could he afford to let grafs who chose him instead of one of the Pfaffen-Kaisers be handled in such a fashion. Prince Tomorrow must take up his travels—to a place where troubled Wittelsbach has room for a grim young man with pretensions to a northern throne.

In the early years of Ludwig's Kaisership, the great fief of Brandenburg fell in to the imperial disposition through the death of the last of the old Ascanier house of Markgrafs. Ludwig naturally gave it to one of his own sons, another Ludwig; boy at the time of about Valdemar's own age, who had endless troubles with small wars, revolts and intrigue (he and the Stadtholders appointed to keep Brandenburg for him), since there were collaterals of the Ascaniers who by no means took the imperial decision kindly. Now young Ludwig was of age; nothing more natural than to strike an alliance, under which he should wed Junker Valdemar's sister, with the promise of help to a throne on one side, a thumping dowry and promise of help against the Ascaniers on the other.

A year ran out with neither promise kept and Ludwig the Kaiser impatient to get on with his proper business of abating France and the inimical Pope who lived there. He let messengers be sent to young Ludwig the Markgraf; Ludwig the Markgraf summoned various notabilities to his castle of Spandau. Under guarantees and bishops' blessings young Valdemar signed over Denmark's claim to Esthonia in lieu of his sister's dower; received two hundred mercenary Norddeutschland billmen and rode to Viborg, while young Ludwig trotted off to win spurs and glory under the banner of Edward of England.

II

This then, was all King Valdemar possessed on St. John's Eve—the name of Atterdag, the two hundred panzenars, the memory of what he had learned at the Imperial court, a taste for song and narration so pronounced that an Iceland saga-man was one of those who rode toward the sunrise with him; and the nimbus of a great and proud tradition, now more than half rejected.

It was Esthonia he signed away—Denmark's heart with it. The guard of the north against destructive invading Slavs, trophy of that crusading second Valdemar, greatest king of the great Skjoldung line. Philip Augustus of France had sought marriage alliance with that Valdemar, the German Emperor recognized him as an equal, Innocent III called him the highest man in Europe, and "No man had any wrong in all the lands he ruled," the German chronicler said.

In those days Berlin was an outpost castle, not infrequently besieged; all the Baltic lands seemed like to be submerged beneath the black tide flowing down from the roof of the world. Then it was that Esthonia saw this second Valdemar come up out of the sea with knights and axemen behind him to end these savageries by striking at their root. On the high crag called Lyndanise, above the beach of Reval, was fought the battle for the fate of the north; beginning in treachery and dismay in the morning, when the pagans forswore an oath of peace to leap in overwhelming numbers from the thickets where they had stealthily gathered. The good bishop was slain with many others, the camp taken, the Christian army more than half broken. Only round the young Prince of Rügen and Valdemar himself was there a stand; in which resistance Danes and German knights fought all day back to back for their lives, which it seemed they must lose.

Yet as the setting sun shot red streamers across the sky King Valdemar called them once more into the breach in the name of a white cross formed by clouds against the flowing glow. "Then rose the hearts of all the Danes; in the morning they had fought like boys and in the afternoon like men, but in the evening like devils." Through the night by the light of sword on sparking armor the pagan Slavs were so beaten that never again did their people attempt the West. The Danes counted that rally a miracle, and said that the white-cross banner ever after borne before their armies had fallen from Heaven; called it the *Dannebrog*, "Danes' cloth"; and sent the name of their king ringing down the ages as *Valdemar the Victorious*, Valdemar Sejr.

That Valdemar built the castle on the height, to which came monks, bearded knights of the Order of the Sword, and ultimately merchants to let in light upon those lands—under that law so good that no man had any wrong. The community he made there has prospered till this latest, littlest Valdemar signs a parchment to tell its people that they are Danes no more.

Geme, plange, moesto more, dolorosia Dania, laughing stock of all nations, from whose head the crown has fallen to this un-victorious Valdemar, under such auspices that before the night of St. John they were already calling him *Valdemar den Onde*, Valdemar the Bad. There were those at Viborg who regretted openly that they had chosen this King Stork who destroyed the Danish heritage instead of raising up a King Log in his cousin, the Slesvig Duke—still another in whom great things were hoped from the greatest of names, but who had honestly earned his by-calling of *Valdemar Dosmer*, the Blockhead Valdemar.

Blockhead Valdemar would at least have been full king in Slesvig; King Atterdag holds in actual rule only one lordship of north Jutland—all the rest gone. North Halland had passed in vague claim to Norway. South Halland, Blekinge and Skaane across the Sound had exercised their Danish right of free choice of kings and joined the Swedish crown. Jellinge, Ribe and Kolding of Jutland belonged to the heirs of a German lord named Ludvig Albrektsen von Eberstein, with the right to coin money, to lay taxes and to enjoy all the privileges of kingship save wearing a crown to bed. Laaland, Falster, Femern and most of Sjælland were in the lands of a Graf of the Holstein stem, Johann the Mild, who was not so mild but that under his orders the last King of Denmark had been whipped to death. Rügen was Mecklenburg's; Langeland and Aerø were held by Lord Laurids Jonssen, but he owed homage only to the Blockhead Valdemar for them. Copenhagen city flew the flag of the Hanseatic League. Most of all, the richest provinces lay under the iron rule of Gerhard of Holstein—Jutland, Fyn and the smaller isles.

Truly a rule of iron; men in iron helmets who made their own laws and let out the land piecemeal, for lords of German extraction and piratical disposition to make what they could out of it. In the past twenty-one years these Holsteins, and especially their Graf Gerhard, had worked out a system of conquest that was intelligent, self-supporting and wholly poisonous. There were intricacies and parchments past counting involved in it; agreements of every type, sworn tonight and broken tomorrow, after the manner of the Middle Ages, but simplified of complexities Graf Gerhard's invention ran somewhat thus:

The King of Denmark was short of money. (A fixed point in this Time of Uproar.) Graf Gerhard gave it to him on a pawn-loan, the pledge being regal rights in (say) Skanderborg *herred*, lordship. In Skanderborg castle itself, the best of the province, Gerhard installed a garrison; the lesser holds at Aale, Silkeborg, Vissing and Fistup, he pawned out in turn to knights or barons among his followers, granting them the local tax and police powers. As these knights were landless fighting men, with no possessions beyond the ability to swing a sword and set a battle line in order, Graf Gerhard not only was able to drive hard bargains with them, but found them willing to make hard bargains—they could collect from the peasantry. Some of them, indeed, extended the system another step by granting sub-sub-pawns on villages to lesser notabilities. The Graf thus had money enough to oblige his good friend the King when the latter wished to relieve his further difficulties by placing another lordship in pawn. If by a miracle which occasionally happened, the King assembled money enough to redeem one of the main pledges, this by no means extinguished the rights of the sub-holders, who had laid out good money and must be repaid. Meanwhile, they owed a feudal allegiance to the Danish crown, but owed it only through Graf Gerhard.

The Jutland yeomen footed the bill.

III

So had the crown fallen from Denmark into the hands of the great Graf Gerhard, Johann the Mild of Holstein-Stormarn, Magnus of Sweden, Albrektsen and the German Hansa —but chiefly and ultimately, the Hansa. One must not think of Gerhard's invention as exclusively his own. He was an innovator in bringing purse-power and sword-power together in a single hand, but that was all; the Hansa had long since thought of everything else.

What was this Hansa? Movement and monopoly, civilization in terms of creature comfort; a domineering democracy, intellectually sterile, politically acute, militarily formidable; the Teutonic attempt to build a polity without benefit of Rome, a better world for Germans only; the key to ten centuries of central European history.

The first two Valdemars had never known it, for it was under the gigantic shadow of Valdemar the Victorious that it came into being—Valdemar the Victorious and the riders of the Teutonic Order, a German gentlemen's crusading and colonization club, which transferred its activities from Palestine to the Baltic on the heels of the victory above the beach of Reval. Already at this time, Hamburg, Visby in Götland, and the "Five Wend towns" of Lübeck, Stralsund, Rostock, Wismar and Greifswald, had charters of privilege allowing them to make and execute their own laws—charters lightly granted by the Emperors, who had little force in those northern lands and were pleased to strengthen the cities as a counterpoise to the princes.

Hamburg, Lübeck, Wismar, Stralsund, Rostock—these stand where the great rivers flowing northwest across the German plain reach the sea, natural transfer points. Visby is at the center of the Baltic web, Greifswald looks eastward and, lying under Rügen, is the first sure harbor of refuge for voyagers from the eastern sea. When commerce could rise at all, it rose among these towns and the other river towns westward—Bremen, Bruges, Antwerp. The Germans are a people of combination; the League of the Hansa grew up naturally around these towns, where beam-ends are carved so elaborately, and where there was produced not a single book or picture or piece of music or idea, except for making money. Nobody knows just how it began; perhaps with German merchants from different cities meeting in foreign lands for common worship and mutual protection against the exactions of princes—but twenty-one years after Valdemar the Victorious set the Baltic free by his battle on Lyndanise Rock, the year after he died, Hamburg and Lübeck signed a treaty which is reckoned as the foundation of the League.

It covered common courts and currency, the protection of trade routes and the obtaining of privileges. The Wend towns and Visby joined early, with others to west and south in central Germany. Within fifty years hardly a ship moved in the north or a bale of goods changed hands that the Hansa did not own. When Norway ventured to resist the pinch of monopoly, the League placed her under a commercial blockade that brought mass starvation, and a surrender that left the whole economic life of the country in Hansa control, the merchants of every other nation being forbidden to trade there. The fur trade of the Russias became wholly Hansa;

and during the long century of Denmark's night, the League began to reach for absolute monopoly of the richest trade of the north, the mere handling of which as middlemen had made the Lübeckers wealthy.

This was the fish trade of the Sound. Being dried, these fish provided more than half of Catholic Europe with its only meat on fast days. It was characteristic of the Hansa and of German thinking in general that the indignation of the townsmen over any attempt on the part of Denmark to regulate the income or outgo of the fish markets was by no means impaired because the fish were taken in Danish waters by Danish fishermen. In Hanseatic eyes these people lacked a proper sense of the fact that they were non-Germans. Hansa dabbled energetically in Danish politics to teach these inferiors where they belonged—that is, the best efforts of a geographically diffuse but well organized money power were exerted to keep every centrifugal force in the dolorous kingdom alive.

Sample case (with a warning that it is a sample case and not the universal practice): a certain Bishop Esgers Juel had a claim on the island of Bornholm, but needed money to hire men and ships for an invasion. He applied to the Hansa; there was a meeting of pot-bellied German burghers in Visby, where the bishop's credentials were examined and he was found a good risk. At once the Hansa commercial houses in Bornholm started a propaganda for Esgers Juel, at the same time transmitting all necessary information about his opponents' force and plans. With Hansa money the good bishop rented Hansa ships and hired Hansa men-at-arms in Hansa cities. At the moment of invasion his enemies found it impossible to obtain men, money, ships, information; their blows went into a mattress, the bishop's thrusts cut them to the quick. In no time at all he was Prince-Bishop of Bornholm, collecting a special tax for the glory of God and the defense of the realm to pay his loans in Visby. In token of the Prince-

Bishop's gratitude, Hansa goods were to be imported into Bornholm duty-free.

He enjoyed a peaceful if unprosperous rule till the cash loan was repaid and Hammershus castle, which Hansa had held as security, was delivered up again. About this time there appeared in Visby a certain Prince Kristoffer, who claimed Bornholm as a personal appanage. There was another meeting with burghers who folded fat hands across their bellies to keep the gold chains from clanking. They agreed that Kristoffer's claims were just in right and law—but after all, they were businessmen, and the trouble this prince proposed to make in Bornholm would cause a disturbance of trade, for which they felt they should be compensated. Would he offer a slightly higher cash rate than the bishop had paid, with an undertaking that no goods at all should be imported into Bornholm but those of the Hansa? He would; he did; Bornholm was conquered from Esgers Juel in the same manner and with the same ease as he had won it.

Who paid for that? The Bornholm yeomen.

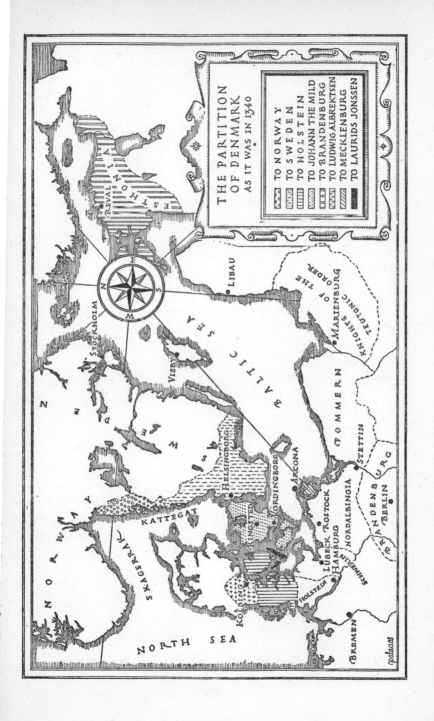

THE PARTITION
OF DENMARK
AS IT WAS IN 1340

TO NORWAY
TO SWEDEN
TO HOLSTEIN
TO JOHANN THE MILD
TO BRANDENBURG
TO LUDWIG ALBREKTSEN
TO MECKLENBURG
TO LAURIDS JONSSEN

ESTHONIA

REVAL

LIBAU

MARIENBURG

TEUTONIC KNIGHTS' BORDER

STOCKHOLM

VISBY

BALTIC SEA

POMMERN

N O R W A Y

S W E D E N

ARCONA

HELSINGBORG

NORDINGBORG

STETTIN

BRANDENBURG

BERLIN

KATTEGAT

RINGSTED

ROSTOCK

LÜBECK

HAMBURG

NORDALBINGIA

SCHWERIN

SKAGERRAK

KOLDING

HOLSTEIN

BREMEN

NORTH SEA

3
The Sense of Form
(1157; 1319-1332)

S O PARTED, SO BROKEN ON THE WHEELS OF HOLSTEIN AND
Hansa, Valdemar Atterdag found his kingdom. Indeed,
there had hardly even been a crown of brass but for the
dismay of this fragmentation; for this and no other reason did
the bishops invoke from Viborg Hill the shadow of that great
and early Valdemar. (One must always have respect to the
medieval sense of form, which lies behind the logic of the
age and the thoughts below logic. The period made its decisions out of a feeling for symbolic symmetry so acute that it
could raise beauty among the tortured spires of a Gothic
cathedral and hamper a great action because a small detail of
pattern was lacking. Example; when that first Valdemar
reached his throne he had a friend in holy orders—Axel, or
Absalon, as he called himself—in whom the King's keen eye
had caught the attributes of leadership. Form demanded that
a churchman who held a high place in the state must be a
prince of the Church as well, else the secular would stand
above the spiritual dignity. But Axel-Absalon, though of pure
life and indubitable learning, was less than thirty, and pattern
said that since Christ had not begun His ministry until such
age, no man should be allowed to take up the apostolic succession earlier.)

This new Valdemar is the last of the direct line of the
Skjoldungs—so was that earlier Valdemar; the Church is

wholly with him—as with the first of the name; like his fore-father, the new King comes at an hour when Denmark is torn from within by disputed succession and from without by warlike tumults. Shall he not save us like the first? "Then hopped all the Danes for joy that they should be delivered from the Holsteiners' hard yoke," says their chronicler. Lund's archbishop and clerkly Odensee might be alone in understanding all the precedents that lay behind a Valdemar at Viborg, but Denmark is a home of saga hardly less than Iceland itself; among the St. John's fires there would be not a few who re-told the old tale of that first Valdemar and how he came to the throne of a broken land:

There was a man named Knud, a younger son of the royal Danish stem with a better claim to royalty than the King himself; generous and knightly, one of those characters the Scandinavian races throw up from time to time, burning with that inextinguishable drive to subdue hard conditions which accounts alike for the Vikings and the settlement of the American northwest. He passed his early years at the court of Lothar, the Kaiser of Germany, learning war and govern-ment; returned to his own land and spent all his heritage in buying the lifetime rule of South Jutland. It was a border march, raided from land and sea by the pagan Wends of the southeast. Knud built castles by the shore, hanged the raiders and set up a peace in the land so strong that no one could break it; he was known as *Knud Lavard*, Knud the Lord.

At this time the other princes of the royal house were build-ing castles; they led the life of mere freebooters as power slipped from the lands of the aged King. Lord Knud forced them to his peace and sustained the bonders who tore down their pirate holds. The people of Laaland and the lesser isles begged him to be their duke; the old King called the estates together and said that Knud should be his co-King and heir.

The old King's name was Niels; he had a son by a late mar-riage named Magnus, who took Knud's preference very ill, though he himself was by no means entitled to the Danish throne, since a lordship in Vastergotland of Sweden had come to him through his mother. During the Christmas feast he murdered Lord Knud in a little wood near Roskilde. As the body of the dead prince was borne through the town his princess lay in a little room with the pangs of birth upon her; the child was named Valdemar. He grew up in a Denmark torn by the civil war that broke out on his father's death and ran for twenty-six years long. In that war fell the murderous Magnus and many others; the crown claim ran out into collateral lines until the day when Valdemar, grown to manhood, and with the Jutland bonders behind him, met the other claimants in Laaland.

One was another Knud, of whom there is not much; he was a young man and handsome; cousin to Magnus' son of the same name. One was Sveyn, called Sveyn Peder, of whom there is a great deal, for he was one of the black-hearted Skjoldungs, which the race throws up equally with Knud Lavards—all the burning energy and fierce persistence, but turned inward, serving no hope but his own. Part of the Sjællanders chose him as King and a bad bargain they made, for he brought the pagan Wends to harry the lands of those who would not have him, and sent offerings to the seven-headed savage god of these men; even appealed to the German Kaiser, offering him the rule of Denmark in exchange for his support. Men began to fall away from Sveyn; in spite of his force in arms it was clear that he could have Denmark only as a pile of ruins when he went to the meeting in Laaland. Sveyn sought to draw Valdemar to his side to revenge his father's murder on young Knud, the son of Magnus, but the son of Knud Lavard replied coldly that the young man had no part in Magnus' misdeeds, and he would hold himself for a lost man if he broke his safe-conduct to the prince for the sake of a man who betrayed Denmark into the hands of savages. The end was that they agreed there should be three kings together, as often in the land of Norway—Sveyn in the provinces beyond the Sound, another Knud, their cousin, in the islands, but Valdemar in Jutland; for Knud Magnusson was newly dead of a sickness, and his claim with him.*

For a feast of peace they went up to Roskilde, Denmark's jewel; and there was a second evil deed of Roskilde done, for Sveyn Peder brought his German stabbers round the hall where the three kings sat at evening meat and let young Knud be killed across the board. Valdemar parried the sword-blow with a cloak rolled round his arm, and though wounded, leaped through a window into night and hiding.

When morning came the men of Sveyn were abroad; he had stuck his own cloak through, and shown it to the Roskilde burghers, with a false tale of Valdemar's treachery. The ways were beset; Sveyn gave orders to bore holes in every boat in Sjælland, but with one friend, who was Absalon's brother Esbern the Quick, the young King made his way secretly to the shore. They found a leaky shallop and put out for Jutland. A frightful tempest, which far to the south wrecked the fleet of Sveyn's allies the Wends, came on the voyagers and cast their craft on a tiny island. But Valdemar won through wound and wreck to the Jutland shore. On Viborg howe on a summer night the bishops crowned him; he rode to Randers and all Jutland rose. When Sveyn came with his Germans and howling Wends, there was a battle on the heath, an end to that bad man, and Valdemar was King—The Great King, who chopped the seven-headed god of the Wends into firewood.

II

Here is the pattern which the crowners of Viborg seek to repeat—lying not merely in the name of this Valdemar of a later day. To their minds, their sense of form, it would be no little thing that the father of the first Valdemar had also grown up at the Imperial court, that the first like the latest Valdemar had

* These three Knuds are a nuisance; perhaps the dynastic table, page 18, will help clear them up.

found the land overrun, that both came to the throne by a hard road through treachery and despair.

The pattern runs deeper yet. Each Valdemar was the last of three brothers, of whom the elder two had reached unhappy ends, each the successor of a King who bore little more than the name of royalty. To be sure, old King Niels, who made Lavard his heir, had seen the crown fade from his head through doddering age; while from Kristoffer, Valdemar Atterdag's father, it had been withheld by his own lords and yeomen in the beginning of the Time of Uproar, twenty-one years before the eve of St. John. He was the Prince Kristoffer who, with Hansa help, took Bornholm from its bishop; one of the kings who borrowed money at so usurious a rent from the great Graf of Holstein. The Danes knew what they were doing when they elected him—a bad job of work, who had a whole series of scoundrelisms on his record, including the harrying of Danish Skaane with the help of the Swedes.

They knew what they were getting, and so were to blame for what they got—but they cannot be blamed too heavily, for the other candidates were as unattractive as he and none of them possessed his standing with the Hansa. Nobody could work up any enthusiasm for Duke Erik of Slesvig, who was a good deal of a fool and illegitimate beside; and the only other men with enough Skjoldung connection to be eligible were the two Holstein grafs, Johann the Mild and Gerhard, who were regarded with equal suspicion by the Danes as foreigners and by the Hansa as too hot to handle. To the prelates, lords and bonders who gathered at Viborg, it seemed that Kristoffer was one of the unpleasant but driving characters of the royal line, just the sort of person to bring the realm out of the dolors into which it had fallen. The Hansa knew this was not so—that he had the character without the ability of Sveyn Peter—but they did not mind seeing a weak king in Denmark and had their own methods of dealing with a bad one. Accordingly the moneyed men swung their large, but only faintly visible influence to the candidacy of Kristoffer and he was elected according to form by the Hof of the Danes.

Not, however, before the estates had taken their precautions against drawing a black Skjoldung of the Sveyn Peter stamp by means of a device borrowed from another nation where they had had trouble with overbearing kings. Before the election Kristoffer was presented with a charter very famous in northern history as the *Haandfæstning,* being informed that his candidacy could not be considered until he had signed it. Of all the documents by which European kings watered down their own absolutism, the Haandfæstning of Kristoffer is one of the most remarkable, by reflection describing both the character of the signatory and of the society that made him subscribe to it. Under it, no man in holy orders might be brought before a secular court unless the spiritual courts had released him; no taxes might be levied on Church property nor might defensive obligations in time of war be sought from its feudal holdings; no priest or bishop might be taken prisoner or his goods levied on without a special letter from the Pope; cloisters might not be charged with the feeding of royal horses or dogs; Bornholm was to be returned to its bishop, now become archbishop of the kingdom; nobles could not be required to undertake war service beyond the frontiers, and if taken prisoner in war, must be ransomed by the King, who would then pay their expenses and a sum for the damage to their feelings; no wars might be undertaken without a vote of the powers spiritual and temporal; the right to tax was severely limited; all export and import duties on the goods of town burghers were abolished and not to be reimposed without a general vote of the merchants (the Hansa at work here); royal courts were deprived of appellate jurisdiction, and appeals from them could be taken to a general court of the nation; the income from fines passed to local noblemen instead of the King; a parliament was to sit once a year. For the benefit of the yeomen it was added that they might not be impressed to carry the royal baggage "to an excessive extent" and somewhat ironically, that Kristoffer was to put down all private wars with the strong arm. As security against violations he must destroy the new royal castles at Ribe, Kolding and Skanderborg.

If the Haandfæstning had ended here and if Kristoffer had been possessed of a concept that had not yet entered the European mind—that wholehearted devotion to the public weal whose product is statesmanship—he would have found it difficult to conduct the affairs of the nation under such an instrument. The feudal system required him to operate through deputies over whom he had been deprived of authority. But Kristoffer did not have even the normal medieval degree of concern for his subjects and the Haandfæstning did not end here. He was forbidden to employ German officers whom he could control. The last King, Erik Menved, had run himself deeply into debt in order to prosecute a series of futile wars; an annex to Kristoffer's coronation oath required that all these debts be paid off at once, along with all the new ones the King had acquired in attaining his position.

Kristoffer began smoothly enough by reconciling with the archbishop, Esgers Juel, who crowned him at Vordingborg as one of the first Danish kings, *Dei gratia*. The castles came down; the accession debts were mostly paid, especially a big one to a certain Knud Porse, a brisk, stirring lord who had been of much help over the election, and who received the entire province of Halland, with the resplendent title of Duke, till then reserved for the royal family. A long quarrel with Sweden was composed, and so was a recent one with the Lords of Mecklenburg, whom Kristoffer outflanked by going down to the Imperial court and making the betrothal that issued as the Brandenburg marriage of Prince Tomorrow's sister.

These moves occupied a couple of years during which the parliament remained unsummoned, the old debts unpaid; the Danes learned that "truth was not in any oath Kristoffer swore." When the King returned from Germany he confronted a thoroughly indignant general assembly which had called itself together, and representatives from both nobles and Hansa presented demands for payment. There was a certain amount of reason in Kristoffer's reply that he had no income from which to pay; if the debts of the realm were to be met, the people would have to help him by accepting new taxes. He suggested one that would be described in modern terms as a general capital levy of 10 per cent.

That so outrageous a tax should be granted by approximately the same men who had lately abolished royal taxation could hardly be expected. They said no; Kristoffer said he'd be damned if he'd pay, the Haandfæstning shivered in a thousand pieces and the obligations of contract were impaired.

The details of what steps the Hansa took are impossible to recover, since the financial men were, as usual, interested in concealing that they had taken any steps, and there were no public audits. Pressure of some kind was certainly applied, for following his stormy assembly, Kristoffer was in distress for money and supplies, borrowing from Graf Gerhard and departing for Skaane. For an experiment in government he now undertook that province was peculiarly suitable, both because of the wealth reflected from the herring fisheries and because the individual landholdings were small. His Majesty announced a tax of one mark on every plow in the province and made an armed royal progress to collect. Those who would not or could not pay went to prison, and their estates went to personal retainers of Kristoffer, usually mercenary Germans. As the money went to maintain the sanctity of contracts with the Hansa, nobody objected very much except the Skaanemen themselves. They raised an armed league of discontent, were soundly beaten for their trouble, and saw a good deal more land being confiscated, when Duke Erik died over in Slesvig.

His heir was the ten-year-old boy whom we have met, grown to manhood, under the name of Blockhead Valdemar.

To Kristoffer, with a considerable armed force in hand and Skaane nearly milked dry, this accession seemed an unparalleled opportunity. He announced that he was guardian for the young man, threw his forces into Slesvig and rapidly took everything but Gottorp Castle, which he held under siege with the boy inside.

III

The whole trail up to this point is through an endless thicket of complicated medieval double-dealing, devoid of ideas and ideals, no light at the terminus. Now there enters a man who had plenty of ideas, even if without any touch of ethics, and a delineable, though thoroughly diabolic ideal. Graf Gerhard of Holstein-Rendsborg had what all the other self-seeking nobles of his time lacked—a genuine social policy. It was centered on fear; on the idea that society is most stable and effective when arranged in a series of steps, whose occupants receive fear from above and exercise it downward. There is no record that anyone ever felt the least affection for Gerhard or that he wanted them to; but they respected him, and he was so efficient in conveying the one emotion he understood that he made a merely bad man like Kristoffer look weak, childish and capricious.

It was precisely for this reason that the great Jutland lords brought him in when Kristoffer attacked Slesvig. There were two of these—Ludvig Albrektsen, who had been the late King Erik Menved's Marshal, and Laurids Jonssen, who had been his Drost, a combination of high bailiff and military officer. They must have had a good deal to do with both King Kristoffer's election and the Haandfæstning, and it seems they extracted their own private charter from him, in the form of an agreement to maintain them in the offices they had held during the previous reign. He left them the titles but gave the Marshal nothing to marshal and the Bailiff no monies to handle.

The two noblemen viewed the proceedings in Skaane with a displeasure doubtless increased by the fact that as Drost and Marshal, they should have had a share of the spoils, but there was nothing they could do about it, since Kristoffer was King, with the support of his German soldiers and the Hanseatic interest, and the Jutland bonders had not been directly touched to protest. They tried a new general assembly without much luck. They tried the Church, but Esgers Juel had died about the same time as Erik of Slesvig and his successor was a kindly scholar uninterested in politics. But with Kristoffer ramping around the Jutland peninsula at the head of an army, it was quite clear that they were the next tall poppies whose heads were due to come off, so they invoked the devil. At a meeting in Rendsborg it was agreed that Gerhard should rescue Valdemar the Blockhead, while they would summon a Thing of the realm, get Kristoffer deposed (with Gerhard's army to back them, it could be made to stick), and elect the boy king.

Marshal and Drost doubtless thought they were conducting a normal medieval political operation, consisting of intrigue with a small admixture of warfare, which would end with the two in possession of the boy-king and practically rulers of Denmark. They overlooked the fact that their fundamental motive was fear and they had appealed to a master of it, who was by no means a normal medieval character. Gerhard mobilized with a speed that made their eyes stand out, and long before the officers of state could gather forces to join the campaign and so establish their claim to adjudicate the result, appeared before King Kristoffer under the walls of Gottorp. The armies met; Kristoffer's was utterly broken, the King himself surrounded by dangerous-looking swords. Graf Gerhard was generous, Graf Gerhard would release him without ransom, on only one small condition—that Kristoffer recognize the conqueror as guardian to young Valdemar Dosmer, who was, after all, his widowed sister's son.

As soon as the document was signed Gerhard flung Kristoffer off to whatever limbo he might choose and himself marched to Viborg, where the Thing of the realm was already in session. Knud Porse had come; so had the archbishop and most of the other great lords. Looking at Gerhard's warlike array, the assembly decided that Kristoffer should no more be King in Denmark, nor his son Erik neither, but Valdemar of Slesvig. But Gerhard was regent as guardian to the young man, legally appointed by a legitimate king. The meeting ended with rewards; ten-year-old King Valdemar the Blockhead was graciously pleased to grant Helsingborg to Knud Porse; Hadersleben castle and district to Marshal Albrektsen; Tranekjær castle and most of Langeland Island on which it stands to Drost Laurids Jonssen—all of them on pawn-loan, naturally, with the monies being turned over to His Majesty's great and good tutor, Graf Gerhard of Holstein.

The nobles were now committed; when Kristoffer called out the levies of Sjælland and Skaane to recover the western half of his kingdom, Marshal and Drost faced him across the Belt with the men of Jutland and Fyn. Kristoffer established his own headquarters at the great stronghold of Vordingborg and began to gather men, thrusting Prince Erik forward to Korsør with the mercenary Germans and such men of Sjælland as had responded to the war-arrow. Erik was cut from about the same cloth as his father; there seems to have been a series of minor nastinesses on his part which built up to an explosion in which the Sjællanders cried they would not fight for Germans against the Jutland yeomen and besieged the prince in Taarnborg castle, inviting Marshal and Drost across the Belt to help them. Sixteen days of the siege brought surrender; "then had Erik the luck to exchange a golden crown for iron fetters" and was dragged off to Hadersleben. His father left most of what force he had in Vordingborg and took ship to Rostock, while Graf Gerhard, for no reason at all, received the title of "Protector of Denmark."

IV

Whatever their other characteristics, there ran through all the Skjoldungs a strain of dogged courageous determination in defiance of all odds and possibilities, so much beyond ordinary persistence that a superlative is lacking with which to describe it accurately. One of the early Sveyns was beaten eight times in the field—twice more than Bruce or Bruce's spider—but came back in a ninth attempt and won all Denmark. King Kristoffer was a thorough villain and something of a fool, but he had all the Skjoldung guts. In return for the island of Rügen, "honorably won by the sword" from the Wendish heathen back in the days of Valdemar the Great, he obtained from Mecklenburg 950 German sergeants. In return for privileges to the Rostock Hansa, he obtained ships to carry them, and came back to Vordingborg.

It was no longer a Danish castle. Graf Gerhard had bought out Kristoffer's commander of the place for four thousand marks of silver, incidentally cheating the man out of his payment. Kristoffer assaulted and carried the castle, but that was as far as he got. To Danish minds it was a clear case of foreign invasion, no matter what the leader's name was. All Sjælland rose to help in the deposed king on the land side, Graf Gerhard appeared with an immense fleet, and Kristoffer had to stand a siege. The Mecklenburg Lord was with the expedition; he "mediated," the terms being that Kristoffer should leave Denmark.

Kristoffer and his men sailed down Vordingborg bight and a couple of hours later landed on Falster, which they attempted to subdue by a *coup de main*. The Falstringer instantly turned out with weapons in their hands, yelling with rage over such treachery, a fleet from all Denmark gathered round and the Lord of Mecklenburg had to make a new armistice, with Kristoffer this time promising never to return to the country.

The Third King

Up to this time Graf Gerhard had appeared before the Danes, when he appeared at all, as a savior who kept the men of Jutland and the islands from receiving the same treatment Kristoffer and his Germans had given Skaane. Now the country began to learn what it was like to deal with a professional ogre instead of an amateur. The protector of Denmark's first care was to cover his southern flank against a renewed effort from Kristoffer by discovering that Blockhead Valdemar's finances were in bad order. The situation could only be saved by letting out the islands of Laaland, Falster and Femern to Graf Johann the Mild of Holstein-Stormarn on pawn-loan. Of course the money received for this did not last long; it became necessary to pawn out other castles and lordships to Graf Gerhard; to sub-pawn them to Holsteiners of one species or another, who raised the money in Lübeck banking houses, paying off themselves and their backers out of the yeomen.

The latter expressed their objections to paying taxes to these Germans at a rate considerably above what they had refused to their own king, and it was in dealing with these objections that Graf Gerhard's social policy became fully developed. The objectors gathered in the old Things, primary assemblies dating from Viking times. But as the Holstein system had broken the ultimate power of taxation into small units and irregular intervals, the protest meetings were local and unco-ordinated, while Graf Gerhard's forces were not only co-ordinated, but also possessed an ingenious and labor-saving procedure, invented by himself. As soon as the protector of Denmark learned that one of his sub-pawnholders was having trouble with the peasantry, he went to the scene with a body of armored horsemen. The objectors were driven into the nearest body of water and the spearmen lined the shore to watch them drown, laughing heartily.

For fourteen years the history of Denmark consisted of these noyades and the struggles of the country to escape its lord of fear. There were endless changes in the political minutiae of the pattern—Blockhead Valdemar abdicating, claiming the crown again, re-abdicating; Kristoffer, that pertinacious man, returning once more, with promises right and left of amended behavior, to be recognized by estates who were ready to accept anything as better than the Holsteiners' hard yoke, and by a Graf Gerhard who perceived that this puppet would be easier to control than the other; Kristoffer, that treacherous man, hewing down a band of bonders who had surrendered after opposing him, and throwing into prison a bishop who came to him with a message; untrusted Kristoffer, limited to the single castle of Nyborg; a rising of Jutland yeomen in primary assembly which catches Hadersleben castle off guard, storms it, and releases Prince Erik; Erik and Kristoffer lying, intriguing, detaching the Holstein-Stormarn Graf from his kinsman, promising and selling the Danish heritage, till they somehow assemble forces enough to try things once more with the sword against Graf Gerhard under the walls of Gottorp castle.

There, on St. Andrew's Day of 1331, November 30, across a wide plain called the Lohede, was the final battle fought. Graf Gerhard had the fewer men, but they thrust too straight and sharp; the Skjoldungs were driven in prone rout and Erik broke his skull as his horse stumbled in a rabbit's hole. Otto, the second son, was taken and sent to a dungeon from which he made but one brief exit in nine years, till he looked like a white worm and his eyes could not bear the light. Kristoffer won out of the defeat to the city of Kiel, but this did him little good, for on an evening in the following summer a couple of drunken Holstein knights set fire to his house, caught him in a fishnet as he leaped from the window, and carried him off as a morsel for the breakfast table of Johann the Mild. Johann the Mild did not think the royal sprat was worth more than being whipped out of his courtyard. Kristoffer died of it; and the realm of Denmark tipped over the edge down into eight years of utter anarchy.

V

The eyes that looked through the swirling smoke of St. John's Eve from Viborg height would see how Graf Gerhard stood, like Sveyn Peder, a figure of incarnate evil whose shadow lay across the land; how invaders from the Wendish lands (were not the great Hansa towns "the five Wend cities," and Mecklenburg "Prince in Wendland"?) had harried the isles for a generation; would see how the kingdom was once more split into thirds, with no kingship in any part; the taxes not to be borne; the Things unsummoned; the old good laws forgotten.

Complete the pattern, then; make us a new King Valdemar.

4

Interlude—The Laws
of King Valdemar

B Y THIS TIME ENOUGH HAS BEEN SAID TO INDICATE THAT
Holsteiners, Mecklenburgers and other assorted Germans were regarded in Denmark with an intensity of
feeling that requires some explanation; a detestation far greater
than that Saxons felt for Normans after Duke William's conquest of England. The obvious reason will hardly do. Holsteiner
and Dane were very little, if at all, different physically, each
spoke a language that the other could understand if the going
were slow, and the nationalities of later ages had not yet been invented. At this same time Englishmen were ruling in Gascony
and Guienne without arousing any particular resentment, and
there was no sense of outrage when the Skaane provinces
transferred themselves to Sweden. Indeed, the normal man
of the period hardly thought of himself as the citizen of a
country so much as the subject of a ruler, involved with that
overlord in an intensely personal contract, which would be
dissolved by the death of either party.

The basis of the Danish emotional explosion was not that
the Germans were aliens of blood, but of practice; that they
were forcibly introducing anarchic and primitive elements
into a society which had very nearly stabilized itself at a high
level. The clash of the two civilizations had many aspects, but
the principal pressure-point was that at which the intruders
encountered the great body of Danish law, so different from
their own. South of the Slesvig line the codification of tribal

customs and the simultaneous Reception of the Roman Law was in full swing, but on a local and limited basis. In Denmark the reduction to written statutes had taken place a hundred years before, as a national project, and with the Roman intrusions indignantly rejected.

"With law shall the land be built," says the first line of the great book called *Den jydske Lov,* or "The Law of the Jutland Men," which was proclaimed with singing trumpets at Vordingborg by Valdemar the Victorious, in the presence of his sons, eight bishops and "all the best men of the country" —after many years of victory and defeat in the changing clang of battle, when in his seventh decade he sat down to make his country great internally instead of by the sword. It was the crown of a long work, the last of three collections which together are known as the Laws of King Valdemar—one book for the Skaane provinces, one for Sjælland and the isles, and this Jutland law, the greatest of the three. Not Valdemar's laws alone—he only gave orders that the codes should be fairly written down and publicly proclaimed, so that no man might be ignorant when the laws were contravened. They are the mirror of an entirely different society from that which the German grafs were imposing upon the country.

The three codes have minor variations, but in those essentials which show forth the picture of their world, they are one corpus. Under the influence of feudalism the rest of Europe had avidly adopted from Rome the principle of status, under which a man's duty to his fellows was regulated by his position in the state. There is not a trace of status in the laws of King Valdemar. Everywhere else, as much by Germanic tradition as by that of the Roman emperors, the king was supreme legislator. But the Jutland law declares: "No man shall meddle with the law, and the king may not set it aside or change it without the will of the land." Everywhere but in Denmark there is provision for serfdom.*

* Actually, some serfs were held in Sjælland, but their number was never important and the procedure was somewhat extra-legal.

Interlude—The Laws of King Valdemar

The last is symptomatic; the whole theory behind the laws of King Valdemar is that "all men are free" if not equal, fundamentally intelligent, kindly, social, and of good will; should be protected in the exercise of their free choice, even at the cost of some security and order. There is nothing mysterious about the production of this type of code so early. The Danes were that kind of people, and if one wishes to be a determinist, the general plan of the law can be seen as growing out of a society highly homogeneous by race and mode of life, which had very early decided it could afford a high degree of personal liberty.

Thus the police power is very weak. The Latin theory that every injury is an injury to the state has no place in this law, nor has the Latin concentration on restraining breaches of the peace by threatening the breaker with punishment, or the Latin doctrine that society rests upon the force which its united parts can apply. The emphasis of King Valdemar's law is on removing the causes for breaches and healing those that do occur by bringing plaintiff and defendant to an agreement. The state has only a supervisory authority over cases, except where it is a party directly in interest; that is, where the act threatens the general security, as murder, kidnapping, persistent theft. The grand distinction of the law is not between civil and criminal causes, but between those which involve the general welfare and those which concern only the individuals involved.

This dividing line may be viewed as a rationalization of the old private revenge principle—that if a wronged party is not sufficiently interested to pursue the matter, no tort has been suffered that is worthy the attention of the state. But there is something more to it than that; where Mediterranean law abolished private revenge by making the state the only avenger, the laws of Denmark look toward bringing wronger and wronged into agreement with each other, on the assumption that if this is achieved, the peace will be kept by all men of good will. Thus punishments are mild to a degree not seen

· 67 ·

elsewhere till the twentieth century, and consist mainly of fines, the largest part of which fall to the benefit of the injured party. That a blood-feud could and should be bought off by a fine is, indeed, a principle among all early Teutonic peoples as soon as they begin to emerge into the light. It is written into the laws of Charlemagne. But the principle disappeared from most of Europe, leaving nothing but traces, under the impact of the quite different theories offered by Roman law. In the Laws of King Valdemar, it is broadened into a code for universal civilized conduct.

Murder, especially murder by fire, treason, and repeated theft are crimes in which the community is the injured party either directly or by implication; "if a man be convicted of these he shall go to the gallows and hang." A few other crimes —mayhem, kidnapping—carry prison sentences, but even here the condemned may "buy his freedom from the King," provided (and note this; it occurs in no other code) he can obtain a pardon from the injured party.

The King's *embedsmand*, or local sheriff, one for each herred, prosecutes these graver cases. In lesser matters he can only act at the request of the plaintiff, in which instance the royal treasury receives part of the fine if it be over three marks of silver. (The income from these fines was one of the main sources of royal cash income; the loss of it through the Haandfæstning was one of the main embarrassments to King Kristoffer's treasury.) The machinery is that of the Thing courts, the primary assembly of each herred. When a case comes up they elect three, six or twelve of their fellows, according to its gravity, to pronounce judgment. These are the *Nævninger*, "named men"; if this jury were evenly divided six more were elected to it, and another six, till one side had a majority. In Jutland and annexed Fyn alone there was a special class of "truth men," *Sandemænd*, professional jurors and inquirers, eight to a herred, appointed by the king. They formed the juries in cases of murder, mayhem, kidnapping of women, boundary disputes, ownership of land and slander. The assembled Thing could always override any judgment.

The embedsmand had no power in making decisions; he only enforced them. But if he had to make a levy on household goods, he was required to do it without public display. There was no ordeal by battle. Ordeal by the hot iron was in the old codes, but King Valdemar had it thrown out (one of his few positive contributions) as too easy to defeat by crafty means. Compurgators, known men of the district, could swear a man free from a charge as in England; but in Denmark they were no more than character witnesses, the accused still had to stand trial before the Nævninger if the embedsmand thought there was a prima facie case against him, or if in what we would call a civil suit, there were compurgators on both sides.

These were the laws of Valdemar the Victorious in their essential features—laws made for honest men, who could still trust one another in the midst of a dispute. They had accumulated little by little for many years; they were proclaimed among the blowing trumpets and streaming banners of Vordingborg a fortnight before the great king died and "The Century of the Valdemars" was closed. They did not prevent private revenges any more completely than the Mosaic code estopped the children of Israel from following after strange gods; but the basic intent was there in one case as in the other, the principle to which practical instances were referred, and on which they were judged. It was a good principle.

II

The opening up of the new world in the sixteenth century had one consequence which it is fairly easy to overlook. It provided Europe with an abundant metallic circulating medium that had not previously existed, and so made possible governmental arrangements that could not otherwise be undertaken. Back in the days when Knud the Mighty conquered England he set up a paid army, the Thingmannalid: "They were so bold that one of them was better than two of any other army's best men, and they all looked like a sheet of ice when the weapons glistened." The institution fell into desuetude under successors less competent and far-sighted than the Emperor of the North and it was not revived until midway along the century of the Valdemars, under the first son of Valdemar the Great, Knud VI.

His father had ended the menace of the Wends, but the Baltic was still full of Slavic raiders (would be until Valdemar the Victorious broke their hearts), and was being attacked from the south by German duchies whose normal condition was war. Knud VI encountered this shortage of circulating medium, a far different thing than shortage of money, and the printing press had not been invented. The country was prosperous; the great Valdemar and his Bishop Absalon had managed it well. But that very prosperity had increased the proportion of merchants, handworkers and especially of farmers in the population, men who were unwilling to drop everything and go for a summer's campaigning, as in Viking days. They were quite willing to meet their obligations toward defense by paying taxes. But there was no cash; they had to pay in kind, and a soldier of the revived Thingmannalid could not make much use of a nice pig, a bushel of herring and a firkin or two of butter.

At the same time the character of the Thingmannalid itself was altered by the change in military technology. The old wars were amphibious operations, in which the Vikings appeared on the battlefield with massive forces of heavy infantry. Horses could not be accommodated aboard their ships; and when continental Europe came to the battlefield with armored cavalry combined with archers, as at Hastings, the new technique easily proved itself superior to the old. Many of the wars of the century of the Valdemars were fought along the southern shore of the Baltic where armored cavalry was indispensable if any head were to be held against the German dukes, who had a great deal of it.

Maintaining a force of such armored knights—or sergeants, as they were called when they lacked patents of nobility—was an extremely expensive proposition. A full suit of armor was outrageously costly, not only originally, but also in upkeep. Men and horses required a degree of training and practice which made them true professionals, with no time for any other activity. The old levy of bonders could not be placed on the basis of supplying these high-priced testudinae, and as Knud VI rapidly discovered, the royal cash revenue was insufficient to keep up an adequate force of them.

Under these circumstances the feudal system was imported into Denmark; but a feudal system radically different from any other in Europe, and one in which King Valdemar's laws lay at the root. Everywhere else, the system was immediately or ultimately the result of conquest, most typically in England, where the lands were partitioned out among a nobility who were social superiors by right of being victorious aliens, who formed a garrison to keep the conquered population down, and who received their landholdings in hereditary ownership. In Denmark there was no garrison; the country had never been conquered. Nevertheless, when the question of a new Thingmannalid came up, the royal estate was relatively land-rich. All uninhabited tracts belonged to it of old right; all abandoned lands that had once been cultivated (of which there were a good many still lying around from the days of the Viking emigration); and of course, the confiscated lands of those who had chosen the wrong side in the civil struggles that closed with the death of Sveyn Peter.

Such lands were allotted to the maintenance of a new class of *hærmænd*, "army men," a few of whom were established by Knud VI, but a great many, the bulk of the whole institution, by Valdemar the Victorious. With the estates went privileges in recognition of the fact that the army men "must constantly risk their necks for the king's and the land's peace," as the

Jutland chronicle put it. The estates were exempt from taxation, those who dwelt on them had no obligation to militia service or labor on roads and fortifications.

So far the Danish system was not too different from other feudalisms, except in being adopted full-grown, while the rest had the naturalness and irregularities of long development. But Valdemar's feudalism had a feature that placed the width of the Atlantic between it and the rest. The estates were not privately owned, and were not hereditary; they fell in to the crown on the death of the individual who served in the king's army, whether he came alone or with underlings. The hærmænd were also called "loan nobility." Birth had nothing whatever to do with entry to their ranks; anyone could join who wished, and a good many bonders did so in order to obtain a hærmænd's privileges for their holdings, in which case the ownership, though not the privileges, followed the ordinary laws of inheritance. Even the embedsmænd, law officers and sheriffs of the ridings, became loan nobles in the absence of cash with which to pay them.

III

The system corresponded exactly to the current national needs, and under Valdemar the Victorious it enjoyed a sensational success. In the reigns of his weak successors of the disintegration, gaps began to appear. As an incitement to ambition, one of the privileges of the hærmænd was that of buying as much land as they were able, which lands were tax-free while held by them, although they fell under the ordinary rule of heredity. Ambitious vassals sought by every means to convert their purchased holdings into the straight hereditary feudal tenures so familiar in neighboring Germany, and some of them found it possible to persuade a feeble king to make a hærmand's privileges hereditary in their families. A century later the hærmænd had become *herremænd*, and the attached obligation to military service was being lost to sight.

In addition there was trouble with the Church. The bishops were very unwilling to furnish hærmand service for lands granted to them by the crown, or even to permit the bonders on these estates to render the ordinary militia service. They waged a struggle against both which convulsed the whole century, and at the same time put out estates on army loans of their own, whose churchly soldiers owed no obligation to the king. The see of Roskilde at one time had no less than forty-three such appanages, which gave a very respectable little private army to the bishop, considering that the forty-three represented something like three times as many full-armed sergeants, besides the usual quota of foot spearmen and bonders with arbalests.

Upon the whole, however, the disruptive tendencies were pretty well held in check by the laws of King Valdemar until the German grafs began to gain a foothold in Denmark through pawn-loans and other devices. To them, the sovereignties they had obtained represented full control in the normal German and feudal sense. They were lords of the high justice, the middle and the low; all the persons on their estates owed them obligations which went with the land; the laws of King Valdemar were so much parchment nonsense that would not stand up against the steel of men-at-arms; and they recognized no appeal, no higher jurisdiction than that of an overlord to whom they themselves owed homage. Since King Kristoffer had been whipped from the courtyard of Johann the Mild, there had been no overlord in Denmark.

What's to be done, then, by the Danish yeoman? Set up a new King Valdemar, restore the old laws and the old days, when no man had any wrong in all the lands he ruled.

5
Cambell and Triamond
(1340; 1157-1159)

THE SEAL WHICH KING VALDEMAR IV ATTERDAG AFFIXED
to his documents bore the legend "For Denmark's
Law," and it was carved in Lübeck. These are the key
facts of his crowning. To the majority he was Valdemar the
Bad, Kristoffer's son, who would bear careful watching, but at
least he was a Dane, who knew what the laws of King Valdemar were, and he had given a promise to uphold them. It
was the only Haandfæstning to which he consented, though
more was asked, and the acceptance of these few words with
the legend on the seal is the measure of the estates' desperation. Even this much had only been obtained by Bishop
Sveyn of Aarhus in the days of the Spandau conference, when
all calculations were overthrown by news from the north.

After Kristoffer's death there had been no longer any king
in Denmark, nor restraint of law or custom on the Holsteins.
They built castles to hold down the realm—Aalholm and
Ravnsborg in Laaland, Hindsgavl in Fyn—and set up again
those that had been torn down by Kristoffer—Riberhus, Koldinghus, Skanderborg. Ludvig Albrektsen's family lost the
semi-regal rights of their father, which fell to Graf Gerhard;
and the Protector of Denmark, having decided that there was
nothing against which Danes needed protecting so much as
against each other, squeezed Lord Laurids Jonssen out of his
continental holdings, back into Langeland. The Bishop of

Slesvig he persuaded to resign; Gerhard's younger brother was elected to the see. "The grafs and their servants took all objects of worth, all jewels and everything that was good to look at, and carried them off to a foreign land—" not robbing bonders only, but the best-born in the realm.

The reaction was widespread, slow to develop and impossible to trace in detail—roving bands of the dispossessed throughout Jutland, with the highest names in Denmark to lead them. Graf Gerhard had never before encountered opposition on such a scale, but the solution he instantly worked out had a diabolic efficiency that is almost admirable. The first step was in diplomacy; he offered Blockhead Valdemar the whole of Jutland beyond Slesvig on pawn-loan for the extremely small sum of 43,000 silver marks (Gerhard held it for 100,000), 18,000 to be paid at once, Duke Valdemar making over his lordship of Slesvig as temporary security for the remainder.

It looked like an extremely good thing, opening to the young duke the dazzling prospect of being master of everything from the Eider to Skagen as soon as he paid off 25,000 marks, which he could easily do out of the taxes from North Jutland. The only inconvenience was that he did not have the 18,000 marks in hand for the down payment. No difficulty at all, replied Graf Gerhard, urbanely; the Duke was merely to let Holstein retain the Ribe and Kallø lordships of North Jutland until the 18,000 were paid.

The Graf's estimate of Blockhead Valdemar's intelligence was low and approximately correct; the Duke was about to sign when he received a visit from Jakob Splitaf, Bishop of Ribe, who had his own reasons for disliking Holsteins in the heavy new taxes that had been laid on church property. The episcopal father pointed out that Gerhard would be getting a neatly unified realm which marched with his ancestral lands, while in North Jutland the Duke would gain nothing but the privilege of putting down a revolution. Moreover, there was little chance of raising money in the uproarious north country, while the easily obtained Slesvig revenues would fill Gerhard's coffers. Blockhead Valdemar flew into a towering rage, not only refusing Gerhard's offer, but also declaring himself the Graf's enemy; attacked, and was beaten off from the castle at Ribe.

It is possible that this was exactly what Gerhard desired as a viable alternative to having the Slesviger pull his North Jutland chestnuts out of the fire. The extraordinary money-tax "for defense of the land" had already been mostly collected, Gerhard counting on the slow reaction-time of popular resentment to enable him to make the Jutlanders pay for their own suppression. As soon as this was done, he doubtless expected to use the army provided by the tax income to eliminate the Duke who, like King Kristoffer, Albrektsen and Jonssen before him, had passed his usefulness. Even while Blockhead Valdemar was considering his former guardian's generous proposal, Holstein recruiting sergeants were out all over north Germany, offering the highest wages ever heard of for men-at-arms. When spring broke, the great Graf appeared at Kolding with an army said to be eleven thousand strong, and probably in fact not much short of that. It was an enormous force for the time and place, though not too many for what Gerhard proposed to do, which was to establish so complete a reign of terror that no one would ever again dare to oppose the name of Holstein.

The band of desperadoes trailed through the fresh countryside in closely supporting columns. Whenever they came to a building of any kind, they burned it; all portable property was carried away; peasants, bonders and herremænd were driven into the woods in common misery, and the land was partitioned out among Gerhard's followers, for he was resolved that no Dane should ever again own anything he could not carry on his back. They were too independent, they insisted upon following leaders of their own choice instead of those who held feudal rights over them.

The Spandau conference was held under the shadow of this campaign. Very likely the assembled notabilities counted on no more than providing Denmark with a shadow-king who could legalize Gerhard's conquests; the Graf's power was beyond challenge, he was friendly to the conference and sent his two sons to attend. The news that made all this foolish was the news of what happened on All Fools' Day.

It was a Saturday night when Gerhard's main column reached Randers and filled up most of the houses. The new moon set early and it became very dark, under which murk a little group of men, with hoods shadowing their faces against the chilly spring air, came along the main street in no particular order. Replying "The Graf's guard" when questioned as to identity, they gathered in a little stone house opposite that where Gerhard was sleeping. At midnight a light was struck behind his second-story window; the Graf rose as usual to confer with his chaplain-writer on letters and orders for the coming day. The business was just finished, the Protector of Denmark was undressing to resume his sleep, when feet sounded on the stairs. He flung open the door to shout his anger and recognized the long, mournful face and straggling beard of a man he had dispossessed, the Danish hedge-knight, Niels Ebbessen. There was just time to reach the window for one shout of "Help!" before steel caught the great man in the back, and as he whirled beneath the burning blow, another blade took off his head against the bedpost. The shout brought Holsteins tumbling forth with hastily seized weapons, but before they could unite or find a purpose, drums were beat through the streets, thatch began to burn everywhere, one or two of the German knights were cut down, there was no one to lead and the "men of Randers" slipped out into the black mists across a narrow bridge between marshes and were free, the bridge broken behind.

Too late Graf Gerhard had learned that fear is a wild dog which bites the hand that feeds it.

This was the news that came down to Spandau, dismaying the Gerhardssons, Heinrich and Nicholas. The former was to call himself "Iron-hard Heinrich" and make good that name under Crécy's dark mill at the side of the Black Prince of England; but in Spandau he was in no position to be hard about anything. Gerhard's constable had the bad luck to be one of those who stood before Niels Ebbessen's blades at Randers. There was no one to lead the largest army in north Europe; with the incontinence that only a thoroughly mercenary force can show, it broke up and went home in fragments with its booty. The Gerhardssons were left with an aroused countryside and an inimical Duke of Slesvig on their hands and no money to put Humpty-Dumpty together again.

Nevertheless, their assets, in the form of the North Jutland castles, the connection with Johann the Mild, and Prince Otto in pickle in one of their dungeons, were not small. The situation called for an agreement, and one was made; Otto to be released and to renounce all claim to the crown, Valdemar Atterdag to be king and to marry the Gerhardssons' sister Rixa, but to outlaw the men of Randers.

It left the new king little more than the shadow he would have been under Gerhard, and without according anything of real value, secured royal support for the suppression of the Jutland revolt. However, the Holsteins had neglected to take the Hansa into consideration, a fact of which they were sharply reminded when the king-to-be reached Lübeck on his way north. As usual we do not know precisely what pressures the financiers brought to bear, but they made it thoroughly clear that they would not tolerate the freezing into permanence of an arrangement which rendered Slesvig as well as North Jutland unsafe for commerce and the obligations of contract. The city men called another conference and summoned to it not only Valdemar Dosmer and the Danish bishops, but also a whole little senate of north German princes, whose position and force made them capable of throwing intolerable weight on Holstein. The Spandau agreement was torn up; in its place a new one was written, of an entirely different character.

Under it, Junker Valdemar dropped Rixa and married his namesake's sister, Helvig of Slesvig, who brought him in dower Aalborg castle and district of North Jutland, with 24,000 silver marks cash. The exchange arrangement which Gerhard had tried to palm off on Duke Valdemar of Slesvig was revived, but with major changes. Slesvig pawned his inherited lands to the sons of Gerhard, receiving North Jutland instead, but paying nothing. King Valdemar would owe him 42,000 marks for the province, which was split into the four districts of Kallø, Horsens, Kolding and Ribe. As soon as the accumulated taxes from all North Jutland amounted to a quarter of the 42,000 one of these districts would fall to the King, free and clear, and so on till all was paid and liberated. But in the meantime the taxes from Slesvig passed to the Gerhardssons as holders in pawn, until Valdemar Dosmer laid down the full sum due. Prince Otto was to be released as before, and bury himself in the Teutonic Order of Knights.

On the face of it, it looked as though Slesvig had made a very bad bargain, and so he had. The explanation is partly that he was as much of a blockhead as his name, partly that he was glad to buy himself out of the war with the Holsteins, to which they could now give their undivided attention, partly that he had no money at all and was forced to raise cash by any means the Hansa proposed. As for the moneyed gentlemen of the cities, they believed they had achieved peace in Jutland by substituting Slesvig for Holstein there, yet left the Holsteiners reasonably happy. For their pains, they received a charter giving them wider control of the Skaane herring market. As the assembled lordly heads left their city, they could congratulate themselves on having found a very useful instrument. If they did so, it was the greatest mistake they ever made.

III

Among those lordly heads there should have been the old duke of a modest, but well-knit principality, Albrecht of Saxe-Lauenburg. For some reason he did not come, but instead sent his son, the young duke, Erich. He lies under the shadow of the years, almost invisible; we only know of him that when his eyes looked into Valdemar's, there occurred one of those mysterious reactions of spiritual chemistry and they were friends, like the two knights on a single horse with whom the Templars symbolized brotherhood. At one point when it seemed that the negotiation must fail before Heinrich Gerhardsson's obstinacy, young Erich leaped to his feet with the cry that Saxe-Lauenburg's riders would follow the Dannebrog to death or glory at Valdemar's word. It was pure friendship, pure chivalry; for though Holstein was a neighbor to Saxe-Lauenburg, the former's ambitions lay all to the north, the latter's southward; there was no line of friction.

A small matter perhaps, with the Hansa and so many others applying pressure to make the Gerhardssons swallow the agreement down; yet for Junker Valdemar, not small. He had found his friend; the symbols were running true, the form was preserved of those ancient days when Valdemar the Great was king.

Or something more than form. The first Valdemar was somewhat less self-forwardly than the earlier Skjoldungs. "No man can rule alone," was a word often on his lips; he made Absalon, who was Axel, his first minister and stay in all things. This was after the several guilds of priests at Roskilde had met in bloody fights, being unable to choose a bishop. King Valdemar bade them that instead of each speaking in open conclave for whom he would elect, the name of the man best qualified should be silently written down. It was done as he wished; the name "Absalon" was found on every ballot, and he was declared bishop in spite of his uncanonical age.

There was little strange in such a choice, since Absalon was lately returned from the university in Paris, with a reputation for learning and piety beyond any in the north. It was thought that he would at once turn to the rebuilding of the church, burned in the civil wars; but Bishop Absalon rather let God's house stand in ruins while he rode to and fro in the countryside, rallying all men to fight the pagan Wends. There is a strange spirit in Denmark. It will lie so supine one might take it for dead, make no effort even to preserve itself, till it hears a Word; then burst forth like a volcanic eruption, defy all the devils hell ever spawned, deploy reserves not of will and courage only, but of mind and heart. King Valdemar called on that spirit; Absalon spoke his Word.

At this time the old Things of Sjælland had been almost given up under the raids of the Wends, who had laid waste a third of the realm. Absalon rode from door to door, calling all men to attend in arms, himself the King's only embedsmand. On a day when there were only eighteen people with him, a bonder came flying to say two dozen ships of the pagans were at the shore. The bishop rode to do battle with them; for shame's sake the eighteen could not but follow and they won an incredible victory.

Heads were lifted at these tidings; it would be in the next year that the Word was given, ever afterward famous as the answer of Absalon. King Valdemar gathered his people in their ships at the island Mesned under the shadow of Vordingborg to turn round on the Wends some of their own harryings. Men said that the pagans were forewarned and had assembled a great host. There was a shortage of provision; this was wrong and the other, until at last the King said the expedition should be broken up. Absalon rowed through the fleet to seek a reason. "We are going home so that many brave men shall not lose their lives," said the King, not without irony.

"Let us try a campaign with the cowards, then," shouted Absalon. "If we fail, there is little loss, and if we win, a gain."

Denmark woke at that word, and poured forth the flood of fighting men who chopped the unpronounceable seven-headed god of the Wends to firewood, but Absalon was more than a warrior merely. After the Danes had marched from side to side of their great island center at Rügen, it was Absalon who let build stately churches in all the lands they had once ravaged. It was Absalon who set up the castle by Amager Isle, built the town beneath it and made an ordinance that it should be a traders' town forever—Copenhagen, harbor of the merchants. It was Absalon who said there should be one church law in all Denmark and wrote it himself—and alas, it was Absalon who provoked the men of Skaane to stand forth in arms when he tried to collect the tithes.

They were perfectly indifferent to his plea that tithes were the law of all Christendom. It was not Skaane law, they said, and drove the warrior-bishop from the province. King Valdemar himself had to cross the Sound with a great host to make a compromise; a thing he did well, for though Valdemar the Great bore a reputation for angers which he had earned by many deeds, the fierce fit ran off him early, and he could persuade so well that it was said he could talk fish out of the streams. The drive of the Skjoldungs was somewhat muted in him, as though the long association with Absalon (whose fires burned even redder than his own) had changed it to something more subtle and meditative. In anger he was a notably few-spoken man and became as time went on still less the friend of many words. It was as though he abandoned his personal style to his minister and friend, himself taking another part of the common intellectual store.

IV

There was no chance that Valdemar IV Atterdag could make such a companion of the young Saxe-Lauenburg duke, who was not only a German, but one fairly deep in his own business. Nor was there another Absalon among the bishops who did so much to bring him to the crown. Lund was Archbishop of Denmark, but his personal see was in Sweden by virtue of the falling off of the Skaane provinces, and he was so deep in economic troubles that he could not even pay the usual fee to the papal Curia for his confirmation; besides, he disapproved of churchmen in armor. Roskilde detested the Holsteins, but his mind did not work along political lines. Aarhus and Ribe were invincibly patriotic, but they were Jutlanders, a region with which Valdemar was particularly anxious to avoid any overt connection for the present, since the situation there had become as intricate as a schoolman's argument.

Under the Lübeck agreement, North Jutland would fall in to the crown if Valdemar only let the province alone to buy itself out of pawn; but a considerable number of Jutlanders were unwilling to wait for the fruition of the process. They had been dispossessed, they had arms in their hands and no means of livelihood but those arms while Holsteiners sat in the castles. The great ogre was dead, and the little ones did not look so formidable; they kept right on waylaying convoys and attacking steads, with Niels Ebbessen at their head, calling himself by the amorphous title of "Leader" in the King's name.

He caught a batch of the Germans setting up a new castle at Stjernaa, cut off their heads and tore down its half-made walls, a considerable victory. Yet however he represented a national uprising, however he led the only Danish military force, Valdemar was required to avoid him. To strike hands with the men of Randers would be a breach of the Spandau

agreement; and though Lübeck might be considered to have
superseded Spandau, Ironhard Heinrich (who so loved fighting) was quite capable of taking the opposite view, declaring
Valdemar deposed and himself hereditary Protector of Denmark.

Valdemar Atterdag's ride to Randers was thus no such echo
of Valdemar the Great as his coronation had been, but an escape from the men of Randers. The town was a seaport in
those days; Valdemar took ship to Sjælland and was almost
lost to sight for half a year, only dimly visible as he is crowned
at Helsingborg among carolling choristers, with his new queen
by his side, or as he makes a treaty with King Magnus of
Sweden. Or (most striking of all) appears at a little Thing
court as his own embedsmand, pleading a case of vandalism
on church property against a bonder named Peder Yels, and
when the Nævninger have rendered their verdict of a four-
mark fine against the said Peder, claims the embedsmand's
due share of the fine, no more.

"For Denmark's Law." The things that the young King
had to do were hard; they would cut to the heart of every
Dane, like the loss of Esthonia, and strike at his life, like the
visits of the Holstein panzenars. In only one way could he
make them bear the burden, and that was to make it clear
that the Laws of King Valdemar had come again, that no
Haandfæstning was needed from a ruler under law, who
pleaded cases in the common courts like one of his subjects,
whose documents were not in the Latin of the shabby-splen-
did monarchs before him, but in honest Danish; who on the
day of the Holy Three Kings, gave out an amnesty for all
deeds done before his coronation.

This was the new administration at a low level. For the
reign to demonstrate progress beyond the last, it was necessary to show Denmark's land was returning to Denmark. The
chances of success were regarded with skepticism—"All they
did at Viborg was to praise the forgiveness of sins and hymn
the glories of the past," said the contemporary chronicler,

who was inclined to look upon the evacuation to Sjælland as a flight.

It would be an error to suggest that Valdemar went thither out of a strategical sense, because the island was the heart and communications-center of the realm; or even because the island held Copenhagen, the one big merchant town not a member of the Hansa, and therefore a probable great source of revenue. The question of the Copenhagen revenues was not to be solved for years; and it is most unlikely that the young King thought of Sjælland in terms of strategic location at the time. To say that he did so would be as egregious an anachronism as discussing his views on nuclear fission. The sense of geography, so familiar to us, was almost completely lacking from the medieval mind, like the sense of daily time. Maps existed only in the form of fanciful pictorial representations of the world. The normal location of a place was that it lay so many days' journey in a given direction from X. No account whatever was taken of intervening territorial holdings or relationships.

Sjælland was chosen merely because it was the area in which Valdemar could operate with the fairest chance of early and showy achievement. Its local arrangements were the most favorable, since all the castles held by Germans were around the coast—Vordingborg, Næstved, Taarnborg over Korsør, Kallundborg, Helsingør—leaving in the center considerable areas that could be brought under the old law without too much interference from the enemy, and with the active assistance of the Hansa, which wished to push its caravans into the interior market towns. Graf Johann the Mild, who held most of the island in pawn, had converted it into a kind of tax-garden, in the hands of his sub-pawnholders, and did not seem to care what happened as long as the remittances arrived on time. Moreover, friend Erich of Saxe-Lauenburg was of much avail; he seems to have told Johann that if the latter proceeded to rough measures against the King's peace, he would have Saxe-Lauenburg riders over his border.

This was, in fact, the key of Valdemar's first half year—
that, altogether unique among medieval kings, he wanted to
keep the peace; achieved at the first breath the realization
that he could not afford rough measures. The Gerhardssons
felt they had been diddled at Lübeck and made no bones
about saying so. They were extremely bitter about events in
Jutland, they liked fighting because it was fun, and they
deluged Valdemar with complaints about the support they
said he was giving to Niels Ebbessen. Magnus of Sweden
thought Denmark was finished (he said so) and was desirous
of having an army in the field against the last Danish king
when the breakup occurred, so that he could claim a better
share of the spoils.

Valdemar himself had no such powerful army of helmeted
men as those who followed these lords, and could not even
count on the support of the bonders until he had convinced
them that he was not another King Kristoffer. The half year
was thus a period of double demonstration—to Magnus,
Johann, and the Gerhardssons that the new rule did not con-
stitute a menace to them; and to the bonders and herremænd
of Sjælland that he did. The Gerhardssons were temporarily
pacified with a new hold on Fyn; it was to fall to them in
full hereditary possession in the event of Valdemar's death.
Magnus was nearer, had fewer distractions, and drove a
sharper bargain. Valdemar had to agree that Skaane and Blekinge provinces were Sweden's forever in exchange for eight
thousand marks of silver.

The documents of this last agreement were never sealed,
the money never passed. Why? It could be that Magnus was
short on funds at the moment and Valdemar refused to do
business on any but a cash basis. So great a sacrifice could only
be made for immediate hard money, with which to hire
armed men and to lift some of the pawn-held castles before
their holders died and the pawns slipped into hereditary possession, which all medieval titles tended to do. More likely—
since both Peder of Lund and Johann of Roskilde were at

the meeting of the two kings—the bishops prevented Valdemar from completing an arrangement so unfavorable to them. Lund was primate of Denmark, but with his see permanently located in Sweden, he was not likely to remain so, and if he were eliminated the archbishopric would fall to Odensee, who was under the tight Holstein domination of Fyn.

The agreement was not sealed, then. Instead Roskilde gave the gold and silver vessels of his church to Valdemar, with the income from the tithes of the islands of Møn and Rügen, which lay in his bishopric. He did more; with the treasury of his church he purchased from the Hansa the pawns on the island fortress at Copenhagen and the castle at the city gate, turning both over to the King. The money would have to be repaid, of course; but to pay it Valdemar now had the regular tariffs of a merchant town where Hansa writs did not run, and the income from the hinterland in its rear.

Inner Sjælland turned from summer to the most peaceful autumn it had known in years, with King Valdemar riding from harvest-Thing to harvest-Thing, pleading cases in his own courts. Over in Jutland it was not so; few crops were reaped and those with the sword, the fire was on the thatch and the wolves came out of the forest to gather round Skanderborg castle, the key of central Jutland, on its island in a lake. There were four thousand of them at Niels Ebbessen's back (say chroniclers not noted for accuracy), certainly enough to make things look less than well for Marchwarden Rastorf, who held the place in the Gerhardssons' name. The attackers had no siege-enginery, but by mere blockade had brought the castle near surrender, when a messenger swam the lake by night and cloud, carrying word to the Holstein lords in Fyn. Iron Heinrich set out at once with six hundred mailed sergeants on horseback; on All Souls' Day he reached the yeomen's encampment, and throughout that day fought against them in clanging battle, steel-clad charges against the stubborn bonders in their leather jackets, with Rastorf sallying to take them in the rear. There befell a great slaughter; for at twilight the Leader fell and his army broke up, back to its forests.

The Gerhardssons smashed his body on a wheel with hammers and threw the remains into the lake; and so in uproar passed the last of the moving figures of the Time of Uproar. Esgers Juel, Kristoffer the king, Prince Erik, Graf Gerhard, Marshal Ludvig Albrektsen, Duke Porse, Drost Laurids Jonssen, who died in bed during the summer—nothing left of them now but names, all dead, down and drowned in the soundless sea of time.

6

Failure (1341)

N O ONE WAS EVER ABLE TO DETECT IN VALDEMAR AT-
terdag that medieval exhibitionism which made Edward of England order the burghers of Calais to wait
on him with ropes around their necks, notwithstanding the
fervor with which the young King addressed himself to the
task of obtaining a royal residence. He traveled so much and
so rapidly (there are two journeys down into Germany during
the first six months alone) that such a seat would have been
of practical value chiefly as a place of deposit for archives
and treasury and a headquarters for an administrative staff.
At this time there was nothing to treasure, very little to ad-
minister beyond a military force which was only a bodyguard,
and Roskilde Cathedral normally kept the archives, so that
a capital would seem to have only theatrical importance. Yet
all Valdemar's efforts after the coronation were concentrated
round the redemption of such a place, and the reasons were
cogent.

In the first place, it was required of him to drive home by
demonstration within the medieval sense of form that he was
the son of the Valdemars rather than of the unlamented Kristoffer, who had lived in so peripatetic a state. In the second
some place of security for the King's person was needed
against flashes of covetousness or temper on the part of the
Gerhardssons, Graf Johann the Mild, or Magnus of Sweden,
who had such powerful forces at their disposal. An instructive
lesson on this point was furnished at carnival-time, when the

Gerhardssons found Blockhead Valdemar on a road without a keeper, threw him into prison and made him pay a stiff ransom—for no other reason than that he was available. Third and most important, if the new reign were to attract widespread support it needed an area where the potency of its measures could be demonstrated. Inner Sjælland would serve very well, but without the cover of a strong castle any material gains would be subject to piracies from the holds remaining in Holstein hands. Now of all castles in the realm, none was more to be desired than Vordingborg. Not only was it a great triple fortress of massive walls and lordly spires; not only was it the gatewarden of the isles by its position and the fine harbor where a fleet might lie; but to it and from it also flowed all the glories of the giant past. Here Valdemar the Great set forth against the Wends into a wild storm, after that the answer of Absalon had been given, saying: "Better to sink famously than live and see our land abused." Here Valdemar the Victorious mustered his crusaders for the east, and here they returned in their battered armor with the Dannebrog borne before. Here were the laws of Denmark given. Second only to Vordingborg was Kallundborg, the guard of the north as Vordingborg is of the south; triple-walled as the other was triple-builded; set on a long tongue of land, the outlook to Jutland.

Johann the Mild held first mortgages on both castles—a man always glad to accommodate. He accepted a stiff down payment on Vordingborg with a proviso that the remainder should be due in one year's time. The Kallundborg situation was more intricate; it is probable that Valdemar would not have bothered with it at all but for pressure from his partners of Church and Hansa. Graf Johann had sub-pawned the place to Duke Porse, who installed a Holstein captain named Hein Brockdorf as his warden. When the Duke died, this bravo took the castle and pledge for himself, but Porse's widow was the dowager Queen of Sweden, and neither she nor King Magnus considered her claim extinguished, while Marchwarden Brockdorf owed more on the pledge than he could possibly pay. He and Magnus accordingly reached an agreement for the division of piracy rights; Swedish soldiers began to collect "taxes" in every part of Sjælland that could possibly be considered adjunct to the castle, while Magnus, who as holder of the Skaane provinces, had the duty of policing the Sound, looked the other way when Brockdorf levied on ships passing through.

The marine side of this business was so very profitable that it cost the Hansa of Greifswald, smallest of the five Wend towns, six thousand marks in the year before Valdemar came to Sjælland. It is not hard to deduce that the city men told the young King that whatever his personal preference for Vordingborg might be, he had better get Brockdorf out of Kallundborg if he wished to stay in their good graces. Accordingly he split whatever money he had (including that from the Roskilde church plate) between the two castles. It was not enough to meet the two down payments due, and though Copenhagen city might be the most valuable of all in the long run, the immediate need was for the castles. Valdemar re-pledged his city to a certain Holstein Marchwarden Stove of Næstved Castle, made his payments and dropped out of major politics to let things ripen.

At this point it is possible, for the only time in his story, to detect a certain naïveté in the young King—perhaps that of his twenty-one years and association with the gentle Archbishop of Lund, perhaps something else, to which we have few clues. To medieval thought, character, as we use the term to indicate a consistent pattern of judgment and ethic which explains a man's actions, did not exist. It was believed that the differences among individuals were produced by the state or status into which they were born, and identical performances were expected from everyone in the same circumstances, unless they happened to be yielding to temptation or to have attained a state of peculiar grace. If we want to know anything about what drove people of that time to do things, we must infer from what they did.

It is a fair inference from Valdemar IV Atterdag's behavior in the first year of his reign that he believed the old times had gone down into the dark with Gerhard and Niels Ebbessen and the morning of another day was really come. His conduct toward Magnus and the Gerhardssons indicates the belief that he could obtain fair for fair. Denmark's law was painstakingly observed; so was the amnesty. It would have been quite easy for him to pay the debt on Vordingborg by clapping taxes on the bonders or by a series of confiscations on landholders who had chosen the wrong side during the Time of Uproar; but he did nothing of the kind.

If this were only intelligent self-interest, there was at least not much difference at the receiving end of the policy; but there is evidence that a good deal more than self-interest was involved. Down at that shaky Imperial court where Valdemar spent most of the fourteen years after King Kristoffer carried his sons off to Rostock, there had been a certain Marsilio, called "of Padua." An exception among schoolmen, in that he had been drinking the heady wine of Aristotle, and in the bottom of the cup had found the jewel of the secular state— not merely a state which formed the doorway between fleshly and mystic life, as in St. Thomas, but an end in itself, the highest form of human relationship. "The government will understand," said this Marsilio, "that only to itself belongs the authority to restrain each person according to the established laws, and to do nothing unauthorized by them without the consent of the subject population, or lawgiver."

Thus spoke: and was heard by Junker Valdemar, for as philosopher before the Wittelsbachs, and verbal hammer for Ludwig the Bavarian against the irreconcilable Pope, Marsilio would have the subsidiary duty of gardener to the tender green shoots of nobility springing up among the meretricious Imperial splendors. His Holiness denounced such doctrine as heretical, for although this particular Holiness had canonized the angelic Doctor Aquinas, he made a point of doing it in a manner which demonstrated that Aristotelians were desirable characters only as long as they let politics alone and stuck to the philosophic proofs of the existence of God and His connection with the human soul.

It is not likely that Junker Valdemar concerned himself with the doctrinal points, still being at an age which did not qualify him for the judicial duel. But somewhere along the road that led to Viborg height, he quite clearly made a discovery: Heresy? Philosophy? Why, this is Denmark's law! In our country truth-men and named-men may stand forth against the King himself to speak the law the Things have made, and if the King (who is only the executive of the lawgiving body, as Marsilio says) persists, then we unking him, as Kristoffer, my father.

Marsilio's doctrine, then, is an exposition and systematization of the laws by which Danes live, a touchstone for their kings and councillors. As a source of Valdemar's naïveté, it is important to note that Marsilio was a Christian philosopher; that is, the observation of his principles led straight to ineffable harmony and perfect peace. So, on the mundane plane, did Denmark's law. It was in response to that law, to the supremacy of the lawmaking body, that Valdemar the Great had turned back from Mesned, when the answer of Absalon was spoken—at the time in anger and tribulation, but the later fruit was joy and glory through all his years and those of his son, Knud VI, with the name of Denmark made terrible around the Baltic shores. In defiance of that law and that philosophy the black Skjoldungs had gone down in inharmonious strife—Sveyn Peder, for example; Abel, who was called Cain as murderer of his brother, the unlamented Kristoffer.

The ideological thus reinforced the practical in urging upon young King Valdemar the most exquisite observance of his engagements; and in all probability, led him to believe that this observance would effectively solve his troubles. For a year he remained in inner Sjælland, doing exactly what the contract called for, making no trouble for anybody.

So rolled the seasons to their beginning, and there were tidings, for the Sjælland taxes were insufficient to provide for the final payments due on the two castles. A messenger from Johann the Mild declared that since the Vordingborg debt had not been discharged on the date due, all monies thus far laid down were forfeit, the lifting of the debt must begin again from the bottom. Hein Brockdorf of Kallundborg said the same, but being a somewhat more pushing man, sent war parties through the Sjælland villages to take by confiscation what he had missed having in cash.

II

To all appearances the young King was now considerably lower than when he had been crowned in brass. Copenhagen was pledged again, all his money was gone, his rule in Sjælland still lacked a fulcrum, and he had been made to look like a particularly dewy chick. But to other powers and principalities this was somewhat less important than the fact that the Marchwarden of Kallundborg emerged as a dangerous villain who lacked the family connections for licensed looting, and who violated union rules by bearing harder than necessary on Hanseatic commerce. The inspiration for the flash league against him undoubtedly came from the five Wend towns, for Lübeck furnished the ships to the combination, and Lord Albrecht of Mecklenburg, Prince in Wendland, furnished at least a token force of men-at-arms. So did Johann the Mild, apparently not unwilling to see the elimination from a castle on which he held reversionary rights of a man who was sliding from him toward Sweden and might easily become independent of both.

Yet the bulk of the force that moved warlike up through the Sjælland ways toward Kallundborg while beech and larch

were bursting bud was Valdemar's own. At its core was a handful of helmeted men," mercenaries out of Germany; around
them the levy of the Danes, summoned according to ancient
custom by sending the war-arrow through the Things. It was
a small host, how different from the days when Sveyn Double-
beard could call forth men enough for the conquest of warlike
England, or Valdemar the Victorious raise an army for the
only truly successful crusade; and its people have mostly gone
down the dark stream, but a few names are still with us.

Item: Peder Vendelbo, whom Valdemar has made his
Drost; a man much stricken in years, who was thought no
worse than the best in all that had to do with war. In King
Kristoffer's day he led a blazing battle at the castle of Hammershus in Bornholm, storming that hold across its battle-
ments after a struggle that went on all day, through the night
and to the second dawn. But since that time he had lived in
eclipse, for he held Kristoffer no honest man's master and
would not serve Holstein or Sweden.

Item: Erik Nielsen of the great house of the Gyldenstjerne,
who bear the golden star of their name—one of the hatchet-
faced Danes, tall and hollow-cheeked; a strange man, very
warrior in appearance, but living so much a life of his own
within the iron shell that it was reported he had been taught
the Black Art by wizards out of Finland.

Item: Stig Anderssen of Bornholm, from a family that had
given more than one marshal to the realm. His seal bore the
simple legend "Stig Anderssen—Soldier," his whole nature
was compressed in that designation, for he dwelt in an orderly
world where all took orders gladly—the people from the King,
the King from the law; no doubts in him at all. He led the
Jutland revolt in the days when King Kristoffer broke his
Haandfæstning, for the King stood then against the law;
served Graf Gerhard when his will was the only law in the
land, but when Valdemar was crowned, came to serve him at
once, since such service was Law; and by that service expected
to gain, for it was lawful that the laborer be paid his hire.

Item: Bo Falk, a Sjælland man who might have been from Provence, for he stepped daintily, danced, sang gestes like a minstrel, bore his lady's favor and would set up his shield at a ford to run spears all day long; a perfect gentle knight, "who from the moment when he first began to ride about the world loved chivalrie"; had journeyed through Germany with harp and lance and sung for the crown of bay on Wartburg height; did his chivalric duty to the Skjoldungs in the days of Prince Otto's fall and even followed that lord to his dungeon.

With these four came the blockhead Duke of Slesvig and the armored bishop of Aarhus in the first war-levy under the young King's golden lions. There are these things to remark— that Valdemar has surrounded himself with older men; that Vendelbo, Stig Anderssen and Bo Falk would not have been there at all, had not the march been one to battle; and that not another prince in Europe would have led to war a host so poor in counts, earls, barons, that only Valdemar of Slesvig bore any title whatever.

At Kallundborg a long fjord thrusts between low shores, behind which gentle wooded hills roll up. A snub-nosed peninsula thrusts out from the northern flank of the fjord; on it stood in those days the castle, behind a deep moat cut across the peninsula, heavy brick walls along the water-edges, tall keep in the center. Ships from Lübeck would have been at the mouth of the fjord as the disorderly stream of men poured from under the forest-cover; ships not closing in because of engines on the high walls, which also covered the approaches to the moat. That channel was too wide, the central bailey was set too deep in, for attack by any siege-engines Valdemar could muster, and there were not enough bowmen to keep the garrison under cover while the gap was bridged and a storm attempted. Therefore a light stockade was run across the peninsula as a protection against sallies, and the little army sat down to a blockade.

Through July they lay there under the conditions of a medieval siege, with a little quarreling, chaffering, and horseplay in the camp, a few trials at arbalest-shooting and the exchange of ribald remarks. The hours turned to August; brown sails rose out of the west beyond Valdemar's ships, at anchor in the fjord. A provision convoy from Lübeck was due; some of the besiegers would be hunting meat in the forest, others gathering toward the shore to see what new tidings there were or what new things the ships had brought. The brown sails were right among the anchored vessels when there was a blast of trumpets, a sudden bright flash of arms, the nettle-banner of Heinrich of Holstein broke to the breeze from all the new arrivals, and at the same moment Kallundborg drawbridge came down and an array of men-at-arms poured across it against the stockade.

Surprised, outnumbered, overborne, the Lübeck men on the ships made but the weakest defense; one after another they were cleared, while the Holstein vessels stood in under pillars of flame from their decks to throw waves of fighting men onto the beach where Valdemar, Vendelbo and Stig Anderssen were trying to rally their men at the shattering stockade. Taken from two sides, unready, their armor in their tents, the Danes gave way; were furiously rallied; gave way again under the double shock and dissolved back among the trees, a good third of them left behind.

Defeat, defeat; in the angry despair of his twenty-one years, Valdemar tried to gather men in the glades to make one effort more at storming Kallundborg out of hand or die under its walls. But the bonders would not follow, the mercenaries saw no pay, the old heads around the crown prevailed, and there was nothing to do but send in a herald and ask for peace.

Oh, certainly, we will give King Valdemar a peace (said Ironhard Heinrich); certainly, since the Church asks it. The conference was at Roskilde; truce in the war the King had unjustly made was granted until fourteen days before Michaelmas, which is the twenty-ninth of September, while a commission sat to decide all outstanding issues. The only condition was that Valdemar leave Sjælland and go to rule the hundred and twenty-five square miles of territory around Aalborg where he was unquestionably King.

7
Hermitage in Jutland
(1341; 1170; 1342)

BY EARLIER AND SUBSEQUENT STANDARDS MEDIEVAL BAT-
tles were both fumblingly conducted and crushingly
decisive. This was not true on the frontiers of Byzantium, to be sure, and it was particularly untrue in Italy, where
a developed art of war had arisen, with textbooks and free
discussion. But the Italian art of war, based on the exclusive
employment of mercenaries who had no convictions of their
own, was a kind of chess game, as formal and futile as a
Chinese tea ceremony. "In a rout celebrated all over Italy,
no one died save Ludovico degli Obizzi and two of his men,
who were thrown from their horses and smothered in a
muddy ditch." From the days when the Lacedaemonian
spearmen marched through the Long Walls of Athens, no
narrative is so filled with shock and incredulity as that of the
Milanese chroniclers who discovered that the French knights
lately come across the Alps did murder on the battlefield. "À
l'estoc!" cried those wild Gauls, and stabbed men in the arm-
pits instead of outmaneuvering them into surrender and profitable service under their captors.

The Italians lived in a land which had never quite forgotten
the traditions of the Empire and where Vegetius was still
read; the Frenchmen came from one which had altogether
lost the Roman military techniques, without developing any
of their own, save in the limited field of battle tactics. It was

not that military brains were lacking north of the Alps. This could hardly be said of a region that produced Richard Coeur de Lion, Bertrand Du Guesclin and Edward Longshanks, not to mention Valdemar Sejr. But the brains, however good, lacked background and apparatus.

A Roman commander of any period from the Punic Wars through Marcus Aurelius found at his disposal an elegantly staffed army, whose soldiers knew how to perform without orders every military task from building a camp to crossing a river in the face of artillery fire. Even the tactics were well standardized. Personal leadership was demanded only in a crisis, and Julius Caesar remained in his tent during one of his battles, conducting the entire engagement by correspondence.

Those Roman commanders were thus left free to concentrate on the larger forms; to think of grand tactics and to develop an art of strategy. They did develop such an art, one of the best proofs being the Roman system of roads and fortified posts, which have not yet lost their validity for the localities in which they lie.

The medieval leader not only lacked the geographical sense necessary for strategy but had no time to develop such a concept. He had to do his own staff and logistic work, a task so onerous that many campaigns, like those of Edward III in France, turned into hunts for victual. Moreover the lack of staffs and strategies was only half the story. There was also wanting any collection of recorded experience, except in the most generalized terms and on anything but the most elementary tactical level. The Roman texts—supposing them to have been widely read, which they were not—were valueless because of differences in weapons and training. The main body of a medieval army was made up of local material, different from every similar body. In the "infantry countries" the Scots and Swiss had pikemen, the English archers, and the Flemish towns billmen, but each type was exclusive to its own area, and a commander facing any of them for the first time was confronted with a novel and rather puzzling question.

Even in Italy, where they studied war, technical debate turned on the question of whether armored horsemen were best employed in heavy masses or in small bodies to give successive shocks. Until well after Poictiers, when some English condottieri drifted across the mountains, no Italian considered archers at all; there were no archers to consider. For the same reason, the Italians never thought of how they might use or defend against Spanish *jenetours*, Welsh dagsmen, or Norwegian axe-swingers.

The art of war had been so localized and specialized, and was so lacking in literary support, that a medieval commander had to re-create it for himself; find a way of answering problems for which there was no accepted solution. Some monumental errors were made in the process, as when Jean of France at Poictiers tried to avoid the error of Crécy by dismounting his armored men; and some reputations were gained by very simple things, as when Charles of Anjou became known as a military genius of a high order, because he held out a reserve at Tagliacozzo. But in general there was little thinking about large issues because so much thought had to be given to those more immediate.

The brilliant successes of Denmark during the century of the Valdemars were in no small degree due to the fact that these kings conducted overseas expeditions. Their logistic problems had to be completely solved before the expedition could begin, and a tactical combination of heavy cavalry with both light and heavy infantry was imposed by the inability of their ships to carry more than a few horses. Valdemar the Great, Knud VI, and Valdemar the Victorious thus had the use of combined arms thrust upon them and were forced by the conditions of their wars to spend time on questions which the average medieval leader was too busy to think about.

Valdemar IV Atterdag was by no means so fortunate, and not alone because his game was played on the home grounds.

· 101 ·

Carl A. Rudisill Library
LENOIR RHYNE COLLEGE

The armies of those earlier Valdemars were still studded with those gigantic axemen, sons of the Vikings, who "stood like a rampart of ice" and did not fear any cavalry the world ever saw, for they could hew off a horse's head. In the interval since their time, the armored knight had considerably improved his equipment, and since he had become a full-time laborer, his skill as well.

In the meantime Denmark had ceased to be an infantry country. As the bonder turned from a part-time Viking to a full-time farmer, his own skill with weapons had declined; no longer was the bright byrnie kept hanging between sax and axe on the wall. This individual military depression had been still further and very rapidly augmented during the Time of Uproar by Holstein and Hansa, the latter of whom preferred to sell luxury items instead of weapons and the former of whom did not wish the bonder to buy anything. At Skanderborg, Iron Heinrich's six hundred, plus the castle garrison, beat at least five times their number of bonders, while in the old wars the proportions had been so thoroughly reversed that the Persian word for Europe became the name of that little group of footmen who never could be ridden down—*Varangistan*, the land of the Varangian Guards. By our Valdemar's time, nothing of the old remained but its spirit; the physical condition of warfare in Denmark had homologated to that general in Europe.

II

One of the most striking aspects of that condition was that when a battle decided anything, it decided everything—a consequence of the system on which armies were organized and the method by which they were raised. The only skill that could be counted on as a constant in medieval war was that of the armored horseman, and he was the only soldier whose equipment was standard. It has become the fashion to disparage this very formidable individual, which is an error in pragmatism. Compared to his opposition, the armored horseman dominated the warfare of his age more thoroughly than any type of fighting man the world has seen.

A knight in panoply of battle presented to an opponent an armor-plated surface arranged in a series of parabolic curves which offered very little bite to any weapon. (The popularity of the mace, which could crush, as against pointed or edged tools, is one effect of this.) With lance in rest, equipment, horse and person formed a locked system which delivered at the point of impact almost exactly three times the punch of a modern military rifle-bullet.* Anything that point hit was transfixed or went down. Even after the knight lost his lance or his momentum, he could deliver from the stirrups a blow with sword, mace or gisarme that very few men were prepared to withstand.

Indeed, the qualities of the armored knight can be inferred from his defeats. The English beat him only by hitting him from the flank with missile-weapons as he charged. The Swiss beat him by catching him in a narrow alley between mountain and lake, where he had no room to charge. For all their drill and steadfastness, the pikemen of the mountains were to receive at Marignano a dreadful lesson in what happened when the gendarmerie had space to swing down on them. To sum it up, the armored horsemen forced infantry to make use of geography—the edge of a wood, a set of hills, a defile.

Yet this invincible and invulnerable rider was a very rare and expensive article. His horse alone, the big destrier he rode in battle, was worth 120 sheep or 10 oxen, and this takes no account of the lighter horses for ordinary occasions, his armor, or the hire of the various individuals who followed in his train. It took a long time for a knight to acquire the technique of handling his various weapons, and the men who did it were few. When the knightly levy of a nation became involved in such a disaster as Poictiers or Bannockburn or the March-

* The knight's relative speed was very low, but the prodigious mass more than made up for it.

feld, the war was over. There were no reserves to call up, no possibility of retrieving such a defeat for years to come. A new generation of master fighting men had to grow up, or to be found through ransom, alliance or hire. This was so well known that most medieval commanders who had good control over their men avoided the chance of battle until it could no longer be escaped, or until they had overwhelming superiority.

As soon as the Gerhardssons began to fight King Valdemar, therefore, they made the odds against him insuperable. There is no direct information on how many knights he could muster, but the total must have been very small, since neither the land-grant method of employing them nor that of hire for cash was open to him. He had to depend upon such loyal romantics as Bo Falk. The logical tactical answer was for the King to use his small force of panzenars and his somewhat larger one of armed bonders in incidented country, where the Holstein men-at-arms could not get at him without dismounting. But whether Valdemar had worked this idea out or not, he would have found it impossible to apply.

The restraining factor was the castles—the need to obtain possession of those castles which, as long as they were held by the rapacious Holsteiners, were an absolute bar to any recovery in Denmark, even to any normal life. If the loss of the down payments showed how far fair methods were likely to carry the King, the appearance of Heinrich before Kallundborg demonstrated that Valdemar would not be allowed to carry things through with the strong arm. Hein Brockdorf was an international outlaw. Heinrich of Holstein was not a party to any agreement, pawn or treaty regarding Kallundborg. His appearance there was the first invasion by Holstein-Rendsborg of those territories east of the Belts which had been assigned to the sphere of the Stormarn branch ever since Graf Gerhard had appeared as general of the Jutland league to drive out King Kristoffer. Heinrich had simply stepped in.

To make it perfectly clear why, it was that this time that the Graf assumed the title of "Iron-hard." Such an act was a royal prerogative in Denmark, an announcement that Heinrich was just one step from proclaiming himself king by right of conquest; an announcement, moreover, that any attempt on Valdemar's part to obtain possession of castles anywhere in the realm would be opposed by mailed horsemen under the Holstein banner.

III

Interlude—The Curious Castles of Denmark. It was the castle factor that rendered the odds against Valdemar insuperable—at least to such an extent that the Hansa withdrew its somewhat tepid support from the young man for the time being. In addition, Magnus of Sweden proclaimed that the priests of Roskilde bishopric were under his special protection, which was another left-handed method of claiming part of the heritage, since Roskilde bishopric included all Sjælland, with Møn and Rügen. If the young King could not attack castles without having to battle Holstein riders, he could not hold together any stable force whatever. He was reduced to the status of Niels Ebbessen, king of the thickets.

The special military problem of the Danish castles was closely wedded to Valdemar's general problem of returning Denmark to herself, and it is worth looking at the senior partner. Danish military architecture represents a special and virulent case of the fact that the means of defense had so outrun those of attack by the fourteenth century that siege operations had become next to impossible.

This was due basically to physical geography, which had produced in Denmark a system of castle-building different from every other. The normal medieval castle grew around a Norman keep, a tall stone building with sharp angles, which in the course of time acquired outer curtain walls and exterior protective structures. Unless this stone castle occupied the whole top of an eminence, like Carcassonne in southern France, there was a ditch outside the curtain wall. The struc-

· 105 ·

ture was set on rock to prevent mining and was usually placed on the highest piece of ground available to dominate assault by wooden towers. Preferably it was where it covered a main highroad. The keep was always set against one of the outer walls, so that if a portion of this curtain were taken it might not serve as a cover for operations against that central bailey. The strength against battering-rams was the thickness of the wall.

Now none of the conditions which brought forth this structure were present in Denmark, save in the island of Bornholm, where Hammershus was a typical keep-and-curtain-wall castle. There were no rocky heights; there was no stone for construction except soft sandstone; and all the more important traffic went by water, so there were few roads to be dominated. Moreover, the back history of defended places in Denmark was not the same as elsewhere. In that country they had grown up less as coigns of refuge from land raiders than as offensive stockaded bases, with easy access to water across which raids might be conducted, like the strong points the Northmen set up along the shores and rivers of England. Defended places in Denmark were lived in all year round; required more space; were more civilized.

The upshot of this was that from the very beginning, the castle-builders of the realm used water instead of stone as the main defense, and made their structures extensive in groundplan, with numerous interior buildings which could serve both as living quarters and separate strong points in case of an irruption through the outer wall. The material of towers and walls being necessarily brick or sandstone, it was important to keep catapults, rams and movable towers at a distance. Therefore the site was so chosen to present a margin of water or soggy ground out beyond the curtain wall to beyond the limit range of such siege engines—say five or six hundred yards. Thus Silkeborg and Skanderborg are on islands in lakes; Kleitrup, Kallundborg, and Vordingborg on peninsulas jutting from seabeaches; Borningholm and Gunderslevsholm in the midst of marshes.

Construction began with a corduroy causeway of logs, covered with earth. The castle was then traced out, and along the line to be occupied by the curtain walls and central towers (none of which towers was ever against the outer guard), huge piles were driven, made of the trunks of the largest trees available. All over the inner ground small piles went in, as close as they could be set; over all the piles a lattice-work of interwoven branches was laid, and earth, stones, broken brick, any rubble at hand, was mixed in and pounded down, the ground of the castle being finally surfaced with brick. It was usual to erect an earthen mound for each tower atop this brick base. Finally, after the castle had been built, a mound was set up outside the outer curtain wall, and both sides of this mound were faced with slippery clay.

Of all the arts, architecture was that which the Middle Ages carried furthest and on the most rational basis. The castle-builders of Denmark early discovered that the corners were the logical points of attack and, their method of construction on made land allowing them to adopt any ground-plan they chose, they built towers or re-entrant angles into their corners long before Valdemar Atterdag's day. The necessity for large quantities of timber in the piles and as supporting members for brickwork caused wide lawns to be cleared out of the forest around the castle. When this has happened there is something more than an approximation of the system through which Marshal Vauban revolutionized the art of fortification in the seventeenth century, with his octagons, bastions, fields of fire, and walls which are as high as the ditches are deep. More than an approximation; for Vauban had been in Denmark and had seen medieval castles still capable of resisting artillery attack before he laid down his famous "second system."

But this is not the point. The point is that the Danish castles could be taken by no means known to the Middle

Ages except blockade, and to blockade them the attackers had to camp on the wide glacis before the walls, where they were subject to the counterstroke of armored horsemen. Iron-hard Heinrich had armored horsemen and proposed to use them in support of any castle that Valdemar attacked.

IV

On the young King's part there followed a period of intensive reaction in intellectual chemistry, a transvaluation of values. Inductive reasoning had not yet been invented, and in the saga of the earlier Valdemars, there was no great comfort for Valdemar the last. There had once, indeed, been a day when Valdemar the Great and his Bishop Absalon were so ringed round by a danger from which no man knew the path of escape. It fell out after that Rügen had been conquered and the bloody god, whom the Danes called Svantevitz because their tongues could not compass his other name, was chopped to bits. There is a shallow sea behind the islands Wollin and Usedom called the Haff; around its shores dwelt great numbers of Wendish pagans, and it seemed good to the King to lead a fleet against them. The more part of the Danes desired to stay at home that season, rebuilding houses between the empty gables or setting beams to the Archbishop's fine new churches. Therefore the King took but a small fleet, with which he entered the Haff, turned east and harried Wollin up to the gates of the town of Julin, where a bridge connected the island with the mainland. There was a fight with the Julin men here, but the Danes won it, broke down the land end of the bridge and sailed on northward to the lesser island of Gistow, where they found a night's rest and fodder for the horses.

Absalon said they should now push out into open sea through the eastern gap at Dienow, but when the day arose, so did a wind which blew water from the shoals that lie there so the ships could by no means get through. Now was the King's fleet deep in trouble, for Kasimir, the war-leader of the Wends, had sailed down the Oder with fifty ships to block exit by the way the Danes had come, and at the Julin bridge the shores were crowded with weaponed men, who would sorely hurt those in the King's ships, since they must pass through one at a time.

King Valdemar called his chief men together. They much blamed Absalon for his unlucky plan to slip out by the eastern sound and were somewhat despairing, for these Wends were by no means painted savages, but had weapons as bright and cities as stout as the Germans round about them.

Said King Valdemar: "It ill becomes men and soldiers in an hour of need to belabor others with reproaches like a lot of women; and now I do not think that the man who has made so many good plans for us will fail to have one this time."

All were silent; but Absalon said that these enemies who now looked so dangerous, should not be hard to beat after all, since they had made clear what their own plans were. His judgment was that all the mounted men should be set ashore on Wollin and come down the beach with the King to lead them. As for the ships, the heavy-armed men with helms should be crowded into the seven leading vessels to break through at the bridge against the Wendish ships, while those that followed immediately should carry all the bowmen, and those in the rear, none but rowers, so that King Valdemar's troop might be taken aboard. It seemed to those present that the men of the seven ships had the hardest part; they asked who would lead them. "I," said the Bishop, "since I will not seem braver with my mouth than with my body."

Kasimir the warlord was then holding a feast to celebrate his coming victory, passing cups of gold from hand to hand along the beach. When his men saw the Danish ships approaching, they hastily embarked in their own vessels, while the Julin men ran down to hold the neck of the outlet. The shot-weapons of the latter would not bite on the full-armed men who followed Absalon, while the arrow storm from the other Danish ships somewhat shook them. When King Valdemar stormed their flank with his riders, they would not sustain the shock, but fled away behind the walls of their town, while all the King's men were taken into the ships. Among the Wendish ships there was a falling off of courage at the sight of their friends so beaten down, and Absalon's assault was very fierce. The first rank of Kasimir's ships fled or were cleared, whereupon all the rest departed in panic, so that the Danes not only escaped the trap, but carried home much honor and booty; which shows that when swords are bared, nothing is to be taken as certain until they are bloodied.

v

Valdemar I's solution was local and tactical; Valdemar IV's difficulty was general and strategic. It may be that he worked out his solution without thinking very much of the son of Knud Lavard, and it is fairly certain that he arrived at this solution by degrees and not in a flash. But it is also clear, it must have been clear to Valdemar Atterdag at the time, even without inductive reasoning, that the normal medieval solution of providing himself with more armored knights would not do; that he must find something as far from the ordinary as the combination of archers in ships and men on horseback.

The available armored knights to whom he could grant holdings in exchange for service were German mercenaries. They were thoroughly detestable to his own people and could only be bought by imitating those procedures of the Holsteiners which the King was trying to abolish. There were a good many Danes who bore the name or right of herremænd, but they belonged almost wholly to two groups—those who had been impoverished by Graf Gerhard's social policy (like Niels Ebbessen), and those whose holdings had become so large that they were counted lords. The latter had too much to lose in a cause that did not show signs of quick and great success; the former lacked training and equipment to make up a body of armored cavalry. Moreover, when Viborg district of North Jutland fell in to the crown during Valdemar's Aalborg period, it was evidently in a state that precluded the formation of an army through grants of new knightly holdings. Such a tenure implied the existence of laborers who would work the land for the knight's maintenance while he was away at the wars, either by the device of serfdom or that of taxation.

In any case, the Danish knighthold was not one where the herremand had all his work done for him. He was at least supposed to give close superintendence and some physical labor.

> "Better can I tie a silken band
> Than play the farmer on lea and land,"

sings Sir Ove in the ballad, to the heiress who has come to ask the King for a husband, and is promptly answered:

> "O sit on my wagon all by me;
> So good a farmer I'll make of thee!
> Take plow in hand, lay the furrow featly,
> Take corn in hand and scatter it neatly,"

with the immense approval of His Majesty, who himself gives away the bride.

Twenty-one years of uproar and Gerhard had so stripped the Jutland districts that it was something of a miracle that the taxes had sufficed to release Viborg. They probably would not have done so from anyone but Blockhead Valdemar who, after his imprisonment and ransom, had grown so morbid on the subject of the Gerhardssons that he was willing to let his royal cousin have anything to keep it out of their clutches. But even with title recovered, the whole countryside needed rebuilding.

The difference between the young King and most medieval rulers is that he did something about it. It is to this Jutland period that there must be dated the first of those steps, each alone small, but in their mass prodigious, by which Valdemar made his kingdom pull itself up by its own bootstraps and more or less in spite of itself. He told the men of Viborg Thing plainly that the hard taxes they had borne must be continued until the rest of the realm was free—which even so, could not be accomplished by means of the present income of the crown. He did not propose to increase taxes. To augment his income he expected the same scale of taxation on a more productive country, made so by the re-cultivation of lands that had fallen fallow and the clearing of new tracts from the forests. All men dispossessed by the Holsteiners, all younger sons who had no place, were expected to take up such lands and make the most of them. The royal treasury would back these pioneers by providing roads and gristmills wherever needed.

The King meant what he said, too, and enforced it by the police power. In Jutland there was a good deal of growling, they began calling him "Valdemar the Bad" again, and in the land's yearbook, the chronicler set down with some bitterness: "In Valdemar Atterdag's time all good customs were abolished in Denmark; neither soldiers, bonders, nor merchants had any rest; no time was allowed for eating, sleeping or repose; but all were driven under threat of the king's hard displeasure to heavy drudgery."

There is in this the signature of a new Valdemar, a somewhat harder man than the young King who had believed that Christian philosophy could be made a rule of action; or perhaps only an increase into full stature of that other Valdemar who killed his man at eighteen. The degree of change can easily be overestimated, and it is important to note that the steps of the Jutland period were tentative. But there is another straw of the same hour to show how the current of Valdemar's mind had begun to set in the direction of escape from

traditions which allowed too little scope for effective action.
As his own embedsmand, he prosecuted before a Thing court
some brothers of the Johanniter Order who had swindled
a Copenhagen merchant.

He might as well have denied the doctrine of transubstanti-
ation. In all medieval polity hardly any right was so incon-
testable as that of the Church to handle its own penal problems. As late as 1856 ecclesiastical courts in some Central
European areas were claiming jurisdiction in all cases involving contracts made under oath, whether churchmen were involved or not. Presumably in this instance (we are not told)
the good brothers pleaded benefit of clergy and the Thing
court disqualified itself; but the question had been asked,
and it was Valdemar who asked it.

VI

The hermitage in Jutland thus saw Valdemar well on the
way to the solution of a personal problem—how shall I rule?
—and a solution to the economic difficulties of the realm had
at least been adumbrated. There remained the military problem of castles that could only be taken by blockade and an
opposing force of armored horsemen who could break up
any blockade. Once more direct evidence of mental process
is lacking; we only know what he did, not precisely why he
did it. But the evidence that exists; the fact that the King
spent every spare hour listening to the songs and sagas of the
history of Denmark; that he had available the admirable
text of Saxo Grammaticus, who wrote of the first Valdemar's
raids as an eyewitness war correspondent—these speak with
the tongues of men and of angels to say that in the victories
of Valdemar the Great, Valdemar Atterdag found a method
of breaking the closed circuit of invulnerable castles and invincible riders.

The castles were sea-castles. He founded a navy.

8

First Revolution
(1342-1344)

THE ARMISTICE WAS TO LAST THROUGH THE FORTNIGHT before Michaelmas, and it must have been a source of some small surprise to the Gerhardssons that, although the commission of churchmen who sat down to write a permanent peace could come to no agreement, King Valdemar remained quietly among the heaths of Skagen, making remarks about tomorrow being another day and building gristmills instead of attending to the proper business of a medieval king, which was fighting. If it had occurred to them that the young monarch had decided that he needed both help and education before embarking on a career as a battle-captain, this would no more than have confirmed their idea that Denmark had been knocked on the head before Kallundborg and it was now time to carve steaks off the carcass; a process that need not be interrupted by the indignation of the Hansa.

In fact, Iron Heinrich went out of his way to provoke the cities by an edict confiscating the goods of Lübeck and Hamburg merchants who passed through his territories. In return the first town lodged a formal complaint with the Emperor and another with Markgraf Ludwig of Brandenburg—a beautiful specimen of period legalism which never mentioned the confiscated merchants (whose caravans were illegal), but protested that at Kallundborg the Holsteiners had killed some

· 114 ·

of the crew of a city ship not under lease to Valdemar, but on a mere voyage of inspection. This was a constructive attack on the city itself and demanded imperial remedy; but both Ludwigs were down in the Tyrol at the time, deep in a complex intrigue for a marriage between the junior and the greatest heiress of Europe, the famous ugly duchess, Margaret Bigmouth. She already had a ducal husband who was sure to make trouble and the Wittelsbachs apparently felt they could not simultaneously handle another row at the northern flank of the Empire, so they only made comforting noises in answer to Lübeck's protest.

The Hansa never did any fighting on its own account; of the other neighbors whom they might persuade to interfere, Saxe-Lauenburg and Saxe-Wittenburg had been drawn into the imperial schemes, and the Lord of Mecklenburg always operated with allies. The Gerhardssons were therefore satisfied that they had eliminated from the forthcoming partition of Denmark all but one of the powers who might interfere. That one was King Magnus of Sweden; and the Holsteiners now eliminated him also by inviting him to share the profits. The Swede had lately obtained possession of the sea-fortress at Copenhagen by buying out the pledge-holder, and there was very little left of Denmark from which territorial gains might be obtained, but the great fisheries of Skaane could conceivably be made to yield their profits to Sweden instead of to the Hansa. Magnus sent emissaries to Visby, of which he held the overlordship, largest of all the Hansa towns. There was a local revolution; the burgomaster lost his head; the new government joined the alliance of Sweden and Holstein. Just before the herring-run, Magnus' men appeared at Skanør and Falsterbo, arrested all the Lübeck burghers present, sequestered their goods and announced that in the future the fisheries would be conducted by Holsteiners, Swedes, and Visbymen.

For the five Wend towns and especially for Lübeck this was bankruptcy and the end of the world. Worried burghers toddled through the streets to the Rathaus, where the city government voted the altogether unprecedented step of going to war on its own account, as head of a league against "all who have trod on the rights of the King of Denmark and those who still tread thereon." The city had no military leaders of its own, but Valdemar sent down his Marshal, the grizzled von Lochen. Lübeck furnished him with a war-chest and sent into south Germany to hire fighting men; and then they bought out the prince everyone else had overlooked— Graf Johann the Mild.

This individual was anomalous in his surroundings. There is no record of anyone seeing him on horseback in battle, yet as a conqueror and exploiter, he ranked second only to Graf Gerhard, without having to bear any personal onus. His method was more intricate; the help he gave was financial and permissive, and he always extracted the fullest value from it. Knights of the Holstein-Stormarn service had helped King Kristoffer to his throne; Graf Johann received pledge-rights to castles in exchange and let them out to those same knights, who collected from the surrounding countryside and paid most of their take to their overlord. Other Holstein-Stormarn knights helped eject Kristoffer and more castles fell into Johann's hands, till by degrees he had brought nearly all Sjæl- land, all of Falster, Møn and Femern under his dominion. Now he could hardly be expected to go to war with his cousins of the Rendsborg line, but he could and did rent to the Hansa his castle of Segeberg as a base of operations. It is possible that some of his men also joined von Lochen— we do not know.

II

The war of the Gerhardssons began with Iron Heinrich falling on the diminutive stretch of Lübeck territory that served the city as a kitchen garden, burning it from end to end and driving the burghers within their gates. Whether he intended to push matters to a siege is uncertain, but he never got the chance. The news that reached him under the city's walls at Pentecost (which fell on May 18 that year) was that von Lochen at the head of two hundred fully armed Bavarian knights bearing the banner of Denmark had broken into the home territories around Rendsborg and was tearing everything to pieces; and that King Valdemar had raised the royal standard in Sjælland.

Pausing only for a call on Graf Johann (who, of course, sold out to his cousin as soon as he was asked), Heinrich hurried back to beat von Lochen in a battle. He was immediately treated to a lesson in the relative values of tactical and strategic mobility. Valdemar's Marshal slipped past the Holsteiners to Kiel, where ships, mainly Lubeck's, partly Valdemar's own, were waiting. The next news Heinrich had was that the Danish force had fallen on Skanør and Falsterbo in the midst of the herring-run, thrown all the Holsteiners and Swedes into prison and confiscated the catch. Heinrich had few ships of his own to follow and could hardly have done so in any case, for at this moment he was simultaneously subjected to a heavy raid of Mecklenburgers brought into action by Lübeck money and a revolt of the Ditmarschers of his western fen country, roused by Hamburg money.

It is always more difficult to fight defensively than offensively with mercenary armies, since the plunder incentive is wanting; and the campaign now forced upon the Gerhardssons was one of dispersion without battles, a type of operation in which armored riders stood at a considerable discount. Unquestionably they would have won in time; with Graf Johann's help they did get into Segeberg, where they captured the small garrison von Lochen had left, with a couple of rich Lübeck burghers who had to pay through the nose in ransoms. But before Heinrich could pass to the offensive the war had been lost and won.

King Valdemar brought all the men he could muster from Jutland and had his ships drop him off to attack Copenhagen before they ran south to pick up von Lochen at Kiel. The place seems not to have been well provisioned and was soon in straits. Its commander ran messages out to King Magnus and to Marchwarden Stove at Vordingborg. The latter, who commanded most of the Holstein forces in Sjælland, came rushing up to the relief of Copenhagen—by sea, since it was the most convenient route.

Stove and his fleet raised the castle towers on the twenty-fourth of June, Midsummer Day, the anniversary of the coronation, and began landing men at once, while the Swedes in order sallied from their fortress to make it Kallundborg over again. But before steel clashed or trumpet blew the Drogden Deep was filled with sails, and here was von Lochen with the two hundred Bavarian spears, so that a great battle blew up across the slippery decks, beginning at the tower and swirling toward the city walls as the half-manned Holstein vessels broke north under the Marshal's overbearing weight. For a time there was a stand at the Bildebro, "the builded bridge," from which this battle would take its name; there Stig Anderssen had set King Valdemar's men in a block, with arbalestiers along the shore to fire from the wings. The Swedish men were trapped here and a great slaughter made of them— four hundred or more, with all their best leaders. A few of the Holsteiners escaped back to Vordingborg, but most were carried off to prison in Lübeck, and Denmark had her first victory since King Kristoffer bought his throne, a quarter of a century before.

It was decisive; it decided that Iron-hard Heinrich would not be king in Denmark, ever. With the lost ships went any chance that he could get enough fighting men into Sjælland to deal with Valdemar and the general uprising the King immediately proclaimed. That island was not his pledge-hold in any case. He asked for peace; received it on condition that he keep his nose out of affairs in the islands, and whirled away from the story to keep his appointment with the Black Prince of England under Crécy's high mill.

This left King Magnus and his allies of Visby, but von Lochen eliminated the latter by sailing back at once to the herring towns, where he caught the Visby ships in harbor and the Visby men in church and did for them both. The Swedish King's immediate mobile force had been destroyed at the Bildebro, he had no ships for a counter-attack in Sjælland and any force he could raise in the home counties was desperately needed in his province of Finland. The Danes of neighboring Esthonia had attacked him there, so vigorously it seemed likely they might lay the whole province under. Magnus was therefore glad to come into the peace on the terms that Copenhagen should be Valdemar's by right of conquest, while the districts and castles of northern Sjælland that had been in Duke Porse's pawnhold should be released by their own taxes on the same terms as those in North Jutland.

III

King Valdemar was no witness of his first victory, being up under the walls of Kallundborg once more. Graf Johann's shift to the Gerhardssons' side had released him from any peace with that lord's vassals, and at the same time an event at the village of Helsinge made a clear-cut issue of the war. A tax-collecting party of Holsteiners from Søborg castle reached the town when some three hundred bonders and their families were in church hearing mass, the date being the Feast of the Assumption. The taxing expedition had been fairly successful and most of the collectors were drunk. Someone in the group saw an opportunity for a rare bit of sport, so they set fire to the church and ringed it round with swords. Those who ran out were cut down, men and women together; those who stayed in burned to death.

The news of this impromptu massacre went through Sjælland hand in hand with a royal proclamation of war without quarter on everything that bore the Holstein name. The whole island blazed up in a determined peoples' rising, with bonders forsaking their steads and monks the cloister to cut down the Germans wherever they could be found.

There are only the most incidental records of that blind struggle, which lasted for a year and a half. Valdemar established himself at Ringsted in the center of the web and kept moving, shooting out his small group of leaders and armored men whenever there was a chance that a convoy or strongpoint might be taken. It is important to note that the force was very small and now exclusively Danish. Lübeck lost interest in the rights of the King of Denmark as soon as the Gerhardssons let go the Skaane fisheries; and the grizzled von Lochen, Valdemar's oldest helper and best friend, had painted himself into a corner when he attacked the Visbymen at Skanør. A gilt-edged bishop happened to be saying mass when the Bavarian knights rushed into the church and began dragging the fish dealers off to prison. The act was regarded as only less of a sacrilege than the murder of Thomas à Becket. The bishop put von Lochen and all his men under the ban of the Church; and Church support was so very important to Valdemar that he could do nothing but load his friend with presents and dismiss him.

It was a grievous loss, for of the native leaders none was anywhere near von Lochen's equal as a strategist and none but Stig Anderssen his equal as a fighter. Bo Falk, indeed, got himself involved in a pitched battle at Flodsaa Mill, near Næstved, in September and not only lost the fight, but was captured, so that Valdemar had to drop business at the general peace conference, hurry down and pay an expensive ransom before his knightly vassal's head was taken off. A little later Bishop Sveyn of Aarhus got into the same kind of trouble. Stig Anderssen had to be moved right off the board into Jutland, where complications had developed that have nothing to do with this part of the story. As for King Valdemar himself, he once more failed in a siege of Kallundborg and on New Year's Day missed a hopeful effort at surprising Taarnborg over Korsør.

It might thus seem that the Holsteiners were winning, but the set of the unrecorded incidents was steadily down for them, steadily upward for Denmark. As long as the King was in the island, the only way the castle-holders could make collections was by heavily-armed raids; they lost a good many men in small groups on the heels of the Helsinge church massacre and a lot more in ambushes. These losses could not be made good; the unwarlike Graf Johann exercised his usual restraint about doing the one thing that would have beaten down resistance, which was taking the field in person with heavy forces. The flow of scattering recruits was small when the piracy business had to be conducted on a basis of no plunder and perpetually hunting through the forest for bands of Danes who melted like smoke and sniped at one with arbalest-bolts from the copses.

In a deadlock of this kind the main question is morale; victory will pass to the side which puts in the last spiritual reserves. The castle-holders were Teutons, persistent by race and possessed of a sense of personal superiority that made them regard these Danish movements with the indignation one might afford to a revolution of mice; moreover their pocketbooks were at issue, if they lost they faced an unemployment problem. But Valdemar Atterdag was a Skjoldung and the issue for his people was that their rooftrees were burning. The Holsteins cracked first, the decisive events coming during the black winter that saw the failure at Taarnborg. One was not in Sjælland at all, but in Falster, which was practically all under the control of the single great castle at Nykøbing. The sub-pawnholder there (we do not even know his name) had troubles with his own bonders, could not make things pay, and offered to sell out for cash. Valdemar had money enough to take him up.

The other event began at Roskilde, where the King was keeping winter with no more than two hundred men about him. A muffled man was brought in one night, having been searched for weapons, and he was a German. Warden of the gate at Kallundborg, he said; tired of this war; for a sum of money he would sell his ward. Done, said King Valdemar, and led his two hundred by secret ways through the cold winter woods to the great fortress that had now twice defied him. On an icy night when sensible men were keeping close, they found the gate ajar, rushed in with a shout of "Denmark!" and blades gleaming in the firelight—and the morning of the new day saw Valdemar's three golden lions waving at last from the great hold of the north.

IV

Theoretically, the war continued for some months after this double event, but actually it twittered down to skirmishes of reduced tempo, then died out altogether in a peace signed by the King and Johann the Mild. The Graf confirmed Valdemar's possession of Nykøbing and Kallundborg, and threw in Søborg, from which the murderers of Helsinge had come; also promised to make his sub-pawnholders observe Danish law in their dealings with the bonders. The possession of Kallundborg had given the King a secure base for his fleet, from which so much pressure was put on the other castles that the whole Sjælland pawnhold was profitless to Graf Johann. Moreover the Church had repaid Valdemar's quick action in the von Lochen affair, by clapping an interdict on all southern Sjælland which, if it did no physical damage to the Holsteins, at least made them uncomfortable and nearly paralyzed the normal conduct of affairs.

As for Valdemar, he was needed elsewhere and had a whole series of reasons for wishing the Sjælland fighting to end. He had gained about all he could; two of the great castles, a secure base, a foothold in Falster, the revenues of nearly half Sjælland, and the moral demonstration that if allowed to do so, he could bring the other day throughout Denmark. The capture of more castles by military means was a task beyond his present resources; the success at Copenhagen showed it as clearly as the failures at Taarnborg and Kallundborg. What he needed to carry on was more trained soldiers and better leaders, and an avenue had opened up by which he could reach them.

But even this would take time, and time was precisely the thing of which he must be miserly. He had been living among the villages and cannot have missed the fact that though the spirit of the people against Holstein remained high, the society they represented was sliding still farther toward barbarism. Fields uncultivated, looms still (who would weave or reap when the Holsteiners might come tomorrow), food growing scarcer, no more dances in the circle round the village church during the intervals between sermons. The ballad-singing of Sjælland, once the richest of the north, falls silent through this war. Not only had a good many villages been burned, but also the town of Kjøge, which had merchant privileges and was a fairly important place. To continue the guerilla war till the Holsteiners were driven out was to reproduce the social policy of Graf Gerhard.

Valdemar's own social policy, the whole rationale of his kingship, the picture of a successful Denmark which he drew as much from ratiocination as from his intensive interest in the past, rested on the maintenance and expansion of the village culture that was being so grievously hurt. Not only was it the sole visible alternative to setting the country out in lordships—which would merely substitute Danish for German names in the captaincy of the castles—but also, with sea communications, it was the feature that rendered the northern civilization unique; capable of solving its own problems without the application of feudalism. To override that village culture was to substitute for the Danish system the disorderly life of medieval Germany.

It was for the recovery of the village culture that the King had set up his gristmills in Jutland and brought new ground under the plow—a process now energetically extended in the parts of Sjælland that had fallen under his control. It was for nothing else that he labored unceasingly at the revival and reinforcement of the Thing courts and the restoration of the Laws of King Valdemar. The experimental trial of the two Johanniter brothers was a step in the same direction—part of the effort to give that ancient and not unglamorous structure of law new and more solid foundations.

New and more solid foundations were evidently needed. For one thing, they were demanded on the military grounds which always had to be a matter of first consideration in the Middle Ages. It was not for emotional reasons alone that Valdemar wished to take out of the hands of mercenaries the defense of Denmark, which had once won by her own arms an empire that reached from the North Cape to the English Channel. Their price was too high; the invincible carapaced monstrosities wanted more than money. They demanded the whole control of society, a Denmark made in the image of German feudalism. One of the striking differences between the ordinary feudal relationship and the custom of Denmark was that in the latter country, service to an overlord was not a lifetime obligation, but a contract that could be terminated by either party. Since Viking days the Danish freeholding bonder had owned his land clear of anything but taxes. If it fell on his mind to go serve the Grand Duke of Muscovy instead of his own king or his local chieftain, he had every right to do so. It was precisely for refusal to render perpetual service that Graf Gerhard had dispossessed so many Jutlanders, including Niels Ebbessen.

This is by no means to suggest that King Valdemar was thinking in any such terms as a national bonders' army. The bonders had given no good account of themselves in the fighting thus far, and there was no sign that they would ever improve. For that matter, the King was still too inexperienced, too uncertain of his ground, to have worked out any complete and rational form of military establishment. But everything he did shows it was clear to him from the beginning that a class of free-holding bonders, centering on the villages, was an indispensable element in that quite complex system of life which made up the Scandinavian civilization. They were at once the law-making body and the repository of the law, Marsilio's lawgiver, which kept the whole structure in balance. They provided a reserve of rising men which would supply the herremænd class with needed fresh blood; they were the reserves for any military establishment not based on mercenaries; and above all, they were the makeweight in the state against the rising power of the native lords who were trying to attain the condition of their cognates south of the Eider.

9
Ruffle of Drums;
Enter the Villain
(1180-1181; 1344-1345)

AT THE SOUTHWEST CORNER OF JUTLAND, JUST NORTH OF
the Slesvig line and near the Holsteiners' district of
Ditmarsch, lies Frisland. It is a country of endless
marshes, "the playground of winds, a floor where flows the
evening light, home of mirage and colored airs." The sea in
season covers much of the ground; when it retreats the soil
is not left barren, but gives birth to long, succulent grasses,
beloved by sheep, who on a summer day can be seen in every
direction as far as the eye may follow, scattered like ball-
clouds across the grass.

At the heart of Frisland numerous trickles from northeast
and southeast unite to form the slow stream called the Vidaa.
At this date great ships could come up so far, and the town
of Tønder was founded at their point of deposit, north and
west of the Vidaa. Valdemar the Victorious gave it a merchant city's privileges and built a tall castle on made ground
in the marshes to protect the place, the Tønderhus.

The Frislanders are called marshbonders. They live in high
houses named *varfter*, strongly built to withstand winter gales
and tides from the western ocean. They were well-to-do in
this age (for the small islands of solid ground among their
marshes grew some of the finest corn in Denmark), and very

· 126 ·

independent behind their moat of drowned ground. By some chance of documents, their district had been left outside any pledge-hold; they had therefore paid no taxes for fourteen years, or since King Kristoffer went down for the first time, and they saw no reason why they should begin now. When King Valdemar's bailiffs appeared, the marshbonders hung a couple from the outer beams of their varfter and sent the rest packing.

This was the emergency that brought the King out of Sjælland. It is clear that he perceived it as far more important than the usual peasants' protest against exactions, far more than the trouble Absalon and his King Valdemar had over the tithing of Skaane in a simpler world. The reply of the marshbonders to the King's men was that taxes were paid to buy them two things—defense and good rule, or as we would put it, administration. Well, for fourteen years nobody had given them any defense and they had administered themselves under the old Jutland law. They were satisfied with the arrangement.

The background of this was the revolt of the Ditmarschers against Iron Heinrich which Hamburg had promoted, with the result that the Gerhardssons were forced to compromise. Doubtless the marshbonders thought Valdemar was as much occupied in Sjælland as Heinrich had been with his war, and much weaker. When new messengers demanded not only current taxes, but the arrears for the whole fourteen years and brought a pastoral from the Bishop of Ribe telling them they must pay, they assembled in a great Thing at Langsundoft, two miles south of Tønder, to give an emphatic refusal.

The men of the Thing were armed, according to custom, but they had hardly met before Valdemar dropped on them from the skies with the Sjælland men-at-arms and all the knights of Slesvig, headed by their Duke. The marshbonders could not stand, but they had met this type of attack before, and knew how to deal with it: to wit, by melting away among their tufts and hummocks, where armored men would hardly follow. They did so; but had hardly begun their movement before they were surrounded by a great force of bogtrotters as expert as themselves, men from the offshore island of Sylt, who hated the Frislanders for their pride and hardness of heart. The latter now had to stand; were beaten in a brief battle, and at a Thing in August promised to pay a fine of a silver mark for each house in the marshlands, and to furnish five hundred men with helms to march under the royal banner for any war within the realm. To see that the agreement was kept, King Valdemar set up a new castle at Nøde-fald and placed in charge of it, as Lord of the Marshes, one Klaus Limbek.

Five hundred men with helms was an enormous force to charge against so small a district, and we may take it that this part of the arrangement was intended to be a confirmation of the normal citizens' militia obligation in case the district itself were invaded. It is the other feature of the settlement that attracts attention—King Valdemar, who was striving so hard to revive the village culture in Sjælland and Jutland, setting a semi-feudal lord over a district where that village culture had been conducting itself independently and with more success than anywhere else in the realm.

The act has the appearance of that normal medieval inability to escape from the established pattern which makes the history of those centuries a wearisome round where only the interplay of personalities is significant. But this appearance is factitious. In the first place this Klaus Limbek was not installed at Nødefald as a baron, owing service for a possession, but as an officer of the crown, performing service under its orders. In the second it would be an error to see a movement toward a crowned republic in Valdemar's efforts to revive the village culture, just as it would to find in his proceedings in Sjælland an attempt to bring forth a bonders' army.

His ideas and methods changed later, but at this period he was looking back rather than forward; had come not to destroy, but to fulfill the law. His point of reference was the old Nordic society described in the poetic Edda; a society stratified along functional lines, in which military and political leadership are furnished by a class, whose members qualify for such employment both by birth and training. They were called *jarls* in the Edda, and an erroneous idea of their position has gone abroad, chiefly because of the mistranslation as "earls," a description which was really a title in England. In all Europe except Scandinavia one became an earl, count or baron through heredity, and the title carried with it not only territorial ownership, but also the right to lead armies in battle, to judge cases at law, and even to a certain extent, to legislate.

The Danish "nobility" had no titles, hereditary or otherwise; Duke Porse was a freak and an unsuccessful experiment. The highborn families of Denmark held fairly close together, especially in Jutland; but what one acquired from membership in them was some special training in military and political leadership and the opportunity to demonstrate ability in those fields. There were no hereditary legislators or even hereditary judges. Legislation belonged to the Things and the King, and in the former a noble's voice was worth exactly one vote, except as he could influence others. There was not even an overtone of special economic position for the wellborn. Niels Ebbessen belonged to the great stock of the Strangesons, but he seems to have been a fairly poor man, even before Graf Gerhard took away from him that little which he had.

The theory, often breached, but never lost to sight, was that eligibility to leadership was determined by family, while the bonders chose which individual should lead. The exalted houses of Ludvig Albrektsen and Laurids Jonssen, Marshal and Drost, disappear after the death of the two men, not because they lacked issue, but because the heirs wanted personal force. Even the royal family responded to this rule of choice from below. The crown was genuinely elective. In only four out of twenty-four reigns since the beginning of the tenth century had eldest son succeeded father. No less than three young men of the age of Valdemar the Great are borne on the lists as King Knud V, having been elected by one Thing or another.

II

The bonders were the repository, the lawgiver. They were also farmers with their noses pointed toward the ground, who never traveled abroad or any other whither. In the hour of the first great Valdemar's triumph, with Rügen conquered, the pagan Wends put down, it was made clear to all Denmark why the people should have great men to lead them. This was the time of Skaane's refusal to pay its church tithes. From his seat at royal Ringsted, King Valdemar sent for the leading bonders; when they came, it was not of Absalon and his tithes alone that they complained, but that the King had raised into embedsmænd of their province Absalon's brothers, Sune and Esbern the Quick, with certain others who were not Skaane men at all, but foreigners from Jutland and the isles. It was the arrogance of these men that had brought on the troubles, the bonder-leaders said. If the King would write a wise, kindly letter in which he promised to send these strangers back to their own land, all difficulties would cease.

At this King Valdemar grew very angry; he wrote a letter indeed, but it was hard and threatening, and the Skaaninger sent messengers to say that they would never again pay taxes to the King or tithes to the Church. King Valdemar gathered his men into ships and immediately went to Helsingborg. It was the time of the fair, and many bonders were at the shore, who as soon as they saw Absalon come up out of his ship, began to assemble in crowds and throw stones in every direction. But when they saw the great King, Valdemar, they all found urgent business to do in their tents, or a bargain to strike with someone. Nevertheless, when they were summoned in Thing, they would not yield as to the tithe. Thereupon Absalon wished to beat them down with hard weapons, but the host, who were for the more part Jutland men and fearful lest this tithing custom be set up in their own country, counselled moderation in tones which showed how little fighting was to be expected from them.

The King now sent Absalon back into Sjælland, himself remaining at Helsingborg; but before he left, the Bishop gave orders that all the churches of Skaane should be shut. The Skaaninger said that if this were done they would cut off the priests' legs, and standing forth in arms, plundered all the places that belonged to King and Bishop; but in so doing they counted themselves too high, for the King and Absalon returned with a strong army of Sjællanders and Blekinge men, their own neighbors. The Skaaninger stood for a battle at a bridge across the river Dysiaa, but while King Valdemar fought with them hard at this point, the Bishop led all the mounted men by a ford onto the bonders' rear, so now they were utterly broken and must come in for peace. Yet still they said it was not good Skaane law that they should pay the tithes.

On this point King Valdemar gave them reason, but he said that since God's ministers, who gave the blessed sacraments, must be provided for, each Skaane man should make a voluntary gift of a tenth of his year's income to the Church. So it was arranged and has been to this day, that there are no Church tithes in Skaane, only voluntary gifts. Valdemar made embedsmænd from those in the province after this, since it was seen that although the bonders were reasonable men who would listen to persuasion, they would persuade themselves wrongly and against the interests of Church and realm unless they had leaders who understood the general interest of all and not merely of their own herreds.

III

The question that excited contemporaries and still has a certain amount of meaning is why the King should choose Klaus Limbek as leader of the Frislanders.

For this was Limbek the devil's apprentice, as robustious a rascal as ever came out of the Middle Ages; Caesar Borgia in a blonde wig, hated, feared, and respected, a good companion in a brawl or at a board and a formidable leader in war. He was only semi-Danish, a younger son of a family from near Rendsborg in Graf Gerhard's domain, by no means of exalted stock. In his early days, a roaring adventurer, who got into some trouble in Lübeck which may have involved a murder; fled north and took service with the great Graf in the early years of the Time of Uproar. They may have been characters destined to come together, but the detail is lost of how Limbek found favor with his lord. We know only that Gerhard gave the young man permission to pay court to Fru Ida, widow of the pledge-holder of Tørning castle, a fine titbit, since she had beauty quite equal to her position and riches.

Klaus Limbek found a preferred suitor already in the field. Another man might have called on the Graf's authority; instead he got the lady drunk one night, seduced her and hired a priest to work on her scruples till she married him. It was a successful and oddly happy match; he sold the Tørning pledge for cash, invested the money in hiring men-at-arms and with them was Graf Gerhard's right arm in the battle at Lohede, where King Kristoffer was overthrown for the last time. The great Graf rewarded him with the stewardship of much of north Jutland and personal possession of Kallø castle, one of the great holds of that land, beautifully situated between Aarhus and Randers, so that the flowing lines of commerce that reach both by sea must pass under its shadow.

Klaus Limbek seems to have had ideas beyond the sweep

of Gerhard's social policy, for the first thing he did at Kallø was ride through the district, inviting the more notable bonders to dine at their new lord's table. They received him in the manner Danes would receive Germans six hundred years later, with grunts and doors closed in his face, and there being no precedent for such a situation in the life of a condottiere, Klaus Limbek went home and complained to his wife about it.

"I am only a woman," quoth Fru Ida. "My business is to dress the table and set meat and drink thereon; it is your part to make people sit at it with you and afterward to do whatever you wish." Never a word answered Klaus Limbek, but took ship that same day for Lübeck, with a bag of silver marks for his journey-companion, and when he came back to repeat his invitations to dine, a company of steel-armed spearmen rode with him. "He saw no more doors except from the inside," says the chronicler.

When Graf Gerhard came north with his army along the road that led to Randers and Niels Ebbessen, Klaus Limbek held somewhat aloof and thus escaped the condemnation that fell on all Holsteiners during the Jutland rising. His word was the only writ that ran in Kallø district during those days, and it was a good word; not that there was any change in the feelings of the men who had been shepherded to their food by spearmen, but they came to find that Klaus Limbek in the impartiality of his power was strong enough to execute any judgment he gave and bold enough to give a judgment against any.

Kallø district was the first of the four in North Jutland to fall to the crown through tax-payments, and power was already slipping like oil through Limbek's fingers when Valdemar took Kallundborg, an event which altered many people's opinions as to what another day would bring to Denmark. On the heels of that event Stig Anderssen visited Kallø castle, and the next tidings were that Klaus Limbek was in Valdemar's service as Governor of Sjælland, while the King conducted his campaign among the marshbonders.

From the first it was a strange service and a strange relationship that developed between King and King's man. Limbek's reputation for heavy-handed but sharp-edged justice certainly made him ideally suitable for the command at Nødefald, in the center of one of the more litigious of existing races. ("It's going to rain." "No, it isn't." "Let's have a lawsuit about it"—runs the local proverb.) But when the lord of Kallø came before Valdemar, his only oath of allegiance was to be true to himself; and some special explanation seems to be needed for the sum of the King's actions. Not only had he placed a district on the borders of Holstein in charge of a rather dubious customer who was half a Holsteiner and a pillar of Graf Gerhard; he went even farther. Valdemar was about to disappear into the southern isles and eventually to Esthonia. He left Klaus Limbek still Governor of Sjælland and effectively regent of the kingdom during his absence.

It was an intricate feat of character-reading on the young King's part, yet one to which he was more or less forced. The journey was a vital necessity (for reasons which will presently appear), yet the Holsteiners of Sjælland, refusing to recognize the verdict against them as complete, had reintegrated to push forward the struggle on quite a new basis. While the King was in Frisland, Marchwarden Stove of Næstved gathered all hands from Vordingborg and his own castle and began to set up a new structure southwest of the latter, on some sandbanks, where the Black Brothers had a cloister. The place was outside the pledge-hold line; the Black Brothers protested in the name of religion and the Danes in the name of the treaty, and were told by Stove to mind their own business. When Limbek attempted to surprise the workers on the new structure, he was beaten off, and it became evident that Stove and his companions had brought in many more fighting men from the south. Apparently they were embarking on a system of reconquest through the construction of mutually supporting castles.

The question before Valdemar was that of finding a commander who could conduct the struggle on a less costly and destructive basis than he himself in the late troubles. Vendelbo was past his time, and in any case, on the outs with the King, who had repossessed a particularly fine royal estate in North Jutland, which the old man had gained by methods that would not bear examination. Von Lochen was gone; Bo Falk lacked the head for a leader and Erik Nielsen of Linde, the heart. Stig Anderssen was best, but troubles in Esthonia had been so pressing that it was necessary to send him there with the title of Captain in Estland to take charge till Valdemar could arrive in person, and the King was himself too young to trust anything but experience and reputation.

He accordingly staked his chips on the idea that Klaus Limbek would be too true to himself to give anything but absolute service when trusted with absolute authority—and he was not mistaken. A hard winter closed down operations after the first defeat. At the break of spring the Holsteiners began an intensification of their program in the previous Sjælland war—strongly armed raids pushing out into the countryside to burn villages. One of them even set the torch to Ringsted, Valdemar the Great's town and ancient home of the Danish kings, while a couple of new castles began to rise.

But they were now dealing with a man who not only understood their kind of war, but also how to make use of the information furnished to him by country people. Klaus Limbek never even tried to solve the problem of the armored horseman; he evolved a strategy to avoid it. While the Holsteiners were on the raid to Ringsted, he slipped round them, fell on Næstved with all his forces, carried it by storm from the comparatively weak garrison left behind, put everyone in it to death, and tore the castle down.

This was not the end. Limbek now secretly assembled his men in the forest around Gunderslevsholm and attacked a big raiding party either just entering or just leaving. There was a savage fight across the lawns at the border of the marshes, with the onset too swift and the space too restricted for the Holsteiners to work up speed for their armored charge. The medieval horseman was an almost purely offensive weapon. These began to go back; the Danes were on the causeway with them, fire in their eyes and yelling. The gate could not be closed nor the drawbridge raised before all were boiling into the castle together, and then Denmark's sword was aloft, for not a man of the Germans escaped.

Klaus Limbek spent no time congratulating himself, but set out at once for Taarnborg over Korsør, whose land communications with Vordingborg had been severed by the Gunderslevsholm victory, while Valdemar's ships held the sea. The place was too strong for a storm, but Limbek placed it under siege, and the Holsteiners had lost too much manpower to work up an army of relief.

IV

Interlude—Forest Idyll. The trouble in Esthonia was a bonders' revolt, complicated by attempts on the part of the crusading Order of the Sword to take over the colony. King Valdemar, who as early as this had learned that nothing anyone told him was as good as what he could see with his own eyes, accordingly set out for the eastern Baltic as soon as he had cleared up the marshbonder business, making a rapid tour of the southern isles en route. Those southern islands are Falster and Møn, Langeland and Aerø, Laaland, Als, Femern and Rügen. Falster had been partly regained; Valdemar found little to fear about Møn, where the taxes were to pay off the pledge and had nearly done so; little to hope in Langeland, Aerø, and Als, which had been the subject of intricate treble pawning operations and were almost unreservedly in the Blockhead Valdemar's possession. Something might be done in Laaland, but of Femern it was useless to think at present, since Graf Johann held it and his communications with it were too good to make attack a practical project.

Rügen remained, pawned to the Lord of Mecklenburg; and there King Valdemar stepped out of history into romance. He had taken a day from care for one of the hunts which were his favorite diversion. The quarry ran far and fast; the King's high-blooded horse outstripped those of his companions so that twilight found him alone and lost in the dark forest, approaching a small chalet by the side of a woodland pool. There was some debate and he must show his signet with the seal of Denmark's lions at the window before he was admitted.

Within, the reason for hesitation became clear. The building held only one person and she a girl, very small but perfectly formed, who greeted the visitor by the name of Junker Otto, and was taken aback when Valdemar named himself Otto's brother, the King. We do not know what debates they had, or whether he learned before her brother's return the clue to her surprise at his name. It lay in their own, for the brother was Henning Podbusk, heir of the great family of Rügen magnates, who had remained somewhat inexplicably devoted to the prisoner-idiot Otto's claim to the crown, and so had severed themselves from all Denmark.

The young king stayed three days; when he left, Henning Podbusk went with him to be King's embedsmand in Falster and Tove (which was the girl's name) to be his mistress. Far in North Sjælland, at the heart of a wood known as that of the Sea-Eagles, Valdemar built a Venusberg for her—Castle Gurre, a doll's house reproduction of the nearby lordly hold of Søborg. Thither he would go on every occasion he could steal from the demands continually pressing on him, to hunt in the forest and to taste the peace he found nowhere else, all his life long.

The Third King

V

Interlude on Interlude—History Is Doubt. The whole story of Valdemar and Tove, or Tovelille, is so surrounded by difficulties that some historians reject it altogether, while others pronounce themselves agnostics. It occurs only in song and saga, never in chronicle; but since the chronicles were written by monks, this is what one might expect.

The difficulties are caused by the fact that there are two series of ballads telling the love story of King Valdemar and Little Tove, one set omitting the meeting in Rügen and quite clearly (the language employed and various references) belonging to Valdemar the Great. It would seem improbable that two kings of the same, not very common name should form romantic attachments for two women of the same, quite uncommon name. It is not at all improbable that Valdemar Atterdag, who attracted legends and songs to himself from every type of source, as a magnet attracts iron filings, borrowed this one from his ancestor.

However, this much is certain: the Henning Podbusk part of the story is all true. He came of a Rügen stem, was a partisan of Otto's, and was won over to King Valdemar during a personal visit. Henning Podbusk did have a sister. King Valdemar did build a castle at Gurre which, though on normal lines, was a miniature, a hunting lodge and not a fighting castle.

As to the other features of the story, it would be rather invidious to comment on the personal morality of a King who had made a political marriage at the age of twenty. Morality is related to current custom in any case; and this was the period in which Gervaise of Tilbury, who was a church father, prayed a girl he met on the road for her favors *"par amours,"* and when she refused, had her burned as a virginity-worshipping Manichee. Yet it seems that there was one person who did not quite fall in with current custom in this case.

Queen Helvig's relations with Valdemar were excellent at the time. She had borne him a son, later known as Junker Kristoffer, and she would bear him several children more before the event that would reveal what thunderheads of tension had been built up, and is a reason for accepting at least part of the Tove story as belonging to this Valdemar.

10
Brief History
of Esthonia
(1346-1347; 1204-1218)

O NE OF THE REMARKABLE REPEATING PATTERNS IN HIS-
tory is the success of maritime colonies with a background of barbarous hinterland. Carthage, Marseille,
Syracuse, Venice, it runs down through many races and civilizations to Boston and Buenos Aires. Esthonia should have
slipped into this pattern, and had begun to do so when Valdemar the Victorious died and Denmark's energies turned inward, while almost simultaneously, men in high wool hats
began to push their shaggy ponies into the country between
the Urals and Vistula's dark stream. Not the least of that
Valdemar's services to later ages was that he set up a guard
through which the Mongols never broke to the Baltic—but
all this was now long ago, and in playing her role of defense
of the west, Esthonia lost her place as little Denmark overseas.

The men who came to the castles by the shore were Germans largely; so were the merchants and city workers of
Reval, where the law that ran was copied from Lübeck's.
German were the feudal holdings, and the lords drove those
under them down to thralldom, so that the chronicler of
neighboring Livonia could write that the land was "a nobleman's heaven, priest's paradise, foreigner's gold-mine and

bonder's hell." Not that the Esthonians were bonders really, only native peasants who had never known anything above abasement. Yet German though these lords were, they often spoke the Danish tongue and were more fierce in their loyalty to Denmark's crown than the king who wore it. They fought hard border wars against the Tartars who had laid the Russian princes under, and when King Erik Menved would have given his subsidiary title of Duke in Estland to his brother Kristoffer, they took possession of all the royal castles and would not give them up till Erik abandoned the design.

This was not a well-deserved judgment on Kristoffer, nor was it pure high-minded loyalty. It was merely that the Esthonian nobles wished the ordering of their own heaven, which they normally had, for the King of Denmark was far away and could spare little force to support his governor, so that all real decisions were taken in the council of well-born men. Yet it had some of the results of loyalty—for instance, during the Time of Uproar, when King Kristoffer sent out a Holsteiner named Marchwarden Breide to be governor. He was the sort of man Kristoffer would choose; tried to sell Reval castle for cash to the Order of the Sword of Livonia, now a sub-order of the Teutonic Knights. The nobles got wind of the project; with the Danish bishop at their head, they rose against the treacherous Breide and clapped him in one of his own dungeons. No more would they deliver the land to Ludwig of Brandenburg when he sent to take possession on the heels of the Spandau agreement that led to Valdemar's coronation.

In the War of the Gerhardssons, these Esthonian lords fought well; but not long after they came sailing home from Finland with their booty, a beacon blazed from a hill behind Reval. It signalled that oppression's cup was full; all over the land the peasants stood forth in that mysterious and terrible surge from the depths which swept across Europe during this century, in England known by the name of Wat Tyler, in Italy by that of Rienzi and in France as the Jacquerie without any other name. Of these revolts the Esthonian was the earliest and deadliest. It had no leaders; there are no records beyond that of an oath which the peasants swore—to kill every German as soon as he was a yard long. The Jacqueries of the west turned to plunder, but this one was all burn and slay; and it posed to the invincible armored horseman a question which he lacked the technical capacity to answer.

When do we eat? The Esthonians had been living in a hell so deep that they were willing to sacrifice life itself in dragging down to their own anarchical level the men who had made such a land. They burned their crops and joined the Mongols. Some castles they took; all the others were besieged, with food running short inside and none in the country round about—and a council of noble lords in Esthonia appealed to Sweden and the Order of the Sword.

The Swedes could or would do little, but the members of the crusading club knew their business, and began to get things in hand. Valdemar sent out Stig Anderssen, a hard man, who beat back the Russo-Mongols, the revolt was put down . . . and now came a check, for the Sword-Order knights said they would not leave until their expenses had been paid and Stig Anderssen had no money to pay with.

This was the situation King Valdemar found when he arrived after the adventure in Rügen, leaving behind him in Sjælland the struggle that may be called Marchwarden Stove's War. He rode rapidly through the land, talked to everybody, and there is record of his fighting one frontier battle against Lithuanian raiders. Stig Anderssen was apparently handling his administration according to Danish law rather than by German feudal custom, and the nobles were not taking it very well. Neither did there seem much chance of elevating the land by the means used in Denmark proper, since the peasantry were of alien blood and there was an endless border war with the Russians. That is, Esthonia was a losing proposition.

Yet the conditions which made it so to Valdemar were

actually recommendations in the eyes of the crusading clubs.
Valdemar posted down to Marienburg to call on Grand Master Heinrich Tusmer of the Teutonic Order. Their conversa-
tion was brief and businesslike, resulting in a treaty which
passed all sovereignty in Esthonia to the Order in exchange
for 19,000 marks cash and 6,000 more to be paid Ludwig of
Brandenburg in extinction of his claim.

What of the townsfolk, largely Danes? The treaty said that
the charters of Reval and Narva should stand, and their laws
not be changed by the Order. What of the Esthonian nobles
and their objections to being anything but Danish? The
treaty took care of this by a clever legal trick. Valdemar ceded
Esthonia to his elder brother, the prisoner-idiot Otto, as
blood-heir—an arrangement not valid in Denmark, where
there was no blood-heir, but unexceptionable in a German
feudal-law jurisdiction. Otto joined the Order, and as it had
a rule against worldly possessions, signed over his dukedom
to the Grand Master; was made commander of Karkus castle,
where he fell, unnoticed, years later, in some combat against
the Lithuanians.

II

Before the end of the year Valdemar was back in Sjælland,
where he found that Klaus Limbek had starved Taarnborg
into surrender, and also that an event of some importance
had taken place along the highroad that strikes from Vordingborg across to Copenhagen. Marchwarden Stove conceived the idea of taking the city by a coup-de-main while
Limbek was busy on the far side of the island at Taarnborg.
The strategy was sound enough, since Valdemar's commander
would have to move almost twice as far for a rescue as Stove
in making the attack, but there seems to have been something
wrong with the arrangements. The Danes learned of the plan;
the King's commander in Copenhagen, an undistinguished officer named Albrekt af Osten, who never again appears in

history, marched out with the garrison and all the local levies he could gather, and set up an ambush near burnt-out Kjøge. The Holsteiners fell into it and were cut down or taken to a man.

Stove himself shared the latter fate, and though he managed to escape after a year in prison, the Germans were left without a commander just as Valdemar returned from Esthonia. The King sent Limbek into Laaland to stir up a revolt against Holstein there, himself taking over much of the Marshal's now veteran and victorious force to lay siege to the great hold of Vordingborg. The double attack brought Graf Johann the Mild out in armor for one of the few times in his life, with all the men he could assemble—a good many, since North Germany was temporarily without a war and hired bravoes came cheap.

Laaland was the obvious place for him to go with what the chronicler describes as "the great host," since that had been little let out in sub-pawns and was an important source of direct revenue. Instead, he suddenly appeared before Valdemar at Vordingborg; and the reason was the first development in the curious relationship between the King and Klaus Limbek, which was to endure all their mutual lives. The Marshal was certainly the ablest man who ever served Valdemar; but he could not endure having any place below the first. When the King sent him to Laaland, he accepted it as an undeserved demotion, got in touch with Graf Johann and offered to join the Holsteiner if the latter could beat Valdemar under the walls of Vordingborg.

Before the battle could be fought, however, a second fleet put into Vordingborg Bight, and to the astonishment of the Holsteiners, here was King Magnus of Sweden, with a host even greater than their own, and the announcement that he was so anxious to arbitrate between the high contending parties that he would join with his army against the first who refused. The odds were too stiff for Johann to do anything but accept; the three armies fraternized and did a little jousting, while the Swedish King considered his award.

It was all in favor of the Danes. Valdemar was to have Vordingborg castle, possession at once, for a payment of six thousand marks, part laid down, part to be paid in a term of months. Of the two main castles in Laaland, Aalholm would go to the King forthwith on terms similar to Vordingborg, Ravnsborg would follow within a year. Sub-pawnholders who still retained lesser place in Sjælland were to be out of the Graf's protection and must make their own terms with Valdemar.

There are these differences to remark between this treaty and the one that broke down into Valdemar's failure before Kallundborg five years previously—that the castles are in Danish hands immediately, and there is money in the till or in easy reach to make the necessary payments. As soon as the seals were on parchment, Valdemar rushed off to Marienburg to dun the Teutonic Order for whatever was still due on Esthonia; obtained it, made his payments on the line, led his army up to Skjoldnæs, north of Ringsted, where on All Souls' Day (how different from that which saw Niels Ebbessen go down) he carried the place by storm from a sub-pawn holder who refused accommodation. It was the last castle in Sjælland to fly a Holstein banner, and a shout of joy went up from all Denmark, for almost at the same hour the Jutland taxes did their work, and the whole peninsula down to Ribe was free from the Holsteiners' hard yoke.

So one of Denmark's major provinces was saved by itself, but the other by the King; but he cared most for Vordingborg, for if little Gurre in the forest was the castle of his heart, the great structure by the sea was the residence of his mind and emblem of his achievement. He rebuilt the old buildings and set up new ones on a steep bank in the bay where a peninsula juts forth to enclose one of the best harbors of the age. It was all done in red hand-made brick, harder than sandstone—a whole city in itself, with a noble cathedral and seven tall towers, many of which still stand to show how different were the ideas of the north from those which sprang out of Latin culture. At Albi, Ely, Angoulême, the high cathedrals were rising, and the plans for Milan had been drawn—Gothic, showing everywhere the pointed arch, exterior buttress, and intricate carving, forests frozen to stone.

At Vordingborg all is straight, flowing line, inside and out. With delight the eye follows plane surfaces so justly proportioned and curves so sweetly drawn that there is no need of decoration. The whole Danish spirit is in Vordingborg; content to make its home in a cottage, but reaching to the skies for peace and protection without a break in the aspiring line. It is the beauty of combining strong and simple elements; might have been built by Doric Greeks. Next to the square battlemented Jomfru Tower stands the octagonal Worm Tower with its pointed roof, and over both the huge round Goose Tower, 34 feet in radius, 132 to the peak of its spire. The theme of towers is carried even to the dwelling-halls, which might so easily be mere barracks; the wings of one sweep out as though they were merely supporting members for the massive square Valdemar's Tower in the middle, the center of the other is almost concealed by round towers rising from its ends. Ruined now, the place is still a thing of beauty; seen from the ships of the new fleet that made its harborage under the walls in the days of King Valdemar, it must have been a glory, that mountain range of red brick towers leading the eye inevitably up to the tallest building in Europe.

III

As soon as he had given orders for the reconstruction of his favorite castle, Valdemar hurried down to Lauenburg with a few companions, picked up his friend, the young Duke Erich, and set out on a pilgrimage to the Holy Land, traveling up the Elbe and through the Brenner Pass to Venice and thence by ship. Jerusalem was by this time in the hands of the infidels, but the Knights of St. John were permitted to maintain a hospice for pilgrims at the Holy Sepulchre. There the young King watched out the stars beside his arms and was dubbed a knight according to the fullest form required by the laws of chivalry, afterward himself conferring the accolade upon Duke Erich; then sailed for home.

Why?

About Valdemar there is always a note of knight-errantry, a challenge to adventure, and certes, there may be some of it in the Jerusalem journey. Yet with Denmark less than half-redeemed, he could have all the adventures he wanted at home merely by asking for them, and the record shows that even when he was being most adventurous, there was a sharp point of policy somewhere under the velvet. The King himself alleged religious reasons when the Church placed him under the automatic ban that fell on all those who visited Jerusalem without the Holy Father's permission: "It was not done out of disrespect to the Holy Mother's keys, but true fear of God." This was adequate for Pope Clement VI, who wrote Roskilde to take off the curse. But it was only the customary exchange of diplomatic communications customary on such an occasion, and in explaining the motives of a King who had drunk deeply at the spring of Marsilio of Padua, and who was widely regarded as an atheist, it fails to satisfy.

The chroniclers of the time gave weight to the idea that Valdemar wished "to see something of foreign lands and customs," which makes a good deal of sense. The mark of Marsilio is on the young King's mind, not only in his approach to some questions, but also in the order of problems that he found interesting. They were both concerned with the state, the commonwealth—the philosopher from the standpoint of determining what the ideal state should be, his pupil with the practical question of giving an altered and enduring form to a state which had broken down.

The Third King

The angle of attack is perfectly clear in the little we know
of the trip. Valdemar displayed an intense curiosity about
the customs and administrative arrangements of the jurisdictions he visited, and on this journey began to appear in the
role that made him famous and welcome throughout Germany—that of arbitrator of disputes. These assigned arbitra-
tions were the usual method of settlement in the period, but
it was also usual for them to stand up only until one party
gathered enough strength for another fight partly because the
award normally was so one-sided as to leave a feeling of
humiliation in its wake. It is one of the most interesting
things we know about Valdemar that his awards had a reputation for permanence of effect. He took the trouble to look
into the background and based his judgments on the thoroughly Danish theory of reconciliation.

The fact is that he was looking for tools. Europe was still
in solution during those years. The methods and assumptions
under which modern life is carried on had not been developed or were agreed to only on a local basis. It was still possible to import into countries which had never heard of them
devices of such major importance as the guild system in in-
dustry or the law of primogeniture in inheritance. Ideological
imports of some kind were clearly necessary for the restoration
of Denmark, for if the civilization of the century of the Valdemars remained sound at the bottom, it had broken down
at the top during the Time of Uproar, and storms were
sweeping through the uncompleted upper stories of the structure. The alternative to finding something new was the installation of the full German feudal system; and to that alternative King Valdemar Atterdag had the most violent
objections.

It would be absurd to claim him as a true social reformer,
or to say that he worked all this out carefully. The procedure
was always groping and it had an overlay of romanticism. The
question before the King was much more limited in its sweep
—that of keeping his crown and recovering the remainder of

its heritage. The feudal system could not be of the slightest assistance to this end, for circumstances had arranged it that the only feudalism possible to Denmark was that of the Holsteiners. The country was without a nobility in the ordinary feudal terms, and to create one would have been very shocking to the custom of Sjælland and the isles, where all the children shared equally in every inheritance.

Jutland was different, to be sure; filled with genuine, if legally unrecognized feudatories. But they had no titles, and it is precisely in the desire to place himself in an inexpugnable position versus these untitled lords that we can trace one of the strands of motivation behind Valdemar's Jerusalem journey.

It made him a knight—and not merely a member of this particularly honorable estate, but a knight of the Holy Sepulchre. It is not easy to convey an idea of the peculiar authority that went with knighthood in a brutal and tempestuous age, for many of whose evils it furnished the only amelioration. The laws of chivalry were often breached and the institution was later watered down to an absurdity for the benefit of politically ambitious manufacturers of soap, but in Valdemar's time it was a living reality. The simple knight, Sir John Chandos, commanded an army in which his underlings were dukes and earls without arousing any sense but one of complete propriety.

The point was that a noble received his powers through being invested with a part of those which belonged to the king—that is, from the secular establishment—while the ceremony of creating a knight had a religious aspect and a quasi-religious significance. The knight was to a certain extent an officer of the Church, and when he passed judgment the sanctions he brought to bear were moral. In his non-military capacity he was a kind of magistrate in ethics, operating in those domains from which the Church had debarred itself, yet in which it was unwilling to deny that morality existed. Thus a priest could not well deal with a case of cowardice, since the mission of religion was peace; nor could any authority but a panel of knights decide whether a given action had been courteous or gallant.

By entering the order of knighthood under such circumstances and in such a manner, Valdemar had secured to himself an invaluable makeweight against the great families, whose controls were paternalistic. In the debatable region where there was no law he could invoke a higher power—for there were very few knighted men in Denmark, Bo Falk is almost the only one we meet. When Klaus Limbek made an armistice with Johann the Mild for Laaland, for instance, the action would not support a charge of treason, since he had taken no oath to Valdemar the King. The Church would undoubtedly have said that any peace to end any war was a good one. But Valdemar the knight could describe the proceeding as unchivalric, and that dash of tar would stick.

IV

Behind all this and far beneath lay the deep underlying medieval sense of form. It is not the first Valdemar that the King follows now, but the other of his name, the Victorious, who stood forth as a knight in Christ on a day when there was need for swords around St. Peter's throne. For the crusade that led to Reval was not one of those undertaken in the spirit of emotional adventure, amid shouts of "God wills it!" but was rather born in deep policy, to hold the north within the circuit of Rome's world.

In those days the strong archbishops of Bremen were moving with a steady drive toward a primacy that should make them as independent of Rome as was Byzantium. Bishop Albert of Riga was Bremen's underling: he had conquered the islands that lie at the mouth of the Gulf from the pagan Livonians, and the town where Düna reaches salt water, from which his see took its name. Therefore the Pope sustained the

Order of the Sword as his rival, and it became so mighty that the bishop must give up a third of the conquered lands to them. Yet this served Rome's need little better; for the Pope was Innocent III, deep in a desperate quarrel with the Emperor, who brought Bremen's archbishop to his side as a weapon against the enemy in Rome.

His Holiness raised Albert to an archbishopric and made an agreement between him and the Sword Order. But now the Emperor so weakened Riga and order both that they found it hard to carry forward the cross. Moreover they were now at Esthonia's borders; in that land dwelt a race hardier than the Livonians and more warlike. They made alliance with the Russian princes; all Livonia was much harried and broken.

The Emperor said this was no concern of his; therefore Pope and archbishop called on King Valdemar, who said he would help them, "for Virgin Mary's honor and the forgiveness of sins," and went forth to the battle on Lyndanise crag. This was now long ago, the pagans were put down; yet the wheel had come full circle.

Ludwig the Kaiser died while our Valdemar, Valdemar Atterdag, was winning Vordingborg; his unquestioned successor was that Karl IV of Bohemia who had once been only a priests' Kaiser. This seemed good to the Pope, but Kaiser Karl was no sooner sure of his crown than he began to run Church affairs in Germany exactly as he pleased. So here's another reason for the pilgrimage to Jerusalem—let the world know there is once more in the north a King Valdemar who serves the cross.

11

The Saint and the
Sodomist
(1347-1349; 1181-1204)

I T IS NECESSARY TO TURN BACK A PAGE AND EXAMINE THE
reasons why Magnus, King of Sweden, who had earlier
been so ready to help in wiping out the last fragments
of Danish sovereignty, should now lay down an award that
placed the solidity of Valdemar's crown beyond attack. The
assigned reason, that he was grateful for Valdemar's permanent cession of Skaane (confirmed at the Danish King's request, by a letter from the Pope) is worth about as much as
Valdemar's own explanation of the Jerusalem journey. Gratitude has seldom been an operative motive in affairs of state.

The fact was that Magnus had become an example of that
impoverishment through overwhelming riches on which so
much Greek myth is based. Before he was three, a considerate
father died in time to let him be brought up as King of
Sweden. Before he was fifteen an equally indulgent maternal
grandfather left him the crown of Norway. Before he was
twenty the Skaane provinces cut themselves off from Denmark and presented him with a third monarchy. His mother
never made any trouble about anything; she was that Ingeborg who became the relict of Duke Porse, but previous to
that she had lived with the man in so publicly scandalous a
manner as to forfeit political influence, and after her second

wedding, she lived in so privately retired a fashion as to be deprived of personal force. Magnus found a well-filled royal treasury; by a not unconnected coincidence the great nobles of Sweden discovered he was delightful. Everyone gave him anything he wanted; he was so handsome that he drove women to a distraction in which they yielded gracefully, attributing their weakness to the enchantments he only half-consciously exercised.

For there was a strain of Finland witch-blood in all the Folkung line from which King Magnus sprang—reaching back to the day when Folke Filbyter, the father of the race, found a demon child in his wolf-pit. He hid her from the dwarfs with whom she used to dance, naked except for anklets of fox fur and dangling chains of glassy beads. She bore him children and ever after there appeared among the tall, blonde Folkungs those who bore the witch-girls' bodily image, small, delicate and with black hair. But blonde and dark alike, all of that stem were touched with a spirit that owed allegiance to difficult gods, and at moments of crisis left them in the irresolution of two contrary natures struggling against each other.

So it was with Magnus. So many women loved him that he carried the by-name of Magnus the Caresser, *Magnus Smek;* but few had any real joy for him, not even the Lady Algotta, who bore him two sons as charming as their father. As King's mistress, she of course bore the reputation of being the loveliest woman in Sweden, but it was not all reputation, for Magnus' taste was extraordinarily good, and he had a fine sense of pageantry. No one could better lead a procession with crown on head and robes falling regally around him; no one could confer an estate on a noble in words better chosen to make the latter feel that his acceptance was a favor to the land; no one could more gracefully handle every type of weapon.

A certain artistic delicacy of feeling usually kept Magnus from exploiting his indubitable talent for arms in any combats more lethal than those of the tilt-yard. But in this also, fortune was his friend. At nineteen there was given to him as wife Blanche of Namur, one of those Flemish countesses who were so often more masculine than their men. The enchantment engulfed her like the rest; the chronicler describes her as "sensible," which means that she did not object to her husband's harem, but devoted herself to fighting like a tigress against uproarious nobles and exterior enemies for the enlargement of Magnus' dominion. A month before the birth of her second son, she was on horseback among the knights, suppressing a revolt in Finland. She even succeeded in bringing a genuine saint into the royal service.

As a child St. Birgitte of Sweden had been a lively specimen, but it is recorded that one day she met the devil walking down a road and never played again. It is unclear whether this was before or after her marriage, at the age of fourteen, to Jarl Ulf Gudmarsson, one of the greatest nobles of the land and a member of the royal council. He kept her busy for a time, producing eight children in as many years, but the tree of vision apparently continued to grow in her mind, and after the death of her youngest child (date uncertain) that tree filled her whole horizon. God and the Virgin Mary appeared to her in broad daylight, issuing communiqués in which Savonarola-like pictures of Heaven and Hell, sex, and highly practical political counsels were mingled in one of the most curious combinations before Swedenborg.

For a time her only converts to a better way of life were among her own family, with whom she lived quietly in exemplary priggishness on an estate at Ulfassa. But when Magnus and Blanche were married, Jarl Ulf obtained for her the appointment as Mistress of Robes to the Queen—very likely in the hope of getting rid of her. He was mistaken; the bishops approved her visions, the secular lords her practical advice, and the court provided her both with a sounding board and a glimpse behind the scenes of Magnus' pageantries. "Instead of the service of God and the regulation of thoughts by His way, there is only evil and corruption," she said.

The visions now changed slightly in character, becoming more specific. Birgitte railed at Blanche for extravagance and at the King for immorality. As her intellectual powers were considerable and her reading as extensive as the age permitted, she had the dreadful faculty of being always right, and she used her authority, at this time, in the direction of extending the powers of the council of nobles. Magnus and Blanche would doubtless have been glad to dispense with her, but were forced to make what head they could by summoning estates of knights and burghers for a matter of six years or so, or until about the time Valdemar took Kallundborg. Jarl Ull now found the atmosphere of sanctity so oppressive that he escaped via a pilgrimage to the shrine of St. James of Compostella in Spain. His wife followed him, and the poor man exercised his only remaining vestige of independence by dying. The Virgin Mary at once took cognizance of the fact that Birgitte was eligible for another marriage in a very special vision:

"As my Son gives the name 'His new bride,' so I now call thee my daughter-in-law. And just as the father and mother entrust and transfer to the daughter-in-law the work of the household, so God and I, who are now old in the hearts of men, announce Our will through you to Our friends and the world."

It was a large commission, in the execution of which Birgitte decided to begin with her home country. For a short time she immured herself in Alvastra cloister to meditate on ways and means of saving the world. Spirits walked her cell with her, as Chrysostom and Clement of Alexandria; not infrequently they transported her to another sleeping place through the walls of stone. By this time the War of the Gerhardssons had taken place, in which Sweden so nearly lost Finland, and the masterful Queen Blanche had discovered that she could not control the nobles without more help than that offered by Magnus. The Queen summoned the saint to return to court and give advice, and the saint was glad to do so; it was one of the things she did best and most frequently.

Her political acumen, now exercised in favor of the royal pair, was as great as ever, but nothing could be more calculated to set Magnus' artistic temperament on edge than having his political counsels handed to him with a sauce of moral maxims. He did whatever Birgitte said in governmental affairs, but the witch-blood took hold and he reacted to the manner in which the advice was given through a series of terrific saturnalias. They reached their climax when the lovely ladies who were earlier his guests had been replaced by handsome boys—and at this point St. Birgitte told the Queen that the only moral thing to do was depose her husband and set up a regency for her young son, Prince Erik.

It was doubtless the politically sapient thing to do as well, but for Blanche the enchantment still held. Instead of eliminating Magnus she tried to regain him via a complaint to a conference of bishops that Magnus had quitted her bed to indulge in unnatural pleasures and asking them to effect a reconciliation. This was no secret; the Swedish nobles began to talk about abdication and Queen Blanche seemed about to lose her game after all when an embassy from Denmark arrived. King Valdemar asked the personal help of King Magnus in bringing to an end the devastating war that was afflicting his country. He would reward such service with the permanent cession of Skaane and a large cash loan.

We are dealing with a pre-Machiavellian world, where intrigue was both naïve and impulsive and the sense of personal glorification very important. King Magnus was delighted; the project not only offered him release from difficulties, but recognition as the great man of the north. The nobles were pleased; they not only bathed in this radiance, but could smell money. Queen Blanche had saved her man.

In fact, of all the people in the royal suite which came to Varberg in North Halland to make the award, only one was discontent—St. Birgitte. In so many words she warned Blanche and Magnus that Valdemar was "the flatterer who pipes to catch a bird," called him "The Wolf of Denmark", and had an unpleasing vision about him. Valdemar remained completely good-humored in the face of these opinions and the saint was treated to the new experience of being ignored. She resigned all her court appointments and rushed off to Rome to announce that it was the will of God and the Virgin Mary that the Pope should return thither from his Babylonish captivity in Avignon; but she would be back.

II

There was a special reason why Valdemar wished to have a contented and weak-minded Magnus in control of Swedish affairs, instead of a regency dominated by the astute Birgitte, whose reach was so very long. He wanted free hands to grapple the problem of Fyn, next to Sjælland the largest of the isles, and, even above Sjælland, the richest at this time, since it had not been devastated by war. It was the seat of one of the most loyal bishops, Odensee; and it controlled the main communications between Sjælland and Jutland, making a really solid Denmark impossible until it was under the crown.

It could only be recovered by violent means, for Iron Heinrich held it under a special form of pledge from King Kristoffer to Graf Gerhard, one provision of which was that Fyn could not be redeemed for cash unless the Holsteiners wished to sell out. But Graf Heinrich was just home from the wars with English gold in his pocket, no particular interest in cash and a great deal of interest in good fighting.

Valdemar did not consider himself a particularly good fighting man, and he had just lost the best leader he had—Klaus Limbek. The story of the break is saga-told and the reasons assigned for it are thoroughly medieval—that Valdemar nagged his man-of-war for an oath of allegiance which the latter now refused on the ground that he had once sworn faith to the Graf of Holstein. Upon Valdemar saying this was no reason, Limbek replied; "If I now break that oath, how can I be true if I swear one to you?" Whereupon (saith the saga) Valdemar fell on a rage and dismissed him.

The story has this justification: a quarrel could readily grow from the fact that within their frames of reference both men were right. Klaus Limbek had sworn to Graf Gerhard; in Denmark such a bond was not transferable, but a Holsteiner would recognize the obligation as due to the office rather than the man. However, it encounters two difficulties; the character of Klaus Limbek, which made any trigger-event unnecessary, and the tradition of the Valdemars, so very sparing in their rages.

There was another man named Valdemar, who was a son of that Magnus, who was son of the old King, Niels; which makes three Valdemars in this part of the story—namely King Valdemar the Great, his son who was later known as Valdemar the Victorious, but at this time a very young man bearing no title save that of Duke Valdemar, and this Valdemar Magnusson, born after his father's death to a lady of Sjælland. The old King and his Archbishop Absalon held that the boy was not at fault for his ancestry. They helped him in every way they possibly could, and as soon as he was old enough, sent him to the university in Paris. He was the best of students, and taught himself also from the book of life, by dwelling now among the poor, now in some merchant's house or with a man-at-arms, which was thought a very strange thing to do. When he returned to Denmark, he was chosen Bishop of Slesvig, though at this time he bore only the title of bishop-elect, since he had not reached the canonical age.

Bishop Valdemar brought order and good government to the see. He founded the Cistercian cloister at Guldholm and set up schools in which the monks were taught. After the death of Valdemar the Great, Knud VI was King; he gave Bishop Valdemar the secular rule in Slesvig as well as the spiritual, calling him "land-protector." The province had been left to Duke Valdemar by his father's will, but he was too young to undertake its government.

All men sat quietly until Duke Valdemar reached his eighteenth year, which was the time for the assumption of his dignities. Then it was seen that the see of Slesvig had fallen into the hands of a black Skjoldung, arrogant and stirring, who could not bear to give away even a little of the powers that had been placed in his hands. He allied himself with the Welfings of Germany, Denmark's foes; menaced Lübeck city into accepting the rule of the Graf of Holstein; took possession of the archbishop's stool in Bremen and coined money which bore his own portrait. When Duke Valdemar tried to restrain these proceedings, the Bishop asked the Pope in Rome to place him under the ban.

His Holiness sent a legate who heard the case, but refused to do anything against Duke Valdemar. This only the more urged on the Bishop, who now went to Sweden, from whence he returned with a great fleet and army, spreading abroad his standard and proclaiming himself King of Denmark. At the same time the Graf of Holstein broke into Slesvig with an army in which were many of the princes of Germany. This was a war that might have gone badly for the Danes; but young Duke Valdemar won the first of his victories in a furious battle against the Holsteins, while King Knud utterly destroyed the Swedish fleet and army, took the Bishop prisoner and shut him up in a dungeon.

Surely, against this man who had so badly repaid the kindnesses done by his kinsmen, Valdemar the Victorious had cause to bear angers. Yet on his own wedding day, he freely forgave the Bishop all that had been done and released him from captivity.

Nor is the theory of a break between Klaus Limbek and his King over the matter of allegiance quite consistent with the rest of the saga. It tells how, after the armistice between Valdemar and Johann the Mild, Klaus Limbek came home to Vordingborg, home from the Laaland war he failed to fight. As he debarked from his ship and rode up the long ramp to the castle, he was met by a boy he knew and cheerfully gave him the greeting of the day as well as a question on how things stood in Vordingborg.

"The pig is fat and the water boiling to cook it, lord," said the lad.

Klaus Limbek gave him one look, turned round and rode back to his ship; but before she could hoist sail to beat out and away, here was a messenger from the King with a safe-conduct, fairly written down. Klaus Limbek read it through; he tore the parchment across and flung the fragments in the messenger's face, crying; "Why did not a dog bring me this? The King's word were enough for me; but as things now stand I dare not go before his face."

So he was gone—down to Holstein, where he becomes visible a little later, sitting on the council of Iron Heinrich. The loss to Valdemar's own council table was not as irreparable as it might have been earlier, since Henning Podbusk had developed into an administrator of the first order, and the regaining of Vordingborg had brought to the royal service not a few of those great men who follow the rising star. Among these is especially to be noted Niels Bugge of Hald, son of one of the lordliest stems of Jutland, called "King Bugge" for his enormous wealth and his leadership of the men of those parts. Graf Gerhard had thought him worth conciliating for his great riches and the strength of Hald castle. The story goes that an English nobleman had been shipwrecked on the coast some years before. Clean against the custom of the time, Niels Bugge took him into his own house, treated him with all consideration and sent him home; which kindness the Englishman repaid by sending a master-builder and a shipload of stone to rear up a hold that should be the strongest in Denmark. Niels Bugge was considered a somewhat highhanded and bad tempered man.

None of the newer lords was likely to replace the dynamic Limbek when the contest for Fyn came to weapon-swinging. But Valdemar's earlier successes and the peace with Graf Johann had bred strains into the structure of Graf Gerhard's piratical Holstein state by causing an unemployment problem among the invincible armored horsemen. When men of their background have all the force there is, but feel the need of money, there is always one thing they can do. The roads and market places of Holstein became actively unsafe, and the younger Gerhardsson, Graf Nicholas, proved incapable of restraining his vassals.

Iron Heinrich was a tougher proposition, but he came home from Crécy to find the disease well advanced, peasants quitting their fields, private wars going on everywhere, the whole territory sinking into an anarchy beyond that of the Danish Time of Uproar for the latter was a case of society settling into a new, if unattractive, mold, while this was utter wolf-law. Heinrich took hold vigorously, smashed up looters in a couple of combats and carried by storm his home castle of Rendsborg, where one of the rebel leaders, named Marchwarden Westensee, had installed himself. The other looters coalesced round one of their number named Hennike Hummersbüttel, but they could not hold the field against Graf Heinrich, who shut them all up in Hummersbüttel's castle of Hohenstegen, a big place, built on a rock.

At this point Valdemar arrived in Lübeck, on his way back from the Holy Land. It must have afforded him one of the more intense pleasures of his life to have ambassadors from Baron Hummersbüttel greet him with an offer to swear fealty to himself and Denmark, if Hohenstegen were supported against the unjust proceedings of Iron Heinrich. Valdemar agreed, with a proviso for his Lübeck friends that road piracies be stopped, and threw a force of men and provisions into Hohenstegen that put it beyond Iron Heinrich's power.

Heinrich complained to the Hansa, the bishops, the Kaiser of Germany, and anyone else who would listen. They found the spectacle of the arch-bandit complaining of banditry ridiculous, and too many of the floating population of mercenary soldiers were locked up in Hohenstegen for him to have any luck at hiring others to beat the place down, so there was nothing to do but make terms with Valdemar; nor would Valdemar make any terms that did not include some release of the Fyn pledge. As the details worked out the total pledge for the island was reduced from 41,000 marks to 31,000; the immediate payment of 10,000 marks of this sum bought half the island's territory and its big castle at Nyborg; and only half this 10,000 was paid in cash, the other half being forgiven in recognition of the Danish King's graciousness in restraining his vassal, Baron Hummersbüttel, from making further wars in Holstein.

There were additional, very complex conditions for the release of Hindsgavl and Ørkel, the other two big Fyn castles, which had underpledge-holders, but the intricacies resolved themselves into the arrangement Valdemar adopted elsewhere, that the taxes should pay off the debt. Hummersbüttel yielded up Hohenstegen; Iron Heinrich wanted his carcass, but as a Knight of the Holy Sepulchre, Valdemar said it would be unchivalrous for him to grant that, and took the man into his service. Twenty years later he was commanding a castle in Denmark, and doing good work.

IV

At the same time the castle of Stege on Møn fell in to crown and realm and the final payment was made on Nykøbing of Falster. The question naturally arises as to where King Valdemar, once so poor that he had to be crowned in brass, was getting all that money. Of course, there was the price of Esthonia, but we know precisely where that silver went, as will be explained presently; and even the heavy drudgery of the people from dawn to dark fails to account for the extent of the royal prosperity, which runs to the release of Falster and Møn, the buying-out of Magnus, and the first payment on Fyn, all in a breath.

The tax income was only important as it came from freeholding bonders, and as early as the King's hermitage in Jutland, it was obvious that so few of these had survived the Time of Uproar that the class would have to be rebuilt. Valdemar had undertaken the task with his gristmills and roads, but this program had certainly not reached the point where it would produce so spectacular an increase in funds.

The fact is that Valdemar had worked out a completely new system of state income. It owed a good deal to the loanhold institution of Knud VI and Valdemar the Victorious, and hence neither offended prejudice nor attracted very much attention at the time. It apparently made it easy for the semi-nobles of Denmark to acquire the status of the hereditary baronage of Germany, and so was eagerly accepted by the parties most concerned. Yet it afforded a peculiarly powerful and sensitive means of political control, as well as a source of financial income.

The nub of the system was that the King did not grant estates or lordships outright to anybody, but allowed royally-owned lands for a period which was theoretically the will of the sovereign. They paid cash rentals for the use of the ground. There was no sense of hard bargain in this for medieval thinkers. Except in the case of freeholding yeomen, there were no permanent titles to land; all feudal tenures were temporary and conditional, usually depending upon performance of military service. Valdemar's cash rentals struck those who participated in them as a peculiarly light and easy method of gaining the use of an estate. They were immensely popular; the parchments making such grants or altering them appear in the archives by hundreds, and the aggregate income from these leaseholds must have been very great, since sums of one hundred marks are mentioned at every step, with a fair sprinkling of much larger amounts.

The granting, inheritance, and exchange of estates constituted the bulk of chancery business everywhere at this time. They were continually falling in to the crown through default of heirs, by attainder of treason, by the clearance of new ground, the examination of old titles which showed them as really belonging to the royal demesne, by abandonment. All of these methods were deliberately and consciously accentuated by Valdemar Atterdag, and in addition he bought estates outright from his subjects. In nearly every case, the estates went out again on leasehold as soon as the royal title was established.

In addition, the King very early made himself the greatest moneylender in the realm. A needy bonder or herremand could always pawn the title to his lands to Valdemar for a few hundred marks. These pawns were to be repaid on the installment plan. They tended to convert themselves into leaseholds, both because such an office as the royal chancery always tries to simplify similar documents in the direction of a single character, and because men who get in so deep that they must pawn their most valuable possession are seldom able to extricate themselves. (There was no such conversion in middle Europe, where land loans were also common; but the lending was done by Jews there, and when Baron Mürich could not meet a payment date, he discharged his debt by burning the Jew's house down—a tactic unlikely to succeed against the King of Denmark.)

Even the free hereditary bonder estates tended to take on the new character; the documents refer to sums due from them not as *afgifter*, which are taxes, but as *landgifter*, which are ground rents. In a polity which had a strong inherent tendency toward absolutism, this might have led to the theory that the earth is the lord's and the fullness thereof, with men enjoying it only during the King's good pleasure. But such a theory was so repugnant to the whole Danish system of thought that no one ever stated it. The real tendency was in the opposite direction—toward regarding *landgifter* and *afgifter* as synonymous on the basis of the latter; toward treating installments due on pawn-loans and land rents as though these were expressions really meaning taxes due to the state, not monies owed to the privy purse of its King.

Valdemar himself powerfully aided this shift to a taxation basis in several ways. He encouraged leaseholders to build on the rented estates, and so to make their rent-paying function a permanent one. He placed in all land conveyances to himself a new phrase, ceding the land to his "heirs, to Denmark's King and Denmark's crown"—thus substituting the institutional for the personal relation. To a great Thing held at Ringsted on St. Knud's Day of 1349 he gave an accounting of the sums he had spent in releasing the realm from Holstein pawnholders—30,000 marks of state revenue plus 10,000 marks that were peculiarly his own, the proceeds of the sale of Esthonia.

The wiping out of the distinction between the King's official and personal incomes was an innovation, but it was the only one in the system. Pawn loans with payments on the installment plan were no new thing; Valdemar himself had bought Jutland back in this manner. The changed aspect of the taxes on bonders' estates was a paper matter. Even leaseholds were not unknown. The change brought about by the King lay in the vigor and consistency with which lands were gathered under the royal title and let out again on rental. There is nothing like this continual drive anywhere else in Europe. Not only did it furnish Valdemar with a treasury which, though it still had difficulties, remained generally adequate to the nation's needs, but it also altered the whole constitution of the nascent noble order that was growing up under the influence of the German lordships and the decline of the bonder class.

In the feudal countries of the rest of Europe, the nobility were exempt from taxation in return for military service; in Valdemar Atterdag's Denmark, this position was reversed.

12

The End of the World
(1332-1350)

DURING THE WINTER THAT SAW KING KRISTOFFER JUMP out of a window and die of the resulting complications, Prince To-Nwan-Timur came to the Dragon Throne of the Yuan in Kingsai. He had every confidence that Heaven had indeed created the earth for the pleasure of himself, its son. The Dowager Empress he executed; the imperial Princesses, his sisters, were placed in his harem; a decree proclaimed that no maiden over sixteen might be married until she had been inspected for enrollment among the royal concubines; and these serious matters having been cared for, the minor business of state was turned over to the Emperor's friend Pe-Yew. Evidence of divine displeasure with something in the state presently appeared in the form of a fiery meteor which struck the earth and destroyed everything within a hundred-league circuit. Pe-Yew quickly perceived that the cause of this visitation was the attitude of the native Chinese toward their masters. He issued decrees that they should no longer use the ideographs for "long life" or "happiness" and that they should be prevented from learning the Mongol language.

These measures proved insufficient. The spring came late, clouds closed in, rains poured down without cease to meet a pestilential mist that rose from the face of the ground. The river districts turned to swamps and the land became filled with the odor of the putrefying locusts which had never darkened the sky in greater swarms. Pe-Yew suggested the issuance of a decree that all Chinese bearing the names of Chang, Wang, Liu, Li, and Chan be exterminated, but before this well-thought-out project could be carried through, the earth began to tremble throughout the empire, all the houses in Honan province fell down, the courses of the rivers changed, the mountain Tsinchou disappeared, and vast clefts opened in the ground. All winter the rains continued, but with the new spring the waters vanished in a burning drought that parched up the shoots from what seed had escaped being eaten. Famines had already begun by this date; even in the cities it was no longer possible to sell a baby for enough to provide a week's nourishment, and bands of robbers were roaming the countryside. The Army of the Eight Banners was sent against them, but there was no food even for the soldiers; they mutinied and joined the bandits.

With the second winter the torrential rains began again; four hundred thousand people perished at Kingsai and a pestiferous wind spread such an odor that many, being overpowered by it, fell down suddenly and expired in dreadful agonies. Those who sought to aid the sufferers were themselves stricken by the infection. They spat blood, their skins developed pustules, which burst with an offensive smell, they fell down in diarrhoea and delirium and seldom survived the setting of the sun. More people died in China than were alive in Europe.

During the next summer this pestilence began to reach long black fingers out across the caravan-routes, progressing at a camel's pace half-way round the world. When Niels Ebbessen struck down Graf Gerhard, it had begun to touch Samarkand and Balkh; when Valdemar took Kallundborg, it was negotiating in the Persian bazaars and struggling down through the Hindu Kush into India; when the victory bells were pealing for Vordingborg won, it joined the crew of a Genoese ship making out of the Black Sea.

The coming of that ship to Europe was preceded by prodigies like those in the East, as though the planet itself were trying to shake man loose from his grip. A tidal wave rose in the Mediterranean and drowned the shipping in Candia harbor. Long streams of lava rolled down the sides of Vesuvius; earthquakes rocked the white cities of Italy; the ground cracked and an odor of brimstone came forth. There were landslides in Switzerland; a great mass of earth fell from the Gota Elv in Norway, causing a flood which drowned out two hundred families. The pastures of Greenland disappeared; masses of ice came floating down from the pole to cut off all communication with Europe, and an expedition which King Magnus sent to the colony was never heard from again. All the sheep in Caithness died of cold gusts which lasted into July, and glaciers formed in the Iron Mountains of Bohemia.

On the heels of these manifestations, as in China, came a summer of terrible floods, during which the ground produced nothing but mould-spores. The drought followed, with a cloud of locusts out of Africa, which ate all the leaves from the trees, then fell dead in stinking windrows across the land. Now a slow and soft wind blew up from the east and held steadily, men said, for weeks; it brought a black fog that hung close to the ground, through which people moved like shadows in a dream, themselves half adream; and through that fog the ship of Genoa came to port with her cargo.

It was no ordinary sickness that could be cured with prayer and a draught from a church bell. It began with fever, thirst, and a sensation of weakness. Outbreaks started on the thighs and arms, there were swellings in the groin, black spots appeared on the body, growing larger and running into each other. The patient became stupid, his tongue was palsied, his breath had a fetid odor, he made clutching motions toward his throat. Presently the little boils burst, discharging a pus; the sick man now recovered his senses for a space, coughed up a little blood, and then died. In many cases people passed through all the stages in twenty-four hours; they seldom lived beyond three days. Those who survived the fifth day usually recovered, but were apt to come out of the sickness brutalized or clean idiot.

The most frightening feature was the terrible contagiousness. To touch those who died of this Black Death, to minister to the sick, to smell their breath, was to take the infection. Messer Giovanni Boccaccio in Italy saw two hogs root around the clothes of a plague-dead man for a little, then stagger a few paces and fall down dead. The peasant who owned the animals came to look at them and broke out with the black spots that same afternoon. The evil floated on the air, invaded lonely hamlets in the hills, which were found years later empty of all save skeletons disposed in an attitude of agony which indicated the route along which life had fled. Whole cities disappeared, like Neu Stargard. In other cities the gay dances of the apprentices ceased and the guilds no longer met for their weekly dinners. There was no herring market at the Skaane fisheries in the year of the plague; Stralsund lost a third of its population; more extraordinary masses for the departed were sung in Roskilde cathedral than during the ten preceding years together. In Viborg Amt eleven parish churches were left without a priest to say mass or a parishioner to hear it. On Bornholm "there were not enough men left to eat a sheep." Wild cattle ran through uncultivated fields around Randers.

What of the living? What was their counsel while the rocks were rending and snow fell in the summer? Counsel of despair; bands of robbers roamed the French roads, sparing none. The forces of order were helpless to control plundering in the cities. The entire population of Mainz went into a collective frenzy, hurling their possessions from their windows, while burghers, priests and knights, men and women, joined in a shrieking dance through the streets till they fell down of exhaustion or the plague. Counsel of hedonism; in Italy the arts flowered gloriously from the poisoned soil and adultery became an art. The court gathered at a villa in the hills where the plague had not come, Boccaccio wrote his

"Decameron," Petrarch lost his Laura and found his voice.

Counsel of sound practical men; it was manifest that the Jews had caused these calamities by poisoning the wells and making a pact with the devil for the destruction of Christians. In Spain, at Toulouse, Cologne, and Mantua, juridical inquiries were opened; a very difficult matter, but by the application of ingenious tortures, representatives of the race were persuaded to admit their conspiracy, and stern measures were immediately taken to bring it to an end.

In most places certain numbers of Jews were hanged and the remainder warned that if their machinations did not cease, they would all come to the same fate. But at Strasbourg the sterner measure was adopted of surrounding the ghetto with a ring of armed men and burning to death everyone in it. This procedure met with so much approval in neighboring towns that the Jews of Speyer committed suicide in a body to avoid such treatment. In Mähren and Württemberg, nay many of the smaller central states, men-at-arms assembled the Jews into caravans and drove them across the frontiers, usually in winter, for it was not good that too many of these enemies of Christ should survive.

To others, even if the Jews were responsible, they were only the agents of an angered God, and salvation lay in reconciling oneself with Him. Bold and selfish men gave their entire possessions to the Church for protection against the malady; the altars were thronged with penitents, who offered money—more frequently than not refused by the priests for fear it would be contaminated. Gold and silver were thrown through the windows of churches and over the walls of monasteries by night. In Hungary there began the movement of the marching preachers, Brothers of the Cross.

They were attired in black mantles from head to foot, with a red cross before and another behind; hoods hid their faces and their eyes were fixed on the ground. Two and two they tramped in columns along all the roads of Europe, bearing velvet banners embroidered with mystic insignia, or long tapers, unlighted. Hanging from each belt was a triple scourge, knotted and the knots studded with points of iron; and as they marched, they chanted to a slow and melancholy beat:

"Whoso would save his soul from stain
Must pay and render back again.
His safety so shall he consult;
Help us, good Lord, to this result.
Ye that repent your crimes, draw nigh,
From the flames of Hell we fly,
And Satan's wicked company.
Jesus Christ was captive led
And to the cross was riveted;
'Sinner canst thou to me atone
'Three pointed nails and thorny crown?
'What wilt thou, sinner, bear for me?'
Lord, with loud voice we answer Thee,
Accept our service in return
And save us, lest in Hell we burn."

When these marching brethren reached a town, they halted in the market place, and while one body of them formed a circle and intoned their dolorous chant, the rest removed their clothing to the waist and lay with their faces to the ground, by their attitudes indicating the nature of the sins they confessed. Thereupon the master of the band moved among those prone, scourging their backs till the blood ran. His lieutenants read aloud letters with mystic words, which they said had fallen from heaven; whereupon they rose and, once again hiding their faces, scourged each other still more, then joined by such of the townsfolk as desired, resumed their pilgrimage to nowhere, adjuring everyone to rout out the impious Jews. Everywhere they were regarded as holy and they were received with awe, even when the black spots of the pestilence showed on their naked bodies. The Pope issued a bull against them, but not for this did they cease their marchings till they fell down dead.

II

It is easy to exaggerate the physical effects of the Black Death and accompanying catastrophes, even though they collectively constituted the worst visitation of recorded history. Except for a few such events as the fall of the Gota Elv and the burning of the Strasbourg ghetto the physical equipment of man's existence suffered little damage. Except for a few such events as that of Mainz, there was no great immediate spiritual damage either. For lack of any more practical ideas, the general feeling was that business should be carried on as usual; and it was so continued, though at a reduced tempo and with less confidence in the result. In the major wars between France and England and Hungary and Bohemia, operations slowed down to the level of outpost combat, but the wars themselves did not cease. After the first great plague year, the Hanseatic cities (which, like all crowded centers, were especially hard hit) took up their commerce where they had left it off. The intrigues of courts went on.

But over the long pull the effect was to leave an indelible mark on the Western European mind; to break up the whole tight little mold of medieval life, with its contentments and certainties. In normal medieval times, the wars with which the chronicles are filled really affected comparatively few people beyond those who went looking for trouble. The system was effective in providing a reasonable degree of security to anyone who sought it sincerely, and security was the reason for which society existed. The personal rights which later ages came to regard as important were not even subjects of discussion.

The Black Death and its accompanying phenomena (whose part must not be underestimated) showed this security to be illusory. The Church had promised protection from acts of God, save as isolated individual events. When the ground shook and the skies rained death on just and unjust alike, it was not surprising that some men should deduce that the fault lay in the protector. The secular power promised protection from man, but proved incompetent to deal with the wave of violent and anarchic hedonism roused by something very closely approaching the imagined end of the world.

It was thus no accident that Plantagenet England, one of the most solid of medieval states, should produce Lollardry and Wat Tyler on the heels of the great visitation. It was hardly even an accident that the Church should rend itself apart in the great schism. It was not only that the world was coming to an end, but the foundations on which all worlds are built were shattering; the basic ideas were no longer valid. If the Creator, despite the utmost one can do in piety, still lets one's wife die of a pestilence, from which had fled the priests whose duty it was to offer spiritual comfort . . . if the baron to whom one has sold liberty in exchange for protection from strong-thieves fails at the moment of utmost emergency . . .

Except for Denmark. Let one not insist too vigorously upon the exception. There were so many exceptions of various kinds that no case was wholly typical. England bore the hard shock well; the very apparatus of ventilation furnished by Lollardry and Wat Tyler enabled her to escape with those minor changes of orientation by which Englishmen always water fundamentals down to the practical level. In Castile and Aragon the reaction was stern, and in the direction of the idea that the faith had been inadequately maintained; a Cid who sometimes fought on the side of the Moors became impossible, and the conquest of Mexico became possible. Italy turned into a refuge of the humanities and China produced a national uprising against the foreign Mongols.

The real difference in reaction was that Denmark under Valdemar Atterdag did not react at all. An extraordinary convocation of bishops was called by the King, under the presidency of Roskilde. It proclaimed that the Black Death could hardly be the work of the Jews in Denmark, since there were none; that it was not the work of the devil, but an ordinary virulent sickness, for which the remedy lay in fortitude and prayer. When processions of the flagellant brethren reached the border in Jutland, they were turned back. A royal edict declared that no Brothers of the Cross would be admitted by sea. Business really did go on as usual in a land which had too lately come too far from night to believe that the world was ending.

13
International
(1349-1350; 1197-1215)

THE POLITICAL OPERATIONS OF THE MEDIEVAL SUB-STATES of Central Europe are an unappetizing compost, in which the main elements are greed, faithlessness and the desire for personal adulation. But it would be an error to assume that there was no overall pattern, no central point of reference. It was almost instinctive, something done without thought; but through that tangle of insincere alliances and conflicts banal to the point of futility, there runs a clue. Consistent assemblages of force are directed against any entity that might impair the general anarchic imbalance which left open to the grafs the only life they knew. A stable state violated the union rules.

Denmark had been dragged down to the sub-state level in the Time of Uproar. By the capture of Vordingborg, with Sjælland and North Jutland, Valdemar was threatening to raise her to the status of Sweden or Poland—an inexpugnable national entity, which might be captured entire (under favorable conditions) but not partitioned. This was dangerous.

Up to the fall of Vordingborg, Valdemar's contacts had been limited to the circle of the north almost as completely as Denmark's had in the days when Western and Eastern Teutonic were splitting into separate tongues. The Holstein grafs looked in the same direction; thought of themselves as Scandinavian rather than German princes, and took no part in the affairs of the Empire.

Valdemar would almost certainly have preferred to continue in this closed circuit for the time being. There was all
Fyn still to redeem, a good part of Jutland and much of the
southern isles, not to mention the Skaane provinces. But in
the plague year the King learned that he had developed from
a local into an international figure. A coalition was formed
against him, and the central figure in it came from within the
Empire.

Albrecht of Mecklenburg was the only Slavonian prince in
Germany, tracing a direct father-to-son ancestry back to the
Princes in Wendland whom Valdemar the Great converted
under the sword. He was energetic, proud, reckless, unreliable and clever; a thorough Slav, whose underlying will-to-
power gave his actions an amount of purpose altogether
exceptional in that age of fantastic projects, quickly undertaken and flightily abandoned. That purpose was to make
his family royal. Albrecht had done all sorts of services for
Kaiser Karl, who had made him a Duke at just this time,
which conferred a certain eligibility toward kingship; he also
had three sons by a wife who was sister to Magnus, the
sodomist of Sweden, and through them, the strongest blood
claim to the triple crown, should that King fail of direct heirs.

The Mecklenburger's method up to this time had been the
typically Slavic one of seeing that all scraps of loose territory
that he could not gather in for himself should fall to Sweden.
St. Birgitte distrusted this generosity, called him "the Snake,"
and never tired of warning Blanche and Magnus that their
brother-in-law was up to no good. He had some intricate
feudal rights in connection with Rostock city, a claim on part
of Falster, and as an adjunct to it, full possession of the tiny
out-island of Bogø.

The new Duke had let this island out to some of his vassals, who set up in business as pirates and made an extremely
good thing of it, since Bogø not only controls the sea routes
from Sjælland southward, including direct access to Vordingborg, but also flanks the sea-lanes through the Sound. While

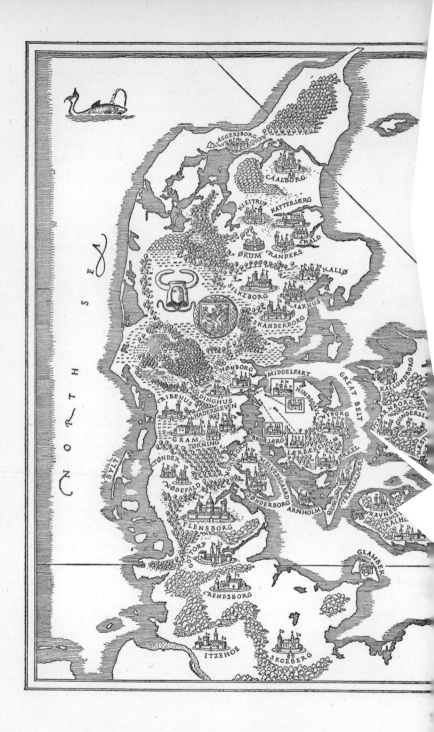

NORTH SEA

GREAT BELT

AGGERSBORG

AALBORG

KLEITRUP KATTEBJÆRG

CHALD

ØRUM RANDERS

KALLØ

SILKEBORG

AARHUS

SKANDERBORG

HØNBORG MIDDELFART

KALLUNDBORG

KOLDINGHUS HINDSGAVL

RIBEHUS HADERSLEVEN NYBORG

TØRNBORG

GUNDERSL

GRAM BROBJÆRG

TØRNING LÆRBÆKSHOLM

NORDBORG

NØDEFALD MELVEDGAARD ØRKEL

TØNDER SØNDERBORG TRANEKÆR

FLENSBORG ARNHOLM

RAVNSBORG

AALH

GOTORP

GLAMBEK

RENDSBORG

ITZEHOE SEGEBERG

SYLT

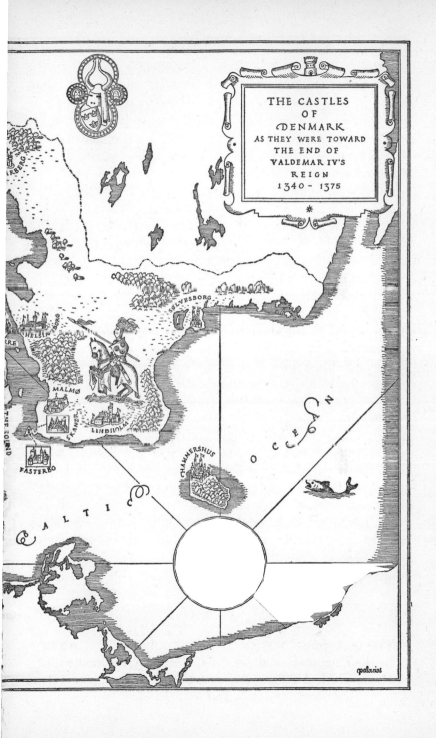

THE CASTLES
OF
DENMARK
AS THEY WERE TOWARD
THE END OF
VALDEMAR IV'S
REIGN
1340 - 1375

SØLVESBORG

HELSINGBORG

MALMØ

SKANØR

LINDHOLM

FASTERBØ

HAMMERSHUS

OCEAN

BALTIC

THE SOUND

qpalacios

the Holsteiners held Vordingborg, Valdemar was indifferent to the little island; the Hansa ships could take care of themselves, and it caused the King no pain to see Mecklenburg and Holstein pirating on each other. But as soon as the lordly red castle belonged to Denmark once more, Valdemar ordered the ships bringing home the Esthonian garrison under Stig Anderssen to stop off at Bogø, where they took the Mecklenburgers by surprise, killed every one of them, and seized their considerable accumulation of booty.

The place was hardly worth bothering about for its own sake, but these were the vassals of Duke Albrecht, a man who set great store by the esteem in which he was held. It is not unlikely that he also felt some nervousness about the King's visit to Rügen, which King Kristoffer had pawned to him, and which he meant to keep. At all events what Duke Albrecht did was to drag Valdemar into the tangled thicket of imperial politics, where almost anything the Danish King did would bring him into opposition with the association for keeping states from growing up.

The fracture line concerned fealty in Rügen, or who owed homage to whom. Normally, this was a question which became practical only at the moment of death—when an estate was inherited by a minor or an unmarried heiress, which gave the overlord a guardianship that he usually managed to convert into outright possession. But police power was also the prerogative of an overlord, so that the heads of sub-states found it clearly in their interest to owe homage to as distant and impotent a personage as possible—as the Esthonian nobles preferred Denmark to Brandenburg or the Teutonic Knights.

II

The background was this:

In the days of the old Ascanier Markgrafs of Brandenburg, the lords of Mecklenburg and Pommern were border-marchers

and vassals of that state. That is, they owed homage to
Berlin. Legally, the arrangement was still in effect, though
there is no record that Ludwig the Younger made any effort
to claim his fealty, or even regarded the question as worth
troubling about till after the death of his father, the Kaiser.
The new Kaiser was Karl IV, of the house of Luxembourg-
Bohemia, whose rivalry with the Wittelsbachs split medieval
Germany wide open. Almost his first official act was to de-
mean the Wittelsbach in Berlin by elevating Mecklenburg
and Pommern to the rank of Reichsprinces, owing homage
only to the head of the Empire.

Ludwig, a dull dog who left most of his business to deputies, merely growled amid the gusty corridors of his castle
at the news. He would have done no more had not Karl
(who passed for one of the subtlest men of his age) possessed
the artistic weakness of being unable to let a good effect alone.
In the year of the plague, when everything was so confused,
there appeared on the frontiers of Brandenburg an old man
with a perpetual look of surprise about his eyes, who said his
name was Waldemar.* He was the last of the Ascanier line;
not dead and buried twenty-five years ago, as generally supposed, but living as a lay monk in the Holy Land in penance
for having allowed lust to entrap him into a marriage within
the prohibited degrees; now returned in an odor of grace
to relieve the state from the burdens placed upon it by the
impious Wittelsbachs, who were certainly responsible for the
Black Death.

Ludwig said the man was a miller's son named Heinrich
Rehbach and the signet by which he proved his identity was
a forgery, but the commons of western Brandenburg cheered
Waldemar through their villages, Kaiser Karl proclaimed him
the genuine article and called on Mecklenburg and Pommern, as his vassals in the north, to support the true heir of
Brandenburg. The date was not long after Stig Anderssen's

---

*Still another Valdemar, but since this one was a German, con-
fusion can be avoided by spelling him with a W.

raid on Bogø. Albrecht of Mecklenburg seems to have set as the price of his services an imperial charter giving him the fealty of Rügen and a similar document regarding Rostock. He was given what he wished and began to move his pikemen into the plague-stricken towns of Brandenburg, with his bull's-head banner borne before.

The best answer Ludwig's advisers could think of was to assemble the anti-Luxembourg electors of the Empire, declare Kaiser Karl deposed, and make a pseudo-Kaiser out of one Günther of Schwarzburg, a Thuringian graf, brave and much respected for his knightliness, but with hardly a piece of silver to his name and little support outside his home city of Frankfurt.

III

Time was when not the vassalage of the isles lay at issue between Denmark and Mecklenburg, but that of Mecklenburg itself between Denmark and the Empire, and the latter proved the lesser party. It lay deep in the golden hours when Valdemar Sejr was king. After the fierce day when he, as young Duke of Slesvig, broke the hearts and armor of the Holsteins in the Bishop's War, the Graf of that land was by no means willing to accept the verdict of the sword. He was a stirring, pushing man with black brows, called Adolf, the third of that name to rule in Holstein. Men disliked him much for his oppression and hardness of heart, but he was a strong lord, holding all the land between the Elbe and Eider. This was called Nordalbingia in those days; the cities of Hamburg and Lübeck lay in it, which brought the Graf much taxes. He had also great castles at Itzehoe, Segeberg, and Travemünde, such structures being then somewhat more rare than they have become recently.

When Adolf had a little recovered from his distresses, he called friends and neighboring princes about him and went up with a numerous army to where Rendsborg stands, on an

island in the Eider. It was his thought to build a new castle
there as a perpetual means of ingress to Denmark. But when
he arrived on the one bank so did Duke Valdemar and King
Knud appear at the north bank with the army of the Danes.
Graf Adolf said these were only bonders who would presently
go home, as they had done before, and bade his men sit still.
Little profit did he have from that advice, for the Holsteiners
sat all summer long and the Danes were there at the end of it,
being for the more part King Knud's new army of hærmænd,
who had somebody at home to reap crops for them.

During the winter Duke Valdemar built a strong and wide
bridge across the river, with a small castle on the island to
cover it. Now Graf Adolf led his men to the south and besieged the city of Lauenburg, this being the only place in
Nordalbingia that did not belong to him. The people of the
town were much straitened, and sent a message placing themselves under the King of Denmark's fealty, but before he
could aid them, they had eaten up all their shoe leather and
been forced to surrender. The taking of Lauenburg was considered strongly done on Adolf's part, since the Danes did
nothing against him.

As for Adolf, he now considered that he might go further,
since King Knud was so peaceable a man that he would not
make war unless attacked; therefore he sent his men to harry
the lands of the marshbonders, over whom he claimed the
rule. There were then two emperors in Germany. Graf Adolf
had hitherto been faithful to the one called Philip of Swabia,
but now he changed his allegiance to Kaiser Otto the Welfing, who had great strength in the northern lands. Graf
Adolf asked him for help against the Danes and Otto the
Emperor said he would give it.

That summer Duke Valdemar sat quietly at home, as near
as anyone could find out, but when the herring-run began in
September, his men fell suddenly on the Lübeck ships at
Skanør, took all of them and threw their people in prison.
On the same day Duke Valdemar himself led his army across

the Eider. Graf Adolf's army was utterly destroyed in battle and he himself driven in flight. Itzehoe castle the Duke took by storm; the burghers of Hamburg and Lübeck said they would do homage to Denmark and opened their gates.

Graf Adolf went to the court of the Emperor and obtained some help. During the autumn and winter he gathered strength about him, and at the time of the Yuletide feast, when Duke Valdemar had gone home to celebrate the holy days, the Graf broke into Hamburg and drove out the Danish guard which had been left there.

Now was it seen that there is little luck in the doings of an unlucky man. Graf Adolf had told his people that the Danes would be keeping festival as usual, with much drinking, and therefore the Holsteiners could do just as they pleased; but as soon as Duke Valdemar heard the tidings, he marched on Hamburg, which he entered unexpectedly by means of the ice-frozen Elbe. Slaughter was made of Graf Adolf's men; he himself was taken prisoner and shut up in a castle with the bad Archbishop.

During this time Otto the Welfing was engaged in a war with the other Emperor, but after Philip of Swabia fell, he became sole Kaiser. One day the court was gathered on the lawns before Braunschweig castle, which was built by a great conqueror and hero named Duke Heinrich the Lion, who set up there his emblem of a lion in iron, looking defiantly toward the east, in which direction the old wars had been made. There was a man named Bernhard the Saxon. He spoke to this beast; "How much longer will you keep snarling eastward? You have gained what you wanted there; it is time now to turn toward the north."

Kaiser Otto took this for the best of counsel; he led out an army and captured Hamburg again. At this time both King Knud and the old Archbishop Absalon were dead, and Valdemar the Victorious had become king. He brought the army of the Danes into Nordalbingia immediately and would have fought a battle with the Kaiser, but Otto the Welfing dared not, for the hærmænd looked mighty grim, and Otto had to think that after a combat with them, he might have to fight with the anti-Kaiser raised up in his rear by his enemy, the Pope, and maybe with the King of the French in addition. This was the first time he had drawn back before an enemy in the field; he was thought to have gained small honor thereby. Neither was there any profit in his taking of Hamburg, for King Valdemar made a winter campaign against the city, building a tower opposite the gates, and closing it in on the river side from the ice. The townspeople themselves were not unhappy when the place was taken.

IV

Otto the Welfing had been very little more than half an emperor, while Kaiser Karl IV could bring a united Germany to the support of his Mecklenburg agents. Valdemar the Victorious had the best army of Europe and the certainty that he was one of the continent's ablest leaders, while Valdemar Atterdag had a pick-up army, some reason to doubt his own military capacity and under-leaders of questionable loyalty. The old King led a strong, united Denmark, and the new a land only half won and staggering up out of night. Behind Valdemar II stood the giant figures of Innocent III and Philip Augustus of France, while the only man our Valdemar could count on was the dull dog of Brandenburg. Yet the medieval sense of pattern required him inexorably to ruffle up against Albrecht of Mecklenburg or be lost. The imperial charter to Rügen challenged not only his chance of future redemptions but his hold on what he had. What if the next step were an imperial document confirming Albrecht's claim on Bogø, or giving the Holstein grafs permanent possession of Fyn?

Valdemar declared himself the enemy of the false Waldemar and landed with the army of the Danes on Poel island, before Wismar, which he harried heavily; hurried aboard ship again and to the mouths of the Oder, where the men of the two Dukes of Wolgast were added to his, and landed in western Pommern. Saxe-Lauenburg and certain of his riders were with him. They stormed the town of Strasburg, which stands where Mecklenburg, Pommern and the Uckermark of Brandenburg meet, and is the rendezvous point where the armies of the two former must focus for an attack on the last. Duke Albrecht, whose march into Brandenburg had been delayed by the feint at Poel, rushed east to regain Strasburg and deprive the Danish King of communications while restoring his own with Pommern.

While he was about it, word came that another army (all these armies are very small) was coming down the Oder under Markgraf Ludwig's younger brother, another Ludwig, called Ludwig the Roman. This seemed the most immediate danger; Albrecht turned sharp round and crushed Ludwig the Roman in a sharp battle at Odersburg, but in so doing, he lost track of Valdemar of Denmark, who slanted southwest from Strasburg, covering his right flank by the Mecklenburg lakes, and fell on the towns of the Uckermark. The feeling for the false Waldemar was strongest there; he destroyed it. By the time Albrecht came face to face with his opponent, somewhere just north of Berlin, the Mecklenburger found himself without a sound line of retreat and facing an army a good deal stronger than his own, for it had not only Valdemar's Danes, but all the forces of Markgraf Ludwig, the Wolgasts and Saxe-Lauenburg.

If not the world's foremost battle-captain, the King had at least shown considerable grasp of the recondite art of strategy, for in a campaign where the only battle had gone against his side, he had now placed his opponent in an impossible position. The marches had been slow, as medieval marches usually were and the summer campaigning season was almost gone. If Albrecht were smashed up in a battle, there could be neither recovery nor assistance from allies till another year. But it was no part of Valdemar's intention to smash Albrecht; the whole

German adventure was a diversion from his objectives in Denmark, and he did not wish to have these compromised by hatreds generated south of the Eider. He offered to mediate all outstanding causes between Kaiser Karl and Markgraf Ludwig, and as imperial deputy in the north, Albrecht accepted.

This is already a long distance from the date when Markgraf Ludwig was lending a landless prince two hundred billmen. What followed opened the gap still wider. Kaiser Karl objected so strenuously to foreigners taking charge of German affairs that he failed to appear at the subsequent arbitration conference. But most of the North German princes with interests in the House of Luxembourg did come—somewhat shaken from their normal combativeness by the effects of the Black Death and so very willing to listen to Valdemar's reasonable proposals for peace that His Imperial Majesty had to save face by calling another meeting at Bautzen in Lausitz during the winter. The moment was propitious; Günther, the pseudo-Kaiser, had just died in bed.

It may be that Karl expected Valdemar to stay home. An error; the Danish King came, inflexibly amiable, irresistibly conciliatory, invincibly persuasive, and—this must not be forgotten—a Knight of the Holy Sepulchre. He talked the dull dog of a Ludwig into giving up the imperial regalia. He persuaded the Emperor that the false Waldemar was done, and it was better to have a friend in Brandenburg than an opponent who might have better luck with another counter-Kaiser.

His Imperial Majesty was charmed; gave Ludwig the investiture of Brandenburg, proclaimed the false Waldemar a cheat, took the real Valdemar to Prague, called him his dear cousin, named him perpetual arbiter of all disputes between the empire and Brandenburg, and awarded him sixteen thousand marks for his services, in the form of a lien on the yearly taxes due the empire from Lübeck city. To be sure, Valdemar discovered that the charm had gone only skin-deep when he tried to collect this money; the subtle Karl had sent another letter to the Lübeckers, telling them to pay nothing.

But this was not nearly as important as the fact that under imperial pressure Albrecht was made to perceive that Denmark was no longer a sub-state. He signed an alliance with the young King, under which he did homage to Denmark for all rights over Rügen and Rostock city; agreed that his son Heinrich should marry Valdemar's infant daughter Ingeborg as soon as she came of age—and in a secret annex agreed to accept ten thousand marks to help the King gain possession of Helsingborg castle.

Helsingør, which is Elsinore, is the more famous foundation, but Helsingborg was infinitely the more important; gate of the Sound and key of Skaane, whose permanent alienation to Magnus of Sweden had been guaranteed by half a dozen documents.

14
Interlude—Carking Castle (1351)

O
N KING VALDEMAR'S RETURN FROM BAUTZEN, HE HUR-
ried off to Gurre in the woods. He may have noted
without thinking on, certain fearful glances from one
to another as he rode up, but nobody seems to have said anything until he had found the doll castle empty of the joy and
peace little Tove had given it. Tove was not there.

Tove was not anywhere. Tove was dead.

Many a question to bring out the full story . . . The girl
had been murdered by Queen Helvig's orders. There was a
man named Folkvard Lavmandsson, the Queen's fancy-man
and lover, with whom she one day fell on a quarrel, in which
words of shame were spoken, so bitter that only death would
pay. Whose death? Not his, he was too dear, and the shame
felt by the Queen was not his making, but that of the white
whore from Rügen. On a day a bath was prepared for lady
Tove; a baulk of timber placed against the door of the bath-
house or a bolt driven home and boiling steam was let in,
while someone ran away from the sound of small hands beat-
ing on the door and screams that did not last long.

Oh, one could have vengeance. "Then did Lord Valdemar
take Folkvard Lavmandsson and place him in a barrel lined
with nails, which was rolled to and fro until the man within
was dead." As for Helvig, Duchess of Slesvig, pledge of alliance, queen and wife till death do us part—she was shut up

in a gloomy vault of Søborg castle. It would be some three or four years before she came out and sat by Valdemar in public places once again. But this was only for a little space; soon enough she retired to Esrom cloister, where she prayed out her life and quietly went mad.

II

How much of it is true?

For this, too, is saga, and so very like a part of the Tove story which indubitably belongs to Valdemar I the Great as to offer grounds for complete rejection. Yet blanket denial will hardly do, either; for there is no Folkvard Lavmandsson in the first Valdemar's story, while in the time of Valdemar Atterdag, there was almost certainly a man of such a name who was executed in the manner described. Like any variation from the norm, the procedure irresistibly attracted the attention of medieval recorders.

There is also no doubt of some serious breach between Valdemar and Queen Helvig at this time, even though its surrounding circumstances may have undergone some retouching. She had been a business partner to the King, and a not ineffective one, presiding over meetings of the bishops and great men while he was absent on his journeys, and bearing him several children. After the date of whatever happened at Gurre, there are no more children, though the Queen was by no means an old woman. Henning Podbusk takes her place as chief councillor and, if not in close captivity, Queen Helvig is at least in house arrest at Søborg.

Moreover, some tragic event is needed to supply the drivesprings for the next act of the drama, and there is a change in Valdemar himself, as marked as that which followed the failure at Kallundborg and the period of isolation in Jutland. It is a tighter, grimmer King in his dealings with the outer world, yet one whose procedures show a touch of romance, even fantasy, not found in the builder of gristmills—as though with half his mind he plunged from an actual existence, too dreadful to be lived, into one of the tales he loved so well.

It is also to be noted that the stories, Tovelille and the rest, come to us from the hands of the last of the saga-writers, men who, like Shakespeare, looked on history as the raw material of literature, something that required embellishment from exterior sources if the essential spiritual values were to be brought out. To the tale of Valdemar and Tove, they add that he transferred his love for her to the tiny castle where they had been happy together—so enduringly that a horn may still be faintly heard as he hunts forever through the dark forest with a huge black hound which is a kobold; and that the hunt will only end when he can come home to Gurre and find her waiting.

15

Second Revolution
(1351-1356)

WHATEVER ELSE MAY BE SAID OF KLAUS LIMBEK, HE was a high man and a doing man, who had small time for petty dealings of any sort. The conditions he found in Rendsborg after quitting the King's service, or perhaps the fact that he found Iron Heinrich even more overbearing than Valdemar, left him disappointed. In the first plague year he came back to Denmark's service, was promptly restored to office as Drost, and accompanied the King on the Brandenburg campaign and the journey to Bautzen. It is possible that some of the intelligent strategy of that campaign came from Limbek's head; it is probable that Valdemar was encouraged to look toward the long-desired redemption of the Skaane provinces by the fact that his ablest officer was once more on the right side.

Before the Skaane project could progress beyond the secret article in Duke Albrecht's treaty, however, the King had to make a quick trip to Fyn to investigate irregularities in the methods of the Holsteiners with regard to collecting the taxes for paying off the pledges on Hindsgavl and Ørkel. It was something about forgiving the local bonders their taxes if they would make "voluntary contributions" of somewhat smaller amount; an arrangement which commended itself to the tax-payers, but which Valdemar failed to find satisfactory, since with nothing that could be legally described as tax money being received, the redemption of the castles would be post-poned to the Greek Kalends. He found that matters were as reported; sent a strongly worded protest to Rendsborg; and to his utter surprise received in return a letter of defiance, which is a declaration of war.

Valdemar moved fast. Niels Eriksen of Linde was sent with the forces immediately in hand to strengthen Valdemar Dos-mer in Slesvig, since he would probably have to bear the first Holstein blow. Klaus Limbek went to rouse the Jutland levies for a counterstroke, while the King himself returned to Sjæl-land to gather men and supplies for a major expedition against Fyn, to teach the bad-tempered Holstein bravoes that if they would not let him buy the castles of his heritage back, they should lose castles and money too. But before the forces could assemble, a torrent of tidings answered unpleasantly the question of how they dared.

Graf Johann the Mild had joined his kinsmen of the Rends-borg line, and they had brought in the two princes of Werle in north Germany. Instead of joining Niels Eriksen, the Duke of Slesvig attacked him, declaring himself the rightful sov-ereign of North Jutland, and the King his enemy for having mistreated Queen Helvig, his sister. Worst of all, Klaus Lim-bek had raised his standard indeed, but in the name of Hol-stein and Slesvig, and had been joined by all the great men of Jutland, with Niels Bugge of Hald at their head. The whole province was up; even the bonders were in it, with the Bishop of Ribe and Erik Nielsen of the golden star, who had once been Marshal; the royal castles were all besieged.

This was a throwback to the evil hours of Kristoffer, and even worse from what happened to Niels Eriksen and the only force that followed the golden lions. He cut his way through the Slesvigers, who were handled with the Blockhead Valde-mar's usual competence, fell back into North Jutland and broke up the force of revolters who were besieging Aarhus. But he was no match in weight or skill for Klaus Limbek, who now appeared with the allied army. Eriksen evidently did not wish to be shut up in Aarhus, but could not afford to fight a battle. He had to retreat, and let himself be maneuvered around the Malvø Vig into Mols peninsula, from which he appealed for help by sea. Before Valdemar could do anything for him, Klaus Limbek was at hand and forced a battle —on a beach, where Eriksen's dispirited men had their backs to the water. The royal army was destroyed and its leader taken.

To see ten years' work thrown down overnight must have been a cruel blow to the King, who had just come through his deepest personal trouble, and the patchwork of allies could hardly be blamed for imagining their game was won. When Valdemar suggested a truce and the arbitration of all difficulties, they gladly consented, naming a graf called Gerhard of Hoya for their side.

Actually this only showed that none of them, not even Limbek, yet understood the meaning of the word Atterdag. Valdemar appointed his friend Erich of Saxe-Lauenburg as arbitrator on his side, and used the time gained by the proceedings to take his bearings. It seemed clear that no one could have formed so wide and sweet a combination but Klaus Limbek, the spider of Kallø—but how deep had he gone? Lacking certain information, the King could only distrust all the members of the great Jutland stems, and he replaced the commanders of the castles in that province with some of the young Germans who had entered his service during the trip to Brandenburg. Inquiry showed Sjælland fully loyal; that island had taken too much from the Holsteiners to join them against the liberating King. On the other hand, a quick trip down into Mecklenburg made it evident that no help was to be expected from that quarter, since Albrecht was just starting a private fight with the Duke of Pommern. In the meanwhile Valdemar placed on a war footing the navy he had almost surreptitiously built, its commander being one Peder Dene, an ex-fisherman, called "Ironbeard."

While the arbitration was going on he took the ships to

Jutland, thoroughly provisioning and garrisoning the royal castles. The award was now announced; Valdemar was ready for its rejection by the allies as utterly unjust—as the friendly Duke Erich had doubtless arranged that it would be, since the King could hardly afford to let rebellion pay any dividends at all.

The rejection fell in early spring of the new year. The chronicles have it that heavy storms in the Kattegat prevented Valdemar from transporting his army to Jutland, but in view of the fact that the campaign actually undertaken shows so much evidence of plan, we may take this for royal propaganda. The King swung south against Langeland, which was Blockhead Valdemar's possession, rapidly carried its dominating castle of Tranekjær by surprise, served Arnholm on Aerø in the same fashion, and then made a lightning raid into the Holstein half of Fyn, where he caught his opponents off guard and took a good many of them prisoner in the open villages where they had cantoned for subsistence.

Before forces could be assembled to strike back, Valdemar placed his men aboard ship, crossed the southern Baltic and suddenly fell on Werle's home principality, which he ravaged frightfully from end to end. The grimness of Gune is in the note that some of the young men who had joined him in Germany now left his service because he cut the ears and noses off men taken in arms in Werle. He wished to make it clear that Germans beyond the Mecklenburg line had no business in Danish troubles.

II

At the same time Saxe-Lauenburg poured his riders into Stormarn, where they hit Graf Johann so hard that he was glad to offer concessions for peace. But both he and the Werles were minor members of the coalition. The real decision had to be obtained from the Gerhardssons. It was; but by a method which left contemporaries in a confusion reflected in their chronicles, because the thing was outside their experience. Valdemar won the war with sea-power.

The existence of the fleet had been the key factor from the beginning. It kept the Gerhardssons and Limbek locked in Jutland after their quick victory at Mols, which might easily have been exploited into such an overthrow as had been inflicted on Valdemar's father. It enabled the King to make the surprise attacks on Langeland, Aerø and Fyn and strike Werle while its defenders were absent. It turned the struggle in Jutland into a profitless business of sieges that brought no result, for with the Jutland lords as his allies, Iron Heinrich could hardly apply his father's social policy, and there was no one with whom he could fight a battle.

Now in the second year, Ironbeard Peder Dene treated the allies to something new in war. As soon as spring broke, the fisherman-admiral took his fleet into the Eider, the Schlei and Eckernfjord and placed these estuaries under a crude, but close and effective blockade, seizing every ship that tried to get in or out. By later standards the vessels were not at all seaworthy, but they were perfectly adequate for this work in protected waters and there was no form of artillery ashore that could drive them away.

They made Holstein extremely uncomfortable. Early spring was always a hungry time among small towns in those days, since only the great Hanseatic cities had important food storage facilities. The roads being what they were, water routes alone were adequate for the movement of supplies. Moreover all this area had been pressed close to the subsistence line by the calamities accompanying the Black Death. The effect of Ironbeard's blockade can be traced; Graf Heinrich disbanded most of his paid troops and attempted no military movement at all during the year. At the opening of the next season, he was not even able to go to the aid of the Jutland rebels when an army under Stig Anderssen landed in the peninsula and laid siege to Niels Bugge's Hald.

To be sure, since the international doctrine of blockade had not been invented, the Hansa treated the actions of Valdemar's admiral as piracy, and signed an agreement with Iron Heinrich against "all who make the seas unsafe." But emergency was immediate and the Hansa lacked means of applying immediate pressure. Before it could get its cumbersome financial and diplomatic machinery into operation, the alliance against Valdemar was already in the article of death. Simultaneously with his second year of naval effort and Stig Anderssen's attack on Hald, the King undertook a secret offensive by offering Klaus Limbek a free pardon and restoration to his office as Drost.

The lord of Kallø was an alien among the close-knit Jutland stocks in any case. After his first successful campaign, his reward had been to see Niels Bugge given the chief command. It is more than probable that there were other indications of disfavor toward this Holstein parvenu, and the King cleverly widened the split by hanging every German he caught on Danish soil, but letting the Jutlanders go. Limbek deserted to Valdemar; Stig Anderssen talked several of the Jutland lords into surrender; Werle was already gone. With no allies but Valdemar Dosmer of Slesvig, and facing the prospect of having his home territories invaded simultaneously from the sea and by a land army under Bo Falk, Heinrich of Holstein agreed to sit down at a peace table.

The treaty was signed at Vindinge Aa in Fyn, and its provisions are noteworthy as marking the true end of the Holstein invasion of Denmark. The Gerhardssons kept Hindsgavl and Ørkel, and Johann the Mild retained Femern island, but on all these there was a firm agreement that the taxes were to pay off the pledge and no nonsense. Johann the Mild abandoned every claim to fealty from any part of the Danish heritage, including some small estates he had inherited from his mother. Kolding and its castle of Koldinghus had been part of the Slesvig pledge to Holstein at the beginning of the reign; they passed to Valdemar at once, for cash. The Blockhead Valdemar secured the return of Tranekjær and Arn-holm, Langeland and Aerø, but had to give up Ribe and the Riberhus, which was the last bit of North Jutland remaining of the old Holstein pawn that had been transferred to him. As for the uproarious Jutlanders, all of them but Klaus Lim-bek received their former possessions. He had to see Kallø made into a royal castle and to go to work for a living.

III

The conference was in July, but it was not until the fol-lowing April that the King accepted the keys of Koldinghus. This was not because he did things at the normal leisurely pace of the Middle Ages. On the contrary; there is no period in the story of Valdemar Atterdag in which he displays more of the inextinguishable energy which was noted as his chief characteristic, and which became even more pronounced after the tragedy at Gurre. He was spending this period riding through Jutland, visiting every hamlet and herregaard, talk-ing to men and women of every degree in search of the reasons behind the revolt, and what correctives could be applied to prevent a repetition.

The great families, yes; the recovery of so many royal es-tates from their hands had hurt them in pocketbook and pride, and so had the relentless exaction of ground rents due. (It need only be mentioned that Peder Vendelbo was one of those hard hit, and that one of his daughters was married to Erik Nielsen Gyldenstjerna and another to Niels Bugge.) But why had the bonders and small tenant farmers, for whom the King had done so much, joined the rising?

Valdemar reached the conclusion that the chief fault lay in the maladministration of ordinary justice. This had begun under the arbitrary rule and still more arbitrary exactions of the Holstein pledgeholders during the Time of Uproar, which in some districts—Ribe and Kolding, for example—had effectively continued for thirty years. In a time when most people could not read and there was no appeal to unquestionable published documents, this gave the force of established precedent to the method of seeking the word or support of the nearest lord.

The first step was to undo old wrongs as far as possible, a task at which King Valdemar trusted no one but himself. At every place he visited he held a general assize, the *Ritterthing,* "Rider's Thing," "Knight's Thing"; gave down judgments in person as chief magistrate of the nation in accordance with the old Jutland law. The processes were sealed with a special seal, the Rider's Seal, which bore the legend "Seal of the Facts" on one side, but on the other, the King's old motto, "For Denmark's Law." Every conveyance of land or goods in the district was examined as far back as the property could be traced before this seal was affixed. "Many who had helped themselves to others' goods were heavily punished, and he saw to it that inheritances which had been seized by violence and wrong returned to the proper heirs."

Offenses against the person it would be harder to find a direct remedy for, but it must be remembered that in Danish law and thought there was not the distinction between these and property cases that developed later; the usual punishment was a fine. Whenever an embedsmand was found to have given bad decisions he was summarily removed, and sometimes not replaced. It is at this time that the title of *Foged,* or steward, begins to replace the older one for law officers among the districts.

On Midsummer Day, St. John's Day, fourteen years from the date when he had been crowned in brass, King Valdemar IV stood before the general assembly of the Danes at Nyborg in Fyn. Klaus Limbek was beside him as Drost; Niels Bugge was there and the lords of the Gyldenstjerna stem, with Bo Falk and Stig Anderssen; revolted Jutland men had come and faithful Sjællanders, the bishops of the realm and a great press of bonders and merchants from the towns.

There should be a new day in Denmark, said King Valdemar. All that was taken from any man in the last war should be returned, and faults of the Time of Uproar forgiven, though so heavy that life and limb were forfeit under the law; in proof whereof he set free the two knights who had netted his father beneath a window, many years before. (How he caught them or when, we do not know, only that they have played their parts without names and are now out of history.) Each year from this one forth there should be another meeting like this, in the same place, with the journeying to it under the peace of St. John for fourteen days before and as much after. Any who molested the travelers, even though they were officers of the King's law, should be responsible to this Danehof.

(Danehof! It was the name of the old Thing of all the Danes, from days far deeper than the century of the Valdemars, the power of the land that made kings and unmade them and spoke the law.)

The laws of King Valdemar should fully run; and if they were broken, the injured party should not try to take revenge for himself, but seek the King's foged; but the fogeds themselves were sharply commanded to be stewards of the law, for the Danehof would judge if they had watched it well. The law should stand over every man; he might appeal from the Thing of his herred to the Landthing of the province, and then up to the King's Drost, his justiciar or the King himself, meeting his opponent for answer before the Hof of the Danes.

So the whole people were made custodians of the people's law. Bishop Peder of Ribe read out the proclamation before the chief men and bonders of the realm, as the Laws of King Valdemar had been proclaimed a hundred years before. When the reading was finished a voice in the crowd below cried out that, after all, these were only empty words and promises that would never be fulfilled.

16
Trumpet Blown, Distantly
(1354-1356; 1214)

ROUND THE NYBORG DANEHOF STANDS SOMETHING HIGHLY
exceptional in the Middle Ages nearly four years of
profound internal peace for all that part of the realm
under Valdemar's rule. Even the Skaane project was shelved
after the Jutland revolt was put down—principally because
Magnus the Caresser had failed to come to terms with his
friends and relatives while Valdemar was successfully agree-
ing with his enemies, which made it dangerous, for the time,
to interfere.

While the Jutland revolt was in progress, the Swede-king's
younger son, Haakon, had reached his fifteenth year and was
proclaimed King of Norway—which, being interpreted, meant
that the crown was placed in commission by the nobles of
that country, a plan so satisfactory to them that the Swedish
nobles were inspired to imitation. The education of the elder
son, Erik, had been in their hands for some years, and they
had managed to deprive him of every vestige of intelligence.
Now they stuffed him full of romantic nonsense (he was to
redeem the Holy Sepulchre from the Saracens, for one thing)
and made him co-king with his father, with the right to sign
any decrees his counsellors drew.

This probably would not have happened had the saint been

at hand to help Queen Blanche, but in the year of the Black Death an unusually brilliant vision informed Birgitte that the cause of the world's trouble lay in the Babylonish captivity of God's vice-regent. She perceived that the Bride of Christ and mouthpiece of the Virgin Mary was too important to be wasting her time on so small a field as Sweden, and went to Rome, vowing not to leave it till His Holiness returned. What influence her presence was supposed to have, it is hard to say, but the Pope to whom her appeals were addressed happened to be Clement VI, born Pierre Roger de Beaufort; he so little regarded residence in Avignon as a captivity that he had purchased all feudal and territorial rights to the principality and was erecting a magnificent palace. The documents regarding Birgitte's visions he gladly accepted (they made good material for encyclicals); he wrote her soothing letters, but he stayed where he was. So did she, working busily on a plan for a new monastic order which should be co-educational, but with its government in the hands of women.

In the meanwhile Magnus was sent to Coventry in his own kingdom, and did not like it. He had an illegitimate son named Bengt—Bengt Algottsson, from being the child of the Lady Algotta, most beautiful of women—a nasty young brat, nearly as bad a job of work as his father, who had him under complete control. Magnus now made this lad duke of both Halland and Finland and Governor of Skaane, which placed these territories outside the authority of his co-king and his co-king's owners. It took only about a year for Bengt Algottsson to embroil himself simultaneously with the Hansa, the chief bonders of Skaane and the Archbishop of Lund, a considerable achievement, but one which the new Duke performed by a single series of acts.

This Archbishop was a new man, Jakob Nielsen, who granted the cities a charter of privilege with regard to the fisheries, in exchange for cash to pay his confirmation fee. Bengt revoked the charter and clapped taxes on the bonders to help meet the trouble he foresaw.

It arrived expeditiously, in the form of an army raised by Erik and the nobles, and presumably financed by the Hansa, since the hallmark of their filibustering was on the operation —that is, Bengt's men deserted him, and he and his father were driven from the kingdom without even a battle. Magnus took refuge in Mecklenburg, where his brother-in-law Albrecht failed to give any practical help, but did offer to arbitrate between Magnus and his older son.

There was little Magnus could do but accept. Duke Albrecht divided the kingdom between Erik and his father, making a proviso that Bengt Algottsson was never again to appear in Skaane, in person or by deputy; and in return for his services as umpire, Mecklenburg was to receive a fee of twelve thousand marks. If Valdemar had not helped Magnus with money and promises, it is likely that the latter would have been deposed.

Yet the Danish King's action here was essentially only a means of preventing Swedish interference in his own realm. The moment Valdemar attempted to use Magnus as a lever for the recovery of Skaane, the tool would break in his hands and the Swedes coalesce around whatever leadership promised the most effective resistance. They regarded the acquisition of the province and its fisheries as a permanent one, and were inordinately attached to it, both on emotional and financial grounds—an attitude which all the intervening years have not extinguished in Sweden, where Valdemar's drive for Skaane is still regarded as a monstrous injustice.

The difficulty was that Sweden was far the better integrated and more powerful nation at this date. Denmark all told had more than twice her population, but half of Fyn, all Slesvig, Femern, Als and Rügen were in German hands, while Jutland was still uncertain, and the great Skaane provinces had been subtracted from Denmark's resources and added to those of her opponent. Moreover, Sweden was tight. Feudalism had been adopted late there, and all of a piece, so that it had been carried both much further and not so far as elsewhere;

a feudalism already moribund when it made its appearance, ready to break down into another and broader polity. There was a really strong landed nobility, but of so recent an origin as to have escaped such causes of decay as the decline of old families, and their lack of contact with less privileged orders. There was a knighthood, also new and vigorous, and a class of burghers, especially in Dalecarlia and Vastergotland, which had suffered no such disastrous syncope as the Danish bonders during their Time of Uproar. Rather they had been brought forward by the crown through charters of privilege (we may suspect here the influence of Queen Blanche, to whose Flemish mind the arrangement would be familiar) as a makeweight against the titled classes.

At the head of this burgess interest, representing to some extent both the farming and the mercantile commons, stood the city of Visby. The island of Gotland, on which it was built, was under the suzerainty of the Swedish crown, but the town itself was a member of the Hansa, and was incomparably its wealthiest and strongest unit, the New York of the medieval world.

At this time it had twelve thousand full burgess members of the corporation, which would mean a population of fifty thousand, half of them Germans. (London had less, Rome only half as many, among the great cities only Paris was larger.) Visby was the port of exchange and deposit for the whole Baltic; the normal procedure was for goods moving either east or west to transship at its spacious quays. In recent years some Lübeck vessels had begun to make the Russian voyage direct, but this did not alter the custom under which the imperial city stood guardian to all travelers as far as Novgorod. The fur trade was entirely in Visby's hands and, as with a fur trade anywhere, enriched the men who conducted it; in the herring trade Visby ranked with the five Wend towns or higher. A change of rule in Skaane would throw into question all the arrangements the city had been able to make through its peculiarly close relationship with ever-needy Magnus.

Valdemar knew that in a contest over the trans-Sound provinces, Sweden would have whatever help Norway could give, and it was now to be feared, the aid of that shifty Slavonian, Albrecht of Mecklenburg. There was a great meeting of princes in Lübeck during the second year of the peace, at which agreements for the suppression of piracy were signed and tourneys held "for the joy of the ladies." Valdemar presided; Mecklenburg's ducal enemies of Pommern were significantly present, and Mecklenburg himself significantly absent. He was paying a visit to King Erik, who had just thrown into prison an ambassador Valdemar sent to King Magnus. The secret treaty about the recovery of Helsingborg was clearly a secret no longer.

II

In King Valdemar's burning energy, one would expect to find a high factor of impatience; but everything we know about him, including the byname, seems to show him almost impervious to the latter emotion. Of all medieval kings, only Louis XI of France bears anything like his reputation for dogged singleness of purpose, and Louis XI's record was marred by gusty outbursts of passion that often brought his projects to the edge of disaster—as in the case of the Constable St. Pol. The answer to the apparent paradox is that in Valdemar's case there was no genuine singleness of purpose. He had a dozen lines of attack on the problem of restoring the Danish heritage and operated along all of them simultaneously, with greater or less emphasis on each as the occasion permitted.

Thus the Nyborg Danehof was hardly over before the King busied himself with the task of making a repetition of the Jutland revolt impossible by setting up a system of royal castles to discount those in the hands of the great families. One of the more striking features of the composition he made with those families is that the only advantage Valdemar took from it was the possession of Kallø, Koldinghus, and Riberhus. He followed this up by building a new castle at Randers, opposite Niels Bugge's Hald, and greatly improving Skanderborg, whence an eye could be kept on Silkeborg.

Now came the making of another Jutland revolt unnecessary. In the first year of the peace, the King called a conference at Roskilde "on how to improve the realm," a phrase which means that the gathering was concerned with economics. It was perhaps the first time in western history that such an event had taken place, but contemporaries do not seem to have found it so very exceptional, perhaps because the leading conferees were twelve bishops—officers who were always being summoned to solemn advisory sessions by kings who seldom did anything they recommended. Numerous herremænd were included and in the later stages, some invited ambassadors from the Hansa. The great lords and the bonders were omitted, with the implication that they formed part of another complex, the political, whose interests had been adequately cared for at Nyborg.

The main fruit of the assemblage was a widespread plan for water regulation, "since King Valdemar did not wish that even the least stream should run to the strand without it had first done service to its best." The program was a supplement to the gristmill building that had begun in Jutland, but now this became more extensive than ever, with mills established at dams on every river in the kingdom, the dams diked along their wings for flood control and provided with an elaborate system of sluices. Like all Valdemar's projects, it was remorselessly pushed through under a new class of officials called *opsynsmænd*, inspectors, with the King himself calling them to account every time he passed through a district. In the midst of a campaign in Fyn during the desperate war that presently supervened he found time to pause, design a dam for a particularly troublesome stream, and leave an inspector in charge of it.

The program altered the face and life of Denmark, transforming it from a land of low-grade agriculture, whose surpluses were grains and pork, to a much more self-contained and profitable economy. The dams eliminated flooding, always the most destructive enemy of grain; the mills made it possible to process corn locally for the main necessity of life, and tightened up the whole village structure. Eventually this led to the rich dairy farming economy which has left Denmark one of the few countries of Europe with an exportable food surplus. The process was very slow and so many other factors became involved that it would be idle to see in Valdemar's foundations anything more than an influence; but a strong influence it certainly was.

One of the additional factors was also due to Valdemar—the system of stone roads throughout the country, which he had begun earlier, but after the Roskilde conference he drove forward as he alone could drive it. Along the roads, around the village, where forest met arable ground, wolf-nets of the King's own invention were installed.

How were these public works carried out?—in their ensemble not less a labor than one of the great cathedrals. It had always been Danish law, one of the survivals from days when there was even less money in circulation with which to meet tax obligations, that fourteen days' work by one man were owed to the overlord every year for every house. The custom had fallen into intermittent observance except on the estates of such forceful personages as Klaus Limbek or Niels Bugge. Valdemar enforced it throughout the kingdom in a manner that more than anything else formed the basis of the complaints about his rigor—"all were driven under threat of the King's hard displeasure to heavy drudgery."

The economic conference closed with the reception of the Hanseatic ambassadors, to whom was put the question of the best means of establishing a common currency throughout the country. It may not have been a wholly ingenuous request, since much of the economic confusion had been caused by the competition of local currencies with the *mark lubs*, the standard coin of the five Wend towns, and every time there was an exchange the cities took a handsome profit. But the ambassadors replied in high medieval style that, though it ill became them to advise a crowned king, if Valdemar really wished a solid currency, the way to obtain it was to establish a single mint for the kingdom, and not allow the size, weight or value of the coins to be changed. There appears to have been a good deal of local and some private coinage (one remembers Ludvig Albrektsen, Kristoffer's marshal), which Valdemar promptly abolished in accordance with advice. At the same time he began minting copper pennies to fill a longfelt want for small change; the first coins of the type in the north, and an item that ranks with flood control and the opening of the roads in the revival of the realm.

Perhaps the Lübeckers suggested the small coins also; Valdemar stood on very good terms with them at this time. Not only had he scrupulously observed his contracts and handled matters so that trade could be carried on without trouble from land pirates or the necessity of illegal caravans; but also he had invested a good deal of cash in their city, mainly in mortgages. The King's drive to repossess his land, in fact, takes a new form during these peaceful years; he is less the legalist and more the business man. Not that the law was neglected; the King notably appears before one of the Jutland Things and wins a case against Stig Anderssen for the possession of three or four estates, once royal, which had been given to the man of war by Graf Gerhard. But the more usual method was now financial. Valdemar buys land-parcels vacated by the Black Death from heirs who already have places of their own, and even purchases a considerable holding in Fyn from a Holsteiner through a man of straw, then builds a castle on it.

The proceeding was likely to exacerbate relations with the

Gerhardssons, for the medieval mind, which could quibble endlessly in avoiding a debt or a service by pleading some complex line of homage, regarded such a financial trick as somehow dishonest and outrageous—the sort of thing a Jew might do. The King was not only indifferent to their anger, but seems at this time quite willing to provoke it. As long as they held the half of Fyn which contained the powerful castle of Hindsgavl, communications with all middle Jutland were insecure, for that place covered the important Middelfart crossing; and the taxes were very slow in clearing the place. Moreover, another of Valdemar's lines of attack was a complete reorganization of the national militia setup; it is possible he wished to test the new army in a small war against the Gerhardssons before undertaking a big one against the Swedes.

At the basis of the reorganization was a determined effort to reconvert the herremænd back into the hærmænd they had been in Valdemar Sejr's day. In spite of vigorous orders this ended in failure. All the King ever got out of these people was money, while the herremænd remained where they were —to become in the next three centuries the builders of those stately chateaux called *herregaarde*, the treasure and beauty of Denmark.

Behind the herremænd was the general levy of the realm, as it had been since the ancient days. The institution had become vestigial among the upper class of bonders, who paid a small yearly tax called the "mustering penny" in lieu of service, and with this Valdemar did not interfere. The middle and lower groups of bonders, however, were bidden to meet on certain days for practice with community-owned arbalests, and the fogeds were charged with enforcing their presence. "If anyone were missing, his foged was to punish him with the highest of fines, so that others might learn to be more dutiful." They were infantry, but they were missile-armed infantry, and if not quite as good as the English longbowmen (with whose exploits Valdemar would be familiar after Iron Heinrich's return from Crécy), regular practice would make them a far better force than anything of the kind in the north.

There was one more, very radical step in the military reorganization. The towns having merchant privileges—the right to maintain markets, a considerable degree of self-government through the guilds, exemption from the corvée and military service—had paid for their indemnities with annual taxes in cash ever since the days of Valdemar the Great and his Absalon. Valdemar IV now exchanged these taxes against ships and their crews for his navy.

The new basis was quite satisfactory to the towns, since they had the ships in any case, and the state of naval architecture was such that the conversion between commercial vessel and warship was a matter of a couple of days' work. The plan was in line with the ancient Danish tradition of service at sea and so offered no affront to the always-active medieval sense of precedent. Receiving the ships instead of money was also more convenient for the King. He did not need the cash, since his rent-hold system was functioning so effectively that he had become the biggest individual banker of the Baltic lands; and taking the ships direct short-circuited the bookkeeping involved in taking money from the towns, then paying it back to them for vessels. Medieval accountancy was a process that usually left money sticking to someone's hands.

There were thus good practical reasons for the change, but the evidence of the rest of Valdemar's military program is that they were less important than something else which lay at the back of his mind. While apparently conferring exemptions in this case, he was actually imposing duties; bringing into being an integrated system, in which the military setup of the realm reproduced the political. In both, the men of the upper social levels—landowners in the country, great merchants in the towns—furnished to the state something they were peculiarly fitted to supply, money and leadership.

On the military side the money was translated into a nucleus army of paid professionals. (An increasing number of German soldiers takes service with Valdemar in these years— a certain Klaus van der Jure, for instance, a pledgeholder who had been paid off, but remained in Denmark as an officer.)

Behind this professional force lay the national militia, both by sea and land, drawn from the next strata of society, who also furnished what we would call in modern terms, the voters —Marsilio's lawgiver. That this organization was not very much like anything in the modern world, or based upon today's political ideals should not be allowed to hide the fact that it was still less like anything in the medieval world.

The medieval state was thought of in its own time as a fundamentally military organization, in which a man's civil status was regulated by his position in the hierarchy of command. The concept had hitherto been violated only in the case of small specialized communities without territorial problems—the free cities of Italy and the Hansa, some of the Swiss cantons. By making the obligation to militia service universal, for country and town, a concomitant of political activity, Valdemar was substituting a complete, rounded structure, whose cement was the law, for the loose system of vertical alliances of which the feudal state was composed.

III

Yet, in a moment, in the twinkling of an eye, the horn of the midnight huntsman of Gurre is blowing, we are out of the moonlight of reason, back into the days when French ambassadors came to Vordingborg with the new short cloaks over their tunics, bearing gifts to Valdemar the Victorious and an offer of marriage to the widowed King. He received them gravely, speaking of his regret that, though a Danish princess might go to France, he had already contracted an

The Third King

alliance with distant Portugal; but in token of amity, gave them a horn of the unicorn, snow-white and fluted spirally.

Could the Valdemar of another day have missed the pattern when once again France stood at Vordingborg when he, like that illustrious bygone King, was widowed and doubly widowed? Tove was dead, like Valdemar Sejr's beloved Queen Dagmar; Helvig a wife no more. As with that earlier Valdemar, one gift of the past was left; for when Queen Dagmar died, Valdemar the Victorious had his only son crowned co-king with him, the hope of Denmark, held to be as high a man as his father—and now this later Valdemar sits beside an only son, Junker Kristoffer.

He was well toward maturity when the French embassy came to Vordingborg at the high tide of Valdemar's peace; a notable young man in arms, one would say one of the warrior Skjoldungs, much loved by his father.

What had been the outcome of the French embassy during the century of the Valdemars? Sent home, with fair words and a unicorn's horn, but the answer was nay; and from that hour Denmark's luck was lost. The new Queen from Portugal was such that her name to the utmost generation became a by-word for a shrew—"Beengjerd—an ugly, quarrelsome woman," the dictionaries still have it. She bore the sons who let in on the land the long decline and Time of Uproar. Men said King Valdemar had better have taken the French alliance. Should Valdemar Atterdag now refuse when ambassadors of the lilies once more came to Denmark with words of marriage and close bond?

Change the old pattern for a new. Yet it would be a more ancient pattern still, a more romantic dream, that King Valdemar IV thought on, as he saluted France courteously and bade the messengers to know that all should be as their master asked. Not the calculating King who dealt in Lübeck mortgages signed the treaty that came forth from this meeting, but the young prince crowned on Viborg height among the St. John's fires. For not only was it set down in the treaty that

· 212 ·

Junker Kristoffer should be the husband of Isabelle, princess of France, but also it spoke of high dealings for which this union was a pledge; and those dealings looked back beyond all Valdemars to the days of Sveyn Forkbeard and Knud the Mighty. On the marriage contract being signed, King Valdemar should receive six hundred thousand Dutch guilders and raising the golden lions, assert the old claim of his house to the crown of England, landing in that country with twelve thousand men.

17
Jutland; the Old Ways
(1356-1358)

THERE IS A CERTAIN FASCINATION IN SPECULATING ABOUT the possible results of King Valdemar's plan for reviving the Viking Age on a grand scale. On the surface the idea looks like romantic folly, for the English army his men would have met was led by that splendid and terrible Plantagenet, Edward III, and his soldierly son, the Black Prince—the pair who had discovered how to exploit the longbow, and were about to use it for the conquest of France. Moreover, the twelve thousand men are questionable; the figure represents something like 4 per cent of Denmark's population at the date, which is a rather higher proportion than any medieval state could support in arms for any but a temporary and defensive campaign. Laborsaving devices and the machinery of communication were too inefficient.

Yet the argument is not all on one side. The English were very involved in France. In that struggle the two Edwards were proving themselves the ablest battle-captains of the age, but they were also demonstrating that their orchestration consisted of but a single instrument and that they did not know very much about strategy. When the Constable Du Guesclin stopped attacking English armies in set positions, they could accomplish little, and when in the next reign, the French made use of their castles, they won the war.

Now Valdemar's special and personal skill as a commander,

visible both in the Brandenburg campaign and the Jutland revolt, was precisely in the field of strategic maneuver and in the handling of castles. He avoided set battles, and he had his navy, while the current British military weakness was, oddly enough to modern ears, on the sea. It was not all one-sided; but the principal reason the grand design was never put to the proof lay less in the military difficulties than in the very fact that the plan had been conceived. Edward of England had a first-class information service, and Iron Heinrich was an old friend of his. The embassies of France and Denmark had hardly been exchanged before the Holsteiner was signing a treaty to serve the English King with a hundred helms and a hundred coats of armor against a payment of two hundred guilders a year.

The occasion arose soon enough. In September of the year following her treaty with Denmark, France was crushed on the fatal field of Poictiers and King Jean became a prisoner. His people cried to Valdemar for the promised aid, and as promptly Edward let loose the Holsteins in a new war against Denmark. Grafs Heinrich and Nicholas had been punished severely enough in the previous struggle to make them cautious, but there were special reasons, quite aside from the two hundred guilders, why they undertook the new one without qualms. They were in correspondence with such Jutland lords as Stig Anderssen and Klaus Limbek (again!) and were quite aware of the profound irritations that had grown up around Valdemar's land policies, such as taking Kallø away from the Drost and the three estates Gerhard had given him from the soldier. We know from the sequel that these two were not the only Jutlanders who felt they had scores to settle with the King.

The chronicle says merely that the Holsteiners promised armed help in Jutland, but the combination which presently developed was so far beyond anything the two rather stupid Teutons ever thought up for themselves that we may suspect it was hatched in the brain of Klaus Limbek. The thing began in the winter with messengers one after another crossing the Belts to complain of the manner in which the decrees of the Nyborg Danehof were being enforced. There were so many that Valdemar felt compelled to call another Danehof at Kallundborg in February to win approval of his actions.

The delegates from the isles were agreeable enough, but the Danehof made it clear that there was fire under the heath among the grumpy Jutlanders, who found the King's new way of administering the law through royal fogeds cold and impersonal. They wanted to return to the old days, when a man could look for help to his chieftain, who was almost necessarily named embedsmand of the district.

That meant trouble, sure enough. Valdemar spent the latter part of the winter provisioning his castles in Jutland and Fyn and sending out another new class of officials, in the form of castle-inspectors, who reported to himself, but who were authorized to make emergency changes. There is no evidence that he was at all surprised when the situation blew up in the fall in a general revolt, headed by Limbek and Stig Anderssen's two sons, Ove and Peder. Anderssen himself remained neutral, but Niels Bugge joined the rebels, as did Palle Jonsen of the great house of Munk, whom Valdemar had lately made his Marshal. The rebellion was followed immediately by declarations of war from the Gerhardssons, Valdemar Dosmer of Slesvig, and Johann the Mild; and shortly after these by more defiances from Erik, the co-king of Sweden, Albrecht of Mecklenburg, and even the Hanseatic cities of Wismar and Rostock, which were in Albrecht's territory.

The number of his opponents made it by far the most formidable combination the King had faced, but the allies soon learned that it is one thing to make an alliance at the paper level and quite another to bring it to common action. The Gerhardssons and rebels did indeed take Tønderhus castle and force the submission of one Thing of the marshbonders in the first rush. The two Anderssens captured Valdemar's new house at Randers (there seems to have been treachery or incompetence—the King threw the castle commander and two of his inspectors into prison and confiscated all their property); while a combined army of Holsteiners and Jutland men crossed into Fyn, drove the royal garrison out of Odensee and burned the place. But with this the drive ran out of steam. The remaining royal castles in Jutland were stoutly held, the rebels could get little help from the bonders, who liked fogeds little, but fighting against the King still less, and the allies lacked ships to bring the war home to Valdemar in Sjælland, where it would really hurt.

Graf Nicholas, who for some reason we do not know, had the field command, accordingly turned against Brobjærg, where the King had set up a new castle in opposition to the Holstein hold of Hindsgavl. The siege had hardly begun when Valdemar came up out of the sea with all his forces; on St Martin's Day, November 11, they drew out into the lawns before the castle, marshaling in sight of the enemy, with helms raised so they might encourage one another. The royal army was somewhat more numerous and of very good cheer.

When they had ranked there befell a hard battle, hard as any Valdemar ever fought, from morning till nearly sunset; but in the late afternoon Holstein broke utterly and under the gray evening their host was wiped out, all those not slain or taken being cut off among the marshes by angry bonders who had borne much from these Germans. Graf Heinrich's son Adolf was among the captured; so was a shield brought to King Valdemar by one of his men-at-arms, who said he had stricken out the eye of the man who bore it and taken him prisoner, but released him to have the wound cared for, on promise to pay a ransom.

"What did he call himself?" asked the King, gazing at the device of a nettle, with a crescent for difference.

"Klaus Holsteiner of Rendsborg."

"He gave his right name; but birds like that should be kept in a tighter cage. That was Graf Nicholas."

II

The other day had come for Holstein-Rendsborg, which would never be so strong again, but while Valdemar was keeping a high Christmas of celebration in Kallundborg, word came that the remaining members of the clumsy alliance had set their project in train. Sjælland was to be invaded from across the Sound by both Erik and Albrecht of Mecklenburg, who would rendezvous with the Swedes in Skaane. About Mecklenburg, Valdemar was not too much concerned for the present. Albrecht was up to his neck in a struggle to obtain the heirless small principality of Schwerin, and good friend Duke Erich of Saxe-Lauenburg had promised to attack him if he launched heavy force against Denmark. But an invasion by the powerful army of the Swedes could be dangerous. After New Year's Day, Valdemar had all the Sjælland castles put in an acute state of defense, called a levée en masse to meet at Slagelse, and ordered a census of food supplies, which would be carried into castles or placed aboard warships.

As the weeks turned toward spring, it became apparent that the Swedish danger had been exaggerated. Erik was having Magnus trouble, and his army still lay behind the great belt of forest that borders the Skaane provinces; possibly he had also failed to consult the Swedish nobles, who showed no great enthusiasm for the war. The levée en masse, which was immediately dismissed, met with such hearty response, the castle system was so tight that Valdemar felt he could turn his back on Sjælland at the start of the next campaign and finish with his enemies in the west. One wing of his fleet, under Peder Ironbeard, went to cruise the Baltic against the ships of Wismar and Rostock as soon as weather permitted. The other took the King and his army to Nyborg just after Easter, extraordinarily early to begin a campaign in those northern latitudes.

Holstein-Rendsborg had been hit too hard at Brobjærg to

afford a field army, and the castles had only their normal winter garrisons, so the chances of taking a big one were good. But with the Swedish-Mecklenburg menace in the background, Valdemar did not wish to become involved in sieges, and apparently decided that the news of his arrival at Nyborg would reach Hindsgavl and Ørkel before a surprise. He gave out that he was going to the latter, then by-passed it, landed on Langeland, took Valdemar Dosmer's Tranekjær in fourteen days and, without losing a moment, used the mobility of his ships to run right around Fyn and try for a surprise at Hindsgavl. A gale blew up; some of the vessels missed their course, the chance of making a quick attack on Hindsgavl was lost, and with it the likelihood that either of the Fyn castles could be cheaply had.

In the meantime, frenzied appeals from the Gerhardssons had stirred Albrecht of Mecklenburg into setting aside his Schwerin project and taking an army up into Skaane for the counterattack against Sjælland. Valdemar promptly dispatched his own wing of the fleet to blockade the Duke in Helsingborg, contenting himself for the time being with marching up and down through the Holstein part of Fyn, eliminating Germans and their possessions. The pause lasted till June, when an embassy arrived from Albrecht to seek peace—not very surprisingly, since the Swedes had failed to come, and while the Duke was shut up in Helsingborg, Duke Erich and his Saxe-Lauenburg riders had entered the Mecklenburg home dominions, won a battle, and were now burning the place out.

The King agreed to negotiate, recalled his ships and had his army set over to the island of Als, which was in the Blockhead Valdemar's domain. The two castles that dominate the island were Nordborg and Sønderborg; they were badly kept, like all the Duke's possessions. Valdemar's sea-borne surprise was complete; Nordborg fell at the first rush to one wing of the army, while the King himself was landing at Sønderborg with the main force. He was just arraying his men under the walls for a storm, when the drawbridge came down, the gates open, and out walked Slesvig's Duchess Rixissa with her three daughters and a plea for mercy.

She was Erich of Saxe-Lauenburg's sister, whom Valdemar could hardly refuse, but her husband had become one of the most venomously persistent of his enemies, and must be debarred from mischief. The terms were that the castle should pay a ransom and be out of the war; no more than twenty men to be within it at any time, and Valdemar Dosmer not to lay his head there for more than three nights running. The Duchess would act as emissary in seeking a general peace.

King Valdemar refused an invitation to break bread in Sønderborg, loaded his men into the ships again, and fell on the northeastern bulge of the Holstein home territory, where his men spread out to harry the place with a thoroughness that became memorable, burning everything that would burn, carrying off the important people and killing everyone who resisted.

Before the Gerhardssons could call forth the levy of their lands for resistance or bring in outside assistance, Valdemar was back with his fleet, sailing across Kiel Bight to Femern, Graf Johann's pledge-hold. Either news of his coming had for once preceded him or preparations had been made against the feared advent. The Femern bonders set up barriers of boats at all the landing-places and barricaded their towns with wagonburgs—"not wishing to become again part of the Danish realm under King Valdemar because of his harshness"— which may mean that Graf Johann got his added name by being an exceptionally easy ruler, since bonders elsewhere found the King giving general satisfaction.

Johann was quite an old man by this time, and had never been a fighter; his territories on the mainland had been attacked by Duke Erich, so he could do nothing to succor the Femern men. But they made a highly creditable stand when Valdemar landed—one that almost cost the King his life, for he was hit by a spear and thrown to the ground. A second and a third assemblage of bonders had to be beaten in field battles; Glambek, the castle of Femern, surrendered when its commander fled. After this King Valdemar held a Thing. The bonders agreed to submit to his rule and to pay a contribution of twenty marks a head.

The Thing was held in September; this being the beginning of harvest-time, the King returned to the Gerhardssons' hereditary lands for a second harrying, in the course of which he took and threw down their castle of Borenburg, then burned Flensborg town, a task he had only just finished when embassies came from all the allies to ask a conference and peace.

III

They might well; of that circle of foes who surrounded Denmark's King a year and a half before, every one but the Swede (who was not really in the war at all) had been badly hurt, even including the two Hanseatic cities, whose commerce suffered a good deal under Peder Ironbeard's raids. Those raids had consequences that would run deep, but one of the surface results was the capture of the admiral himself, when a change of wind pinned a division of his unhandy vessels on the coast near Wismar, where they had been making a shore landing. The townspeople came out and shot flaming arrows into the ships and captured their crews. Valdemar never had to pay any ransom for them, though; Ironbeard got his prison guard drunk one night, stole the keys, and escaped with all his fellow prisoners.

The other effects were more serious. Navy seamen were fairly uncontrollable people in those days, taking most of their gain in licensed plunder, and not being overly nice about who owned what they took. The King's men plundered some Lübeck ships off Wismar; and though he instantly met the bill for damages when it was presented, there was from this time forth a certain coolness between him and the city that

had been almost as faithful a friend as Erich of Saxe-Lauenburg. It was not that the burghers understood in the least
that the King had invented sea power and used it to defeat
in detail enemies of five or six times his own force, though the
invention was quite as important, both in its military and
social results, as the tactical use of the English hunting bow.

Perhaps Valdemar himself failed to understand fully what
he was doing. He acted on empirical lines. With the ingenuity
of a man fertile in expedients, he had founded his fleet to
furnish cement for a kingdom that was falling apart and
could everywhere be struck to the heart from the water. After
he had the ships, he used them to provide the rapid military
movement which his unquiet energy demanded.

Sea power certainly implied blockade as a means to military
pressure, and blockade was anathematized as straight piracy
by the city people, but they do not seem to have been dis-
turbed by the blockade of Duke Albrecht in Helsingborg,
though it was much more severe than that of the Holstein
coast during the previous struggle. Neither was it that the
Hansa perceived that King Valdemar's use of a novel weapon
had given his campaign a consistency and purposefulness utterly unlike the vague ramblings and chance battles in the
rest of Europe, and so made him dangerously strong, a threat
to bring back the days of Valdemar Sejr, when Hansa cities
were subject to Danish rule.

It was rather that Lübeck and Visby discovered, as a result
of the attack on Wismar, that a navy was a dangerous institution in the hands of a king, and an ideological monstrosity.
Moreover a Denmark which could support so powerful a
force out of its own commercial surplus was a threat to their
monopolies. The Hansa had no use for autarkies: "We buy
the English fox's skin for a groat and sell back the tail for a
guilder," was one of their cant phrases. In their tight little
medieval system of ideas, ships belonged to free cities and
were their specific means of maintenance and differentiation
from other forms of polity. For a king to have a fleet was as

òutrageous a violation of the established order as for a priest to have a wife or a serf a golden crown. This violation was accentuated when the ships both came from and protected a stream of commerce that was likely to rival their own.

That is, they objected to Valdemar Atterdag, the banker and maritime agent; and they had still more serious objections to the way he handled his seagoing property. The northern waters were full of free lance pirates, which it took all Hansa's efforts to restrain, though they were outlaws who operated on a small scale. What would be the position in the face of a seapower backed by a legitimate government, which could set whole fleets afloat in time of war—fleets whose seamen were careless about *meum* and *tuum*?

By the very conditions of its existence, the Hansa could only be irreducibly hostile to Valdemar's new institution; and it was. It took a little time for this hostility to develop, to find spokesmen and means of expression, and some of the expressions have been lost from the record. But from this hour forward, Valdemar's dealing with the Hansa became a journey through a tar pit of opposition.

IV

Part of the composition which ended the war was that the King should meet his rebellious vassals of Jutland at Nyborg and come to an agreement with them. Valdemar was somewhat offstanding with these men who had joined foreign enemies against the realm, only sending Junker Kristoffer to the meeting, and he without full powers. It was decided that a delegation of the lords should wait on the King at Slagelse two days before Christmas, with the bishops of Ribe and Odensee as peacemakers. Niels Bugge was the choice of the Jutlanders; he brought the sons of Stig Anderssen, who were his nephews. The King kept them waiting, for not only was there forward a visit from King Magnus and Queen Blanche of Sweden, from which encounter an egg would hatch, but also he let it be known that he considered it beneath his dignity to hurry to a meeting with outlaws and rebels.

This was naturally no salve to haughty Bugge's feelings, and still less were the terms King Valdemar laid down— namely, that the great men must return to their allegiance, paying for the damage they had done, and thenceforth observe the law, not receiving so much as a kitchen garden out of all the estates they had taken during the rising. Niels Bugge and the two Anderssens said they would give an armistice for eight days, while the other lords considered the matter, but it was easy to see they were so angry that little would come of the negotiations. The three lords then left, riding across Fyn since the weather was inclement for ship travel.

At the Middelfart crossing they came upon some fishermen who were digging for bait with pointed forks. Nobody knows what was the sequence of word and blow between those lofty lords and the stiff-necked Jutland fishers, but words were spoken and blows were struck, and the end of it was that Niels Bugge lay dead, and with him the two sons of Stig, the only sons he had.

To men of a period which had a tale of poisoning every time a husband or heir died at a convenient moment, it was perfectly obvious that Valdemar had ordered the slayings. A perfect thrill of horror went through the realm over this method of settling a dispute with men who, though they might be wrong, had only stood up for what they considered their rights under Denmark's law. That horror lives on in the legend that the red burdocks of Middelfart shore have drunk the blood of the murdered men, and will never be quit of it; and in a ballad, still sung:

> "The King has written the Middelfart men;
> 'Now pull Herr Bugge down again,
> But when you let him under go,
> Let slay his sister's sons also.'

Lord Christ, give the Middelfart men shame
That killed Herr Bugge, the well-born man! *
The midway men, Christ strike them sore,
Who slew Herr Bugge by the shore."

Valdemar did all he could to purge himself; took a solemn
oath before the bishops that he had no part in the man-
slayings; swore eternal hate to the murderers and laid a perpetual tax on the three main houses of Middelfart (it was
still being paid in 1873), called the "Bugge-penny"; had Junker Kristoffer swear blood-brotherhood with Bugge's son
Knud, and advanced the young man in his own household.
No use; he was Valdemar the Bad again, the suffrage of Jutland gone from him forever, and with it Stig Anderssen,
soldier, who now joined the rebels from whom he had held
aloof; nor would he ever again be seen in Valdemar's service.

* This is not fumbling translation; the rhyme, or attempted rhyme,
is exactly the same in Danish.

18

Signature of a Contract
(1214-1218; 1358-1360)

ISTORIANS HAVE EXPRESSED THE VIEW THAT BUT FOR
the events of that year's end which saw the fall of
Niels Bugge and Valdemar keeping high feast at
Twelfth Night with King Magnus, the attack on England
would have been made. One of those historians has remarked
that the King should have been grateful to his enemies, who
preserved him from fatal follies. Assuredly, at the time when
a new embassy came from Charles, Dauphin of France, to
say that the promised subsidies were being raised, Valdemar
had no true idea of the power and glory of Edward of England, nor of the weakness of his ally.

No means of information at his disposal could tell him
that the towns of France were in revolt, the nobles falling
away from the crown and a fever of Jacquerie running through
the blood of the land. His contacts were official; he knew
France as the heiress of the west and England as Denmark's
sometime colony, which paid a tax to buy off sea-raiders in
the days of old. The younger Edward was Black Prince of
Wales, but that land had been so lately brought under English sway that the fire in its peat could still be fanned to flame;
Welsh chieftains had promised to follow King Valdemar if
he raised his standard. So had the lords of Scotland, groaning
under the outrageous ransom due to Edward for their captured king. The old Viking state of Sodor and Man sent in
its adhesion.

How much did this count beside the glamor of reviving the high and far-off days of Valdemar the Victorious when Kaiser Otto the Welfing retreated with little honor before Denmark's arms? Innocent III was then Bishop of Rome; he had crowned as Emperor the King of Sicily, named Friedrich. This Friedrich was of the Hohenstaufen line, imperial in Germany for much time; he was more learned than a priest or a philosopher, and a famous warrior into the bargain; men called him "The Wonder of the World" and said that no one ever saw him without wishing to become his vassal. The dukes beyond the Elbe had never set eyes on him, and so considered him a foreigner with whom they wished to have nothing to do.

At this time the King of England and the counts of Flanders were in alliance with these dukes and the Welfings, as was the Archbishop of Bremen, who wished to make himself Pope of the north. Thus the Empire was divided in two parts, and Kaiser Friedrich could not win beyond the forests of Thuringia. He asked King Valdemar Sejr to be the sword of the Church and the Empire in those lands, and said that all Nordalbingia should belong to Denmark, along the Elbe to its confluence with the Elde, as well as the Wendish lands won from the pagans in the days of Valdemar the Great and Knud VI.

This was a somewhat uncanny manner for the Kaiser to deal with a friend and ally, since the Danes already had the rule in these lands without owing anything to anybody for it, and the overlordship by name would only raise strife with the nobles of the Welfing alliance. They held many possessions in Nordalbingia and did not wish to be vassals of a mere king to hold them. Nevertheless Valdemar Sejr, who was a somewhat more splendid man than his father, accepted Kaiser Friedrich's alliance and said he would do his bidding.

In these days a man named Albrecht was Markgraf of Brandenburg. He was one of the Ascanier house, a brisk, pushing man and very handsome; in guest-exchange with the

Saxon dukes and the grafs of Schwerin, and much attached to
the Welfings. He led out his men against the town of Stettin
and other dominions the Danes had taken from the Wends.
The Graf of Schwerin and the Saxons joined him; they were
thought to be much stronger than the Danes, or Kaiser Otto
either. Their armies drove the Prince of Stettin from his town
and harried the countryside.

King Valdemar and his men went into Schwerin, took one
of its towns and threw down all the buildings, then turned
against the Brandenburgers so overbearingly that Markgraf
Albrecht would only stand one shock. After this he abandoned all struggle and fled away to his own land. The
Schwerin and Saxon lords came somewhat late to the field,
but when they came, thought twice about fighting against
the Danes and sued for peace. Now King Valdemar went up
into Slesvig. A great holiday was held there on St. John's Eve,
and the Things of the realm having given their consent, his
son, Valdemar the Younger, was crowned co-king with him
and king after him, in the presence of fifteen bishops, three
dukes, and three grafs. At this gathering King Valdemar said
he would take the cross to the land of Esthonians, which was
thought to be nobly done on his part.

II

It could be that Valdemar Atterdag also dreamed of crowning a son after a victorious campaign—against England, which
would be no more than his forefather had made against the
force of an empire; for with the builder of Gurre, we are never
too far from dream. There was a secret treaty with the twin
dukes of Wolgast at this time, its details unclear because ill-
preserved, but pointing to the thought that they will follow
Valdemar to England with all their men. Yet whether he
meant really to make the attack is one of the highly fascinat-
ing mysteries about the King. His energy was so prodigious,

his powers of continuing a consistent line of action through all beclouding circumstance so much beyond those of any other man of his time, that he often appears to begin projects merely for the purpose of giving his mind something to do, working through the resultant circumstances, or of concealing what real purpose he has in mind.

The plans he brought to fruition are by no means always those which an exterior observer would have chosen as likely to succeed. The Brandenburg campaign, with Kaiser Karl and the North German dukes in opposition, was as chimerical a scheme as England; the revision of the whole land-tenure system in Denmark as impossible. For that matter, so was the recovery of the Skaane provinces, now that Albrecht of Mecklenburg had decided that the interest of his house lay in keeping the Swedish heritage intact and taking it over.

For the peace that ended the war of the alliance against Valdemar was no peace. The terms granted by the victorious King—through Duke Barnim of Stettin as mediator and Lübeck city as guarantor—show how hard he tried to leave his beaten enemies without cause for complaint. Except for the Blockhead Valdemar, who sulkily refused to be a party to any treaty, thereby losing Langeland, Aerø and Als for good, those terms amounted to a *status quo ante*, with the surrender of all prisoners and no fines or ransoms. Since Valdemar was the only party who had any prisoners to speak of, besides being in full possession of Femern and in a position to take the Fyn castles at will, this generosity caused him to be accused of sacrificing solid advantages to the pursuit of the English rainbow. This was not true; the egg that hatched at the Christmas conference with Magnus was the implementation of a nearer and dearer plan.

Skaane, at last. Magnus and his Queen came to the meeting in a mood of bitterness so intense that they were willing to barter anything they owned for revenge on young Erik, the nobles, and Albrecht of Mecklenburg. If Valdemar would help them with money and his fleet, they were willing to pawn

him Helsingborg castle and district.* The bargain was struck
at once and sealed by an act of betrothal between young
King Haakon of Norway and Valdemar's daughter Margrete,
then only six years old. Valdemar instantly ordered his forces
across the Sound—and as instantly discovered that the men
who pulled down Herr Bugge had turned his design to dream.

The Jutland lords would make no accommodation with
the murderer of that wellborn man, and the Holsteiners, with
their prisoners back home and money coming in from Edward
of England, found the opportunity for injuring Valdemar
with the help of his own vassals altogether too good to be
missed for the mere sake of keeping their word. The Gerhardssons complained that the mediator had gone beyond his
powers in ordering the return of Tønderhus to Valdemar,
poured their men into the marshbonder country and laid it
under fee. Graf Johann's men, with some Mecklenburg help,
landed on Femern and took it back before there could be any
question of voluntary return. The Jutlanders sent messengers
to say they would die with honor rather than submit to such
slavery as the King offered them; and when Barnim of Stettin
called on Lübeck to support her guarantee, the town corporation turned up its collective nose at the idea of helping a
King who kept a navy.

Valdemar's Skaane attack was a surprise, delivered before
the normal campaigning season, but under the circumstances
it could achieve nothing solid. The King rendered it still less
effective by (for once) allowing hope deferred to make him
impatient, and crossing the Sound without his usual care to
provision his army in advance. Most of the Skaane Things, as
thoroughly disgusted with the antics of the Swedish royal
family as they had been with Kristoffer, gave their adhesion

* Creating a pretty, and illustrative, problem in the medieval law
of homage if it had gone through. Valdemar would owe Magnus
homage for the castle; but since it was originally Danish royal property, and some of the surrounding estates royal, Magnus, as Valdemar's overlord for them, would also owe homage to the Danish King,
as soon as the latter came into possession.

at once, and Valdemar marched down into Blekinge, where he took the castle at Sølvesborg without difficulty; but then the situation began to catch up with him.

Magnus refused to turn over Helsingborg, and the Hansa became very nasty over the employment of the Danish fleet in the area of the herring trade. It was unthinkable for Valdemar to live off a country he was trying to recover for Denmark, so he had to return to Sjælland for supplies, taking most of his people with him. This was in early April; later in the month King Erik and the nobles appeared in the province with a force so hastily raised and so poorly equipped-that it was known as the "Club-army." Clubs or chivalry, it had only to deal with some of the Thing levies who stood by the new (and very old) allegiance. They were quickly put down after Erik burned one group alive in a church to show that he meant business.

This was a mistake which could have cost the Swedes dearly, for no offense was quite so outrageous to the north (as the Laws of King Valdemar show) as murder by fire. Neither was the act palliated by its locale; and Erik was already in trouble with the Archbishop of Lund, whom he had thrown into prison. But the young King preserved himself from a ban by dying during the summer, followed closely by his Queen.

Public opinion, as expressed in contemporary songs, was uncertain whether Valdemar or Queen Blanche had poisoned the couple (as a matter of fact, nobody did; it was smallpox); but the practical effect was to make Magnus sole King, without a rival or even an heir in sight, save the collateral line in Mecklenburg. This made it inevitable that Magnus should turn patriot and make an agreement with Duke Albrecht, and he did so, signing an alliance to partition "all conquests and prisoners made from King Valdemar on the basis of strength contributed to the common cause."

The fishers of Middelfart had not only robbed Valdemar

of his victory; they had apparently brought back the general alliance against him, stronger than ever.

III

But apparently only, for the King's earlier victories had been decisive and the strength of the restored alliance was an illusion. Nothing could overcome the objections of the Swedish nobles to forwarding Magnus, and at this moment he fell under the ban of the Church because, with income from Denmark cut off, he had relieved his perpetual shortage of cash by taking the Peter's penny from the churches. The last struggle had left the Gerhardssons too weak to make any head. The King turned a wing of his army against them under one Valdemar Sappe, an illegitimate scion of the Slesvig house, who re-took all the marsh country, captured Tønderhus and shut Klaus Limbek in Nødefald.

At the same time, death, which had done the allies a favor in the matter of King Erik, now balanced matters by taking off old Johann the Mild. His son Adolf had succession troubles with the local baronage and did not want to fight anybody on the outside. This left Albrecht of Mecklenburg, who was far too clever to ruffle against so dangerous a customer as Valdemar single-handed, so the latter was able to concentrate against the heart of the trouble, in Jutland.

Part of his force crossed the Belts in early summer and besieged Randers, but Stig Anderssen, who commanded there for the rebels, made a sally and burned out the siege-engines which caused the attack to abort. In September, when it became evident that there would be no thunder and lightning from Magnus, the King himself took reinforcements into Jutland. Some of his ships were lost in equinoctial storms, but Valdemar captured and burned out small castles belonging to the magnates at Kattebjærg and Kalvsholm. The revolters still held nearly as many places as the King, but the royal army was too strong to be met in the field, too watchful to be surprised. By controlling all means of communication in the countryside, it rapidly built up pressures that became intolerable. Negotiations began.

They dragged. There is a good deal of obscurity about the details, but the point around which they revolved was clearly that of Valdemar's personal acquisition of land titles, and his refusal to let them out except on rent tenure. The "slavery" to which the Jutland lords referred in their protest was specifically that of Sjælland, where the new system had been placed in operation earliest and carried farthest. At the time the King's obstinacy was attributed to his unwillingness to make composition with men who had aided the enemies of the realm, and he certainly did take a fairly Rhadamanthine attitude toward what he considered treason, but the crux of the matter was still those tenures.

On this point, he was absolutely unyielding, and it is possible to see why. He had been brought up at one imperial court and had lately made the acquaintance of a second Kaiser at the Bautzen conference. The factitious splendors that enveloped those establishments had not concealed from him their real powerlessness. The heir of Charlemagne and Barbarossa was supreme lawgiver for all Germany—indeed, all Europe in theory—and his justice overrode every other. But his laws were only pious hopes that people would behave better, and the execution of his decisions depended upon the force of the alliances that could be gathered in their support. The Bautzen conference itself had offered a spectacle whose inconsistency no medieval mind could miss; the picture of the supreme judicial officer of the Empire submitting a cause between himself and one of his vassals to the arbitration of a foreign king. If this were not enough, there was the repeated matter of the imperial elections. The last two centuries had seen men of seven different houses on that throne, and the elections themselves were usually accompanied by violence.

King Valdemar would not, as we might, think of this as

demonstrating a lack of stability or continuity in policy. In medieval thought instability was the by-product of a system; one looked at the form of that system and checked events against it. But the King cannot have missed, and the evidence shows that he did not miss, the fact that in its weakness and discontinuity, the Empire was a macrocosm of Denmark during the Time of Uproar. The basic movements in Empire and nation had the same pattern. Denmark was also elective, and elections had been disputed with the sharp edge of the sword. In Denmark also there had been a departure from the old form of the state. And if the Emperor had no real authority but that which he possessed as Duke of Bavaria or King of Bohemia, Valdemar himself could remember a day when he was King of nothing but Aalborg and inner Sjælland.

The cause was the same in both cases—poverty. The imperial title conferred nothing but dignity, the name of King of Denmark meant nothing but the right to wear a crown to bed because, in both polities, the estates of the crown had slipped away, and His Majesty could not afford a force big enough to exercise the police power. In their relations to their underlings, the Jutland lords were, and doubtless would continue to be, restrained by the laws of King Valdemar and the traditions that went with them. But in a system where they were allowed individually or even by groups to rival the royal income, they would inevitably, like the great vassals of the Empire, render the central authority nugatory. It was a period where there were so few outlets for capital that wealth translated itself almost automatically into military strength.

One of the special abilities of Valdemar Atterdag was that he perceived the land tenure question as the heart of the matter. He knew that if his crown and the realm of Denmark were to survive, he must put a halt to the encroachments of the great families of Jutland. There were families elsewhere, to be sure, but two factors made Jutland a special domain. One was the effects of Graf Gerhard's social policy, which had all too successfully depressed the only social group that could stand against the great stems; the other was that Jutland law had one peculiarity. Among the islands all sons inherited equally, and the tendency was toward splitting up large holdings; Jutland had early adopted the unit inheritance, and the effect was toward concentration.

It has been remarked that another of Valdemar's gifts was his ability to find a line of compromise between opposing views. In the Jutland case, he perceived that if he were to continue his land policy, he must give a *quid pro quo*.

We do not know the steps, only that after fetching and carrying that lasted deep into the spring, a great general Danehof was called at Kallundborg for Pentecost, the twenty-fourth of May. Burghers came from the merchant towns and not a few bonders; six bishops; Junker Kristoffer, Valdemar Sappe, Henning Podbusk, Bo Falk, and Niels Eriksen, Stig Anderssen and Limbek at the head of Jutland lords such as Erlend Kalv, Benedikt Alefeld, Palle Jonsen, and Knud Bugge. Even Valdemar Dosmer of Slesvig came.

There were long debates, in which the Jutland bonders set it forth as a grievance that they should be asked "to work in marsh and mud on the upbuilding of the King's castles, till by these endless labors they were brought into deep distress." Others said the King's fogeds were careless in their dealings, taking lands and goods unjustly. The variety and intensity of these complaints must have surprised Valdemar, who had been particularly careful to inquire into the administration of the fogedships every time he was in the province. There is record of the punishment of certain of the stewards who had claimed lands for the crown from men to whom they really belonged. It was evident that the King had not watched things closely enough; that the second Jutland revolt had some basis in bonders opposed to the new ways.

Valdemar was acute enough to perceive that neither his personal interest in dams, roads, and gristmills nor the promises of the Nyborg Danehof were adequate to make the bonders see that their interest lay with the crown. Something was needed that would on the one hand produce a return of the confidence lost by Niels Bugge's murder, and on the other an abridgment of the old Danish right of free choice of a leader, which had carried Skaane off to Sweden and had now twice seen alliances between the Jutlanders and the enemies of the realm.

Valdemar himself thought of this as treason, but he was probably the only person who did so, for outside Denmark the principle of nationality was still so young that the desertion of an overlord was only a broken personal relationship, while in Denmark the vassal was even freer in placing his allegiance. The ancient forms offered the King nothing but the chieftainship system which had made possible the looseness of these bonds. What was needed was an entirely new basis of agreement between crown and subjects; a pattern that should actually be novel while apparently reproducing the old forms.

The result was that remarkable document known as "King Valdemar's Haandfæstning," which is not a Haandfæstning at all, but a double letter. The King and Junker Kristoffer write to the assembled estates that they will defend all rights of bishops, priests, churches and cloisters, herremænd and squires, women and maids, merchants and bonders, as they are set forth in Valdemar Sejr's laws, found in "an old, true lawbook"; that the rights given by the Nyborg Danehof shall stand, and that other Danehofs shall be held yearly.

In return "the dukes, bishops, knights, weaponed men, and all the people of Denmark" set their names to it that "when any of us or anyone else in the land of Denmark shall break these laws, we will all gather and help that he shall be condemned and punished according to law, and especially anyone who robs, burns, or makes anyone prisoner in the realm of Denmark, or calls in foreign lords to harm the realm, shall lose goods and life. Whoever commits crimes against our Lord King, his son, or Denmark's crown, shall be condemned according to the land's law, and be punished by every right man, and to this end will we help with all our might. Likewise we promise for ourselves and for all the kingdom's manhood that the crown and its people shall enjoy all rights according to the laws."

There had been royal charters before, but they were concessions wrung from absolutism by force. This was different. Despite the curious phraseology, there is no mistaking that the document contains a definition and condemnation of treason to an entity which is not an individual but a nation. It is a free contract between King and people, in which the former submits himself to law, and there is nothing like it in the Middle Ages.

But the Middle Ages were breaking up.

19
The Fisheries of Skaane
(1360-1361)

IN THE PREAMBLE TO KING VALDEMAR'S HAANDFÆSTNING IT
is set down that the guarantees given therein shall stand
for Denmark "and the lands that with God's help we
may rewin." Since King Magnus had sent in letters of enmity
after Erik's death and had never signed a peace, there was so
little doubt about the significance of the phrase that it had
some influence in bringing the rebellious Jutland lords to heel.
It meant a war, with ransoms and plunder.

Notable among the reconcilers was Klaus Limbek, who
staged an embracing scene with the King and was appointed to
a command in the army, though not to the highest place, which
seems to have been divided between Erich of Saxe-Lauenburg
and Junker Kristoffer. The Kallundborg Danehof was thus a
mobilization as well as a constituent assembly; hard on its
heels the whole strength of the nation was gathered for the
effort, with the bishops and towns contributing extra ships to
the forces. As soon as the meeting was over, King Valdemar
personally led fleet and army forth, landing near Malmø, which
he carried by storm on July 4, then re-embarking the main body
for Helsingborg, which was placed under siege.

Lindholm city threw open its gates and voted a present of
money to the King, and everywhere the Danes were received
as deliverers, with joy and ringing bells. Many of the chief
men came out in arms to join the invaders; Valdemar spent

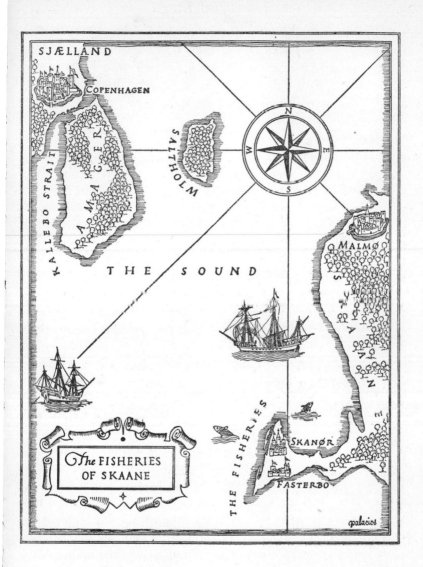

SJÆLLAND

COPENHAGEN

KALLEBO STRAIT

A M A G E R

SALTHOLM

N
W   E
S

THE   SOUND

MALMØ

S K A A N E

THE FISHERIES

SKANØR

FASTERBO

The FISHERIES
OF SKAANE

palacios

much time talking with them, while Erich and Kristoffer handled the operations. Not that there was much fighting to anticipate; Magnus had thrown himself into Helsingborg at the first alarm with what men he could gather, and young King Haakon of Norway was trying to raise more, but not many could be roused in his country, while the strength of Sweden was withheld in one direction by the Danish fleet and in the other by the great forest.

King Valdemar had summoned ambassadors from the Hanseatic cities to discuss taxes and privileges in the great fisheries when they should come under his rule. He was to meet these men in Copenhagen castle, but when the envoys arrived, the word was that the King begged their pardon. He was hunting that day and would meet them on the one following. Then the tale was that he had gone up to open the siege of Helsingborg. The embassies came along to Helsingør, where they found him in conference with Albrecht of Mecklenburg, who had a letter from King Magnus, authorizing him to negotiate a peace.

The reports of the Hanseatic ambassadors say that Valdemar advised their people to stay away that year from the herring areas "which Magnus holds with unright," but said nothing more on taxes and privileges. They feared he was trying to pull the Swedish kingdom to pieces. Presently they became convinced of the Dane's real desire for peace and were glad to assist at a conference of arbitration. Duke Albrecht represented Magnus; the Danish delegation was headed by Erich of Saxe-Lauenburg and the Bishop of Borglum. The board decided that Helsingborg should be surrendered to Valdemar. Magnus thereupon evacuated to Rønnebro, a little farther north, where he began to collect an army to continue the war, and where Bengt Algottsson was murdered. Not another word about the fisheries.

Thus the official account, which breaks off sharply as the ambassadors go home, leaving a residuum of the unexplained. Everyone is acting out of character except Duke Albrecht, who has evidently been reached by the King, for he immediately claims (and does not get) the ten thousand marks due under the old secret treaty for helping Valdemar into possession of Helsingborg. Magnus was never any intellectual giant and it is rather surprising for him to imagine that his interests could be trusted to the snake of Mecklenburg, but this part of the affair can be explained on the basis that he did not have Queen Blanche at hand to stiffen his backbone, had received a bad shock in the suddenness and severity of Valdemar's attack, and was well aware that there was no chance of making a successful defence of Helsingborg. Even the murder of Bengt Algottson, which Magnus at least did not prevent, can be explained. The young man was descended from Valdemar the Victorious on his mother's side, had spent his exile in Vordingborg and was believed to be acting in the Danish interest.

What really causes difficulty is the conduct of Valdemar and the Hanseatic delegates. The King's punctiliousness about keeping appointments was more than once remarked about him. This time he not only fails a meeting, but even refuses to discuss the business for which the meeting was called. One can only conjecture what happened, what he learned in the six weeks between the Kallundborg Danehof and the abortive meeting at Copenhagen, that made him change his mind about coming to terms with the cities.

One line of this conjecture is in relation to the Hansa itself. It was about this period when the cities signed formal alliances, took the group name of "Die Deutsche Hansa," and divided themselves up into *Kreise*, "tertials"—a western group under the presidency of Cologne, a Wendish-Saxon group presided over by Lübeck, and a Prussian-Swedish-Livonian group headed by Visby. The ambassadors who came to Copenhagen assuredly made it clear that they were not acting for individual towns, as formerly, but whole congresses of cities as units, and very powerful units.

The Third King

There is an ominous note of cartel in the agreements among the towns; they permitted no competition in any area or market among cities of the same tertial. The Golden Bull of Kaiser Karl, which was the fundamental law of the Empire, had forbidden exactly such associations, but the cities formed them anyway, then asked the Kaiser what he was going to do about it; and the Kaiser found himself unable to do anything. At the same time the western towns had forced an abject surrender upon Bruges, which only wished to run its own affairs. The King would have learned of these events about this time, and the idea of giving so arrogant a united body a treaty foothold in the Skaane fisheries cannot have been attractive.

Moreover, the body, once united, was almost guaranteed to be hostile. The Lübeck circle contained two cities that had lately been at war with the King; he turned over the Wismar prisoners to Duke Albrecht as the price of his services on the arbitration board at Helsingborg. Valdemar was quite aware of what he could expect from Lübeck, in spite of recent good relations. Back in his first year, when he was still only a shadow of a king, the city had calmly ordered him to exchange Copenhagen to the Swedes for Falsterbo, so that her own market-privileges in Skaane might be increased. What tone would she take now that she had ten or fifteen other cities behind her?

The leadership of a tertial by Visby was even more portentous; not only a Hansa town, but a vassal-city of the King of Sweden, furnishing him with support. The new arrangement could mean that all the cities of Prussia, Pommern, and Livonia were linked to the Swedish interest, since the system placed the diplomatic affairs of a group in the hands of its presiding member. It was not very likely that Visby would find acceptable anything Valdemar cared to offer with regard to the Skaane fisheries; and this may be one of the reasons why he chose to offer nothing.

II

Another reason for the failure to come to terms may be the conditions Valdemar found in the Skaane market when he got there. The same passion for first-hand information which sent the King to Jerusalem and led to the summoning of the great Kallundborg Danehof is evident during the Skaane campaign. He lets Duke Erich command the forces, while he devotes himself to the service of intelligence. After the capture of Helsingborg, Valdemar spent nearly an entire year in riding through the recovered provinces, not in royal progress, but halting at the meanest hamlets, where the chronicles show him talking with bonders, knights, and priests, questioning them closely about the customs of the land, as well as on their personal lives. At the time of the broken appointment in Copenhagen, he could have had no such elaborate personal knowledge of the trans-Sound provinces as this process gave him; but he certainly found out enough to make him suspicious of the offer which the Hanseatic embassies were known to be bringing.

That offer was a flat payment of one thousand silver marks for the confirmation of the cities' rights and privileges at the fisheries. The question was where the line of rights and privileges lay. It was no such simple matter as a mere permission to bring ships to the herring market and there exchange money, goods, or services for their product. The fisheries of the Sound constituted one of the greatest fairs of the whole Middle Ages, of which a knightly French pilgrim named Philip de Maizières has left an arresting picture.

"Between the kingdoms of Norway and Denmark," says he, "is an arm of the great sea which separates the island and kingdom of Norway from the continent and kingdom of Denmark. This narrow strait stretches fifteen leagues and is only two leagues in width, and God has ordered it that the herring voyage from one sea to the other through this strait in only two months of the year, that is, September and October, in so great number that it is a great wonder. Now comes another wonder; according to old custom there gather in these two months boats and great ships from all over Germany and Prussia along this strand, for to take the herring, and the general opinion is that not less than forty thousand boats meet here to do nothing but fish for herring, and in each boat there are not less than six men and in many, seven, eight, or ten; and beyond these forty thousand boats are there five hundred ships, which do nothing else but to put the herring in salt. And it is a fact that the men from all these vessels in these two months dwell along the coast in huts of wood and branches along the fifteen leagues of shore in the kingdom of Norway. They fill the ships with salted herring and after two months and eight days no one can find either boat or herring in the whole strait. This is a great gathering of people to take so small a fish, since if one will reckon up, one finds that more than three hundred thousand men in these two months do nothing but catch herring. Now one may know the graciousness which God shows to Christendom through these great numbers of herring, by means of which all Germany, France, England, and many other lands have nutriment in Lent, since poor folk can have a herring where they could not have a large fish."

The good knight's geography is somewhat fanciful and he probably exaggerated the number of ships and men, though not by very much. An accurate census two hundred years later, when the fisheries were sliding rapidly toward extinction, showed seventy-five hundred vessels of considerable size along the shore. But Philip of Maizières only sailed through and listened to what people told him, missing completely the events behind the beaches, where the herring were shoveled from boats into carts and taken to booths where "gutting-women" cleaned them and passed them to "packing-women" for disposal in casks. Behind these fishing-booths was a vast city of other structures, where the ships that came to be filled with herring deposited every product of east and west—Russian furs, iron and ironwork from Sweden, woven cloth from the Netherlands, wines of the south, French salt. There were cookshops and eating shops, taverns and workmen's huts; also others. A monkish chronicle from Erik Glipping's day takes pleasure in the fact that of all the Rostock ships which sailed to Skaane that year, the only one lost had a cargo of forty prostitutes.

Each city had its special area or "factory" at this combined festival and business convention, and the legal-financial problems that arose were in the last degree complicated. The ancient rule was that all wares might come free to the Skaane market, taxes being paid when they left it, except in the case of foreign food and drink consumed on the ground, which bore a sales tax. By old rule also, Danes who bought goods in the market might carry them free into their own country, and Danes paid less tax than foreigners on the movement of the herring which were the center of the whole affair. On the other hand, one of the earliest claims of the Hanseatic merchants was to have their own judges, who handled cases arising in a particular factory according to the law of the home city; and this had in some degree been conceded.

But this was only the background. During the early years of the Time of Uproar the royal authority was so very weak, the administration so uncertain, that the visitors had come to regulate everything pretty much as they pleased. In the year after Valdemar took Kallundborg, King Magnus, as overlord of Skaane had a meeting with the burghers, at which bills and counter-bills of complaint were filled, and those bills show how things were going.

On the side of the cities it was objected that some of their people had been arrested for carrying weapons to the market, though they had only the single sword or spear that it was legal to bear; that when a German had fled after killing a man of Skaane, a fine had been assessed against others from the same factory; that the Swedes were exercising the strand-right of taking everything from wrecked ships; that Swedish nobles were remiss about meeting their bills—and so on.

King Magnus' griefs were quite different in character and much more fundamental. The men of the cities were collecting for themselves the sales tax on consumed goods without allowing a penny of it to reach the crown. They were fishing illegally from large boats, which sailed away without paying export duties on the fish. They smuggled wine continually; gave short weight; justice against them in tort cases was unobtainable, because even when these involved a Skaaneman and a foreigner, they insisted upon the judgment of the extraterritorial courts. They drove Skaanemen from the fish with arms. They stretched factories beyond the permitted limits and set up inns where imported beer was served instead of that brewed locally. They used their control of the market at Bergen to insist that shipments between Sweden and Norway should travel in Hansa bottoms instead of those of the nations involved. They engaged in the retail cloth business, whereas their charters allowed them to deal in it only at wholesale.

The noteworthy feature of Magnus' meeting was that nothing was said on any of these points in the resulting agreement. That is, the practices complained of presumably went on, and to them was presently added the fact that the Hanseatics often escaped the payment of any tariffs whatever on goods they brought to market. King Valdemar certainly learned a good deal about all this after his landing at Malmø; at least enough to make him certain that he did not wish to take one thousand marks for a blanket confirmation of "all rights and privileges" to this new and very strong association of cities. The ambassadors were accordingly sent home with fair words and empty hands while the King went down into Skaane to get the detail of what he had previously skimmed.

One of his visits was to the great market at the height of the herring-run, where he laid down a systematized group of tax regulations, covering everything. A tax was placed on each booth; a tax on foreign boats used in the fishery; a head tax on all those who would sell in the market; on the carts that carried the fish to salting and goods that left the market for any destination. Fines paid for breaches of the peace were to fall to the crown, whether assessed in the King's courts or those of the outlanders. Even barmaids had to lay down two coppers before beginning work and another for each jack of ale or mead they served.

The individual amount paid was very small; something like the 1 per cent ad valorem normal in the north during the middle ages. But it was rigorously collected, and when King Valdemar cast up his accounts at the close of the herring run that year, he found himself with six thousand marks, more than the realm's income from any other single source. The Hansa ambassadors appeared again after the break of the new year with a variation on their previous theme—this time, four thousand marks cash for the same confirmation of all rights and privileges. The King refused.

III

Interlude—The Trail Goes Dim. We are in saga again, at precisely this point where light would be most desirable. To be sure, many of the objective facts stand out sharply enough. The utter fury of the Swedish nobles over the loss of Skaane has not vanished from the page. They compelled Magnus to force Haakon, King of Norway and Prince of Sweden, to break his betrothal with Valdemar's daughter Margrete, and to undertake another with Elizabeth of Holstein, sister of the Gerhardssons, an old maid as much beyond the young man's age as Margrete was below it. The inability of the Swedes to implement this fury for themselves and the reasons for their powerlessness are visible enough. The loss of the Skaane revenues must have produced a financial crisis that precluded the raising of any large force in a hurry, and whatever army they did raise could not get at Valdemar without the aid of a fleet strong enough to challenge the Sound against the Danish navy. There is no question but that the Hansa, and especially the tertial headed by Visby, was mighty angry at Valdemar's failure to grant a charter of privileges in the herring market.

But now what? Did the proud city of Gotland offer Magnus ships and men? We are not told. What we are told is that in Visby town there dwelt a man named Niels the goldsmith; a good man of his hands, who had become rich through his craft. He had a daughter, thought to be the most beautiful of women, always well-dressed and somewhat haughty. Many young men sought her in marriage, but she found none good enough for her, nor would her father compel her to take any against her own will. This was a cause of much anger among the other Visby merchants; they ceased buying the wares of Niels Goldsmith and laid fines on him unjustly.

This was so little to be borne that Niels quitted the city with his family and went to live in the southern part of the island; but he himself took ship to Denmark. King Valdemar received him well. He urged the King to attack Visby, saying that the greatest wealth could be won there, since the town was so rich that the housewives spun with golden wheels and the pigs ate from troughs of silver. King Valdemar thought this was good advice, but said that the Visbymen would keep stout guards over so valuable a treasure. He therefore went in disguise in a small ship to Gotland, where he had guesting at Niels Goldsmith's house. There the girl who had refused the young men of Visby fell in love with him; all that he asked about the town and island, the people's leaders and how they set their array in order, she discovered for him. In return, he said that when the Danes came to Visby, she should hang a white flag before her house that it might be respected.

. . . Thus far the saga. It would explain part of the year

which Valdemar is supposed to have spent in Skaane, the period being somewhat overlong for what he did there. It is also psychologically in accord with his usual desire to see everything for himself; but by no means so close to the clout in making him act from romance instead of policy, for his truly romantic actions, like the love affair with Tove, he kept in a different department of his life. Also it would be odd to find him launching an attack on Visby out of desire for plunder; he never did that elsewhere.

The certain thing is that a year from the landing at Malmø, the Danneborg was given to the breeze at Vordingborg and all the host and fleet of the Danes set sail for Gotland.

20
Come to Judgment
(1361-1363)

E RICH OF SAXE-LAUENBURG WAS WITH THE FLEET; LIM-
bek, Henning Podbusk, Junker Kristoffer, and Valdemar Sappe; they landed first on Öland and swept out
that isle after a fight in which its castle of Borgholm was
stormed. On St. Mary Magdalene's Day the host reached
Gotland at Kronewall, five miles and a half south of Visby.
The burghers had made a mocking song against King Valdemar and thought it beneath them to oppose him at the shore,
but ranked at a marsh called the Fjälemyra, half-way between
the landing point and their town, using the bog to cover their
flank, as they were somewhat deficient in mounted men. The
onset came on July 24, no room for maneuver, only hard fighting in the old style. The short northerly night came down on
a battle still undecided, with many slain on both sides and
the wounded crying in the dark. At dawn the Danes fell
on again; the day was more than half gone before the lines
of the Visbymen began to tease out and they to go back,
not in rout but sound retreat. Valdemar Sappe saved the day
by his courage and address; the King knighted him on the
field among the broken bodies.

The Danish army was too exhausted to pursue till it had
had a day's rest, but the townsmen were equally too shaken to
have much success with their effort to pull down the subur-
ban buildings which would give an attacker access to their

walls. Accordingly they made another stand on the outside, and there the losses of the Fjälemyra told their tale. Visby broke under the Danish onslaught, with eighteen hundred of its people killed, whom King Valdemar laid in a grave-mound under a cross whose inscription is still visible: "In the year of Our Lord 1361 the Tuesday after St. Jacob's Day fell the Gotlanders before Visby gates under the swords of the Danes. Pray for them."

The wall above was very famous, stretching from shore to shore, 45 feet high and 10 feet through, with 48 square saddle-towers, 90 feet high, astride it, but there was no more fight left in the defenders. They made no resistance when Valdemar ordered a section of the wall beaten down, so that he might ride in across the breach as a conqueror, with trumpets blowing. There was a method in this; when the corporation offered as ransom the three biggest ale-casks in the city, filled with gold, jewels, and other objects of worth, the King accepted the gift, but not as ransom.

He meant to make an end; as conqueror he seated himself in the market place, with a naked sword across his knees in sign that he would punish rape or violence, then gave the place up to loot. The song says that only one house was spared, the one that had a white flag before it, and that afterward, townsmen who had noted this fact built a new tower at the shore and buried Niels Goldsmith's daughter alive in its foundations. That may be; the assured fact is that the pillaging was so thorough that Visby was erased, in universal bankruptcy, from the list of cities. Grass began to grow on the great quays, now empty of ships; the place lost its weight in the League of the Hansa; her people gradually scattered; in a couple of centuries she had sunk to the provincial "town of roses and ruins" and five thousand population. New York had become New London overnight.

Around the circle of the Baltic the event produced somewhat the same shock that the fall of the modern metropolis might yield today. A wave of intense bitterness against Valdemar ran through the cities of the League. Their sense of urgency stands out of the fact that August had not ended when delegates from all three tertials gathered at Greifswald —phenomenal speed, considering the state of communications. The meeting made trading in Denmark a capital crime for any Hanseatic merchant. Nor was it a paper decree; machinery for enforcement was provided in each city, and homecoming ships were required to carry clearance papers showing they had not visited the forbidden land. It was decided not to hold the Skaane market at all that year; each city might send one ship thither, but under municipal direction and only to bring home her nationals who were there in semi-permanent residence.

The delegates were presently joined by an embassy of eleven Swedish nobles. The bishops of their country had given King Magnus the Peter's penny to carry on a war which had become a crusade. Sweden would put into the field two thousand knights and men-at-arms, with an appropriate number of supporting troops and ships, and had tightened the agreement with Heinrich of Holstein by giving him possession of Kalmar castle. The nobles represented, however, that with Gotland and Skaane in his hands and the Baltic full of his ships, Valdemar of Denmark was too heavy for Sweden to tackle alone. They wanted direct military as well as financial help from the Hansa.

To this the cities of the Prussian-Livonian tertial demurred. There was some disorder in their councils with Visby so badly hurt and a contest on for a new presidency; and they feared that if they got into war, the uneasy lords in the hinterlands would attack them. They pointed out that it was contrary to the tradition of free towns to make war on their own account.

Lübeck, which had broken with this tradition in the War of the Gerhardssons twenty-five years before and obtained satisfactory results, signed an alliance with the Swedes, bringing the main members of her tertial along—the five Wend towns, with Kolberg, Anklam, Hamburg, Bremen, and Kiel. Some of the Dutch cities, important for their shipping, were persuaded to join. Together they agreed to find 27 cogs, each capable of carrying 100 men and 20 horses, with 25 snake-ships having both sail and oar-power, all the necessary crews, 2740 sword-weaponed men and a great store of engines for sieges. Erich of Saxe-Lauenburg, caught between Lübeck and Hamburg, they threatened into neutrality. They tried to draw Albrecht of Mecklenburg into the alliance, but were less lucky there, as Valdemar had countervailing inducements to offer.

Being commercial men and Germans, they had to make a transaction of the whole business. The treaty of alliance gave the high command to Johann Wittenburg, Burgomaster of Lübeck, and as a guarantee that Sweden would come up to the chalk, Magnus placed Hansa officers in charge of the castles at Bohus and Marstrand. When the conflict had reached a satisfactory conclusion, Magnus was to have the Skaane provinces, but the castles of Varberg, Skanør, Falsterbo, and Helsingborg would belong to the League, and in the meantime, Hanseatic privileges were extended in both Sweden and Norway. The Swedish nobles signed these rather onerous terms; they were in a mood to have pawned their souls for revenge on Valdemar.

The rendezvous of the forces was set for the late fall, but an obscure row developed between Magnus and his son Haakon, which ended with the former being made a prisoner, and the latter named co-king in Sweden. By the time this was straightened out the season was so far sped that it was dangerous for ships to be out, so nothing could be done that year.

The Third King

Spring came late; it was the first days of May when the armament of the eastern cities, even larger than promised, sailed north under Wittenburg to meet the ships of Hamburg, Bremen, and the Dutch towns in the Sound and to harry the coasts of Skaane. One wing tried a raid on Vordingborg and was well beaten.

It had been the intention to push on from here and destroy Copenhagen, whose growing commercial importance was a source of annoyance to the League, but some of the Swedish lords offered the idea that the forces by land and sea could better cooperate against Helsingborg, and when this place was taken, everything else of importance must fall. The objective was changed thither and the place laid under siege.

The castle stands on a high hill, with the city crouching at the water's edge below. The Hanseatics closed it round tightly, and while waiting for Magnus and his army, set up batteries of siege engines, including the first cannon seen in the north, which "rained stones on the walls day and night." Inside the commander was Peder Nielsen of the iron-beard,* Valdemar's naval officer. He made an active defense, with frequent sallies, and there was a good deal of fighting under the walls, with the Germans usually getting the worst of the exchanges and making no great progress in battering the structure.

In the meantime, what was Valdemar up to?—the leader who had disconcerted so many opponents by striking sharply before the normal season for war had begun. He had plenty of warning and the passive side of his preparation was well done, such as provisioning and garrisoning the castles. Iron Heinrich did not even try a campaign on the southern border, but worked out of Kalmar toward the reconquest of Öland. But now it almost seemed as though the King had forgotten war for fantasy. While the stones were falling round Peder

---

*It is not absolutely certain that this was the same Peder; but the evidence is as good for as against, and I have chosen to set it down that way.

Ironbeard's head and men dying at the sally-ports, Valdemar was down in Vordingborg, celebrating a marriage between his daughter Ingeborg and Duke Albrecht of Mecklenburg's son Heinrich, with violinists nodding their heads and pacing out their own tunes, merry tumbling mimes and many a flower strewn out before.

It was a strategic feint. While joy ruled Vordingborg by day, by night Valdemar was negotiating with the captains of the Dutch ships, offering their cities charters of privilege in Danish commerce as against the Germans. In late July the deal was closed and the Hollanders sailed home, out of the war. By this time the siege had been going twelve weeks; Magnus and Haakon had patched up their difficulties, roused their forces, and were coming, slowly down through Halland, while messengers urged them to speed. At Helsingborg the mobile defense had so upset Wittenburg's arrangements that he was forced to anchor most of his cogs offshore and use the better part of their crews in the siege-lines. He would have plenty of warning before a land army of relief could come down, and he provided against naval counterattack by setting out chains of snakeships as pickets south of Copenhagen and at the entrance to the Kattegat, with cruisers out as far as Falsterbo in one direction and Kallundborg in the other.

No doubt this should have been adequate. The trouble was that Valdemar knew all about the arrangement, and his inactivity produced exactly the effect he wanted—a perfunctory performance on the part of the guardships. The consequence was that when he burst out of Vordingborg with all the armed forces of Denmark aboard his ships, he captured the cruisers in the southern Sound and then snapped up the chain of snakes without one of them escaping to give warning.

The first news the men of the League had was the appalling sight of the whole Sound filled with Danish ships bearing down to attack them. The King landed some of his men and drove home on sea and shore together; Peder Ironbeard came roaring through the gates in another sally, and the Hanseatics were overwhelmed on both elements. Twelve of their twenty-seven big cogs were taken, with immense stores of food and weapons; several more were burned and the survivors fled north, some reaching Bremen but only one or two returning to Lübeck through the Belts. Along the shore the men of the cities were driven into their encampment, with so many of them captured that Valdemar had to build a new tower at Vordingborg for their reception. It was called the Goose-tower because he crowned it with a golden goose for a weathervane in honor of the men within.

Wittenburg's army was now blockaded in its camp. Valdemar might have stormed the place or starved them out, but he still had the Swedes to reckon with, and in any case never liked to press an opponent to desperation, so he offered terms; which being accepted, they laid down their weapons and went home, to fight no more in this war. Himself, he remained at Helsingborg to superintend the evacuation. The bulk of the army, under Junker Kristoffer and Sir Valdemar Sappe, moved up into Halland. There was some maneuvering on this front whose details escape the eye; then Magnus began to retreat, probably short of provisions. The Danes followed sharply and just over the borders of Smaland, in the edges of the great forest, forced battle on the Swedes and won so complete a victory that the ransoms paid by their great men totaled over thirty thousand marks, or more than the sum for which the whole of Esthonia had been sold.

In the meanwhile Burgomaster Wittenburg had reached Lübeck. He was ill-received, the town corporation first throwing him into chains and then cutting off his head, before writing an accusatory letter to Magnus, saying that because he had not met his obligations "they suffered the greatest, most irreplaceable, and immoderate defeat and overthrow." This placed the onus of the defeat where it belonged, but did not do much to solve the practical difficulties of two autumns running without herring to sell. The commercial loss was enormous, and actual want of victual is reported from Lübeck, which depended heavily upon the fish staple, not only as an article of exchange, but also for food. The result was an extraordinary meeting of the central tertial and a decision to permit Danes to bring fish to the markets of the Hansa towns, providing they were accompanied by a certificate that no Hanseatic citizen had anything to do with their capture or preparation.

Under the circumstances, it was not difficult to widen this rather peculiar armistice into a kind of peace, a sullen peace on the Hansa side, surrounded by recriminations and strictly limited to a duration of a single year. The meeting was in Rostock, on November 10; the terms were the release of all prisoners, commerce to go on as before, and a general congress for the resolution of grievances to be held on May Day. The Prussian-Livonian tertial complained bitterly that its interests had not been cared for, that all its cities were left at the mercy of the Danes, and that some of its ships had been seized and sold in the harbors of the five Wend towns to help pay for the war.

III

King Valdemar's highly favorable terms to the Lübeck tertial should by this time cause no surprise in view of his constant effort to keep beaten enemies from being enemies again. It is possible that there was also some design for introducing confusion into the ranks of this powerful confederation of cities, by unexpected favors to one member of the complex. But before this or any other line of policy could take effect, all policies were changed by a reshuffle of the dynastic cards into an arrangement far from favorable to Denmark's land and throne.

It began with the Holsteiners. Iron Heinrich was not in the armistice with Lübeck. While Helsingborg castle was bearing the shock of the engine-stones, the marriage of his sister Elizabeth to King Haakon was celebrated with great pomp at

Plön castle in Holstein. It was a proxy wedding, in which a local noble named Herman von Witzen took the place of the groom, since Valdemar's cruisers made the seas unsafe for bringing the affianced pair together.

When news of the armistice came in December, von Witzen and the bride set out in a Lübeck ship, but a storm cast the vessel on Bornholm shore. The Archbishop of Lund, who ruled in the island, was a good friend of Valdemar's; he sent word to the King and kept the lady in Hammershus castle— as a Christian duty, he explained, because the Baltic was too dangerous to be traveled in winter. In the meantime the Norwegian nobles had been making some very rude remarks to their King on the score of his connection with the Hansa, which was cordially hated in their country ever since the starvation of Bergen.

Valdemar learned of this, and also that Magnus was once more in trouble with his own estates as a result of his defeat during the summer. There was a special peace conference of the three kings in January, while Elizabeth of Holstein was keeping her Epiphany in Hammershus; on the first Sunday after Easter, Haakon and Margrete, Valdemar's daughter, were married by Lund in person, and across the banquet table Magnus passed the title deeds to Skaane, as his present of the occasion to the father of the bride. She was ten years old at the time; they took her to Sweden to be brought up as wife and queen. It is related that one of St. Birgitte's daughters had the task, and did not neglect to apply the switch to her ward.

Medieval marriage alliances were notoriously feeble political levers, but this time Valdemar might have reasonably congratulated himself that he had achieved something solid in the disposal of his daughters. The Norwegians were solidly behind an alliance with the conqueror of the Hansa. As for Albrecht of Mecklenburg, his house had been brought into the line of the Danish succession, and he surely would not be too anxious to abate his son's prospects.

But when you touch them, they vanish. Haakon's marriage and the deeding away of Skaane brought Sweden's gall-cup to the brim. When the news spread, the nobles held a Thing at Upsala, before which Magnus Smek and his son were summoned to answer for high crimes—namely, the old King's evil life, that he had laughed at the Papal ban, that he had allowed Gotland to be harried and Skaane alienated without defending them, that he had allied himself with the kingdom's worst foe. There was no reply; the nobles therefore declared the Folkung line deposed from royalty, and chose as their King, the young Duke Albrecht, son of Albrecht of Mecklenburg. When he came he was cheered through the streets of Stockholm and proclaimed King of the Swedes and Goths at the ancient Stone of Mora.

This was not all. In the same summer died Junker Kristoffer, only son of Valdemar, Denmark's King.

21

"And Those Who Fall
Will Die for Naught"
(1231-1252; 1364-1368)

QUEEN BLANCHE DIED A DAY OR SO BEFORE THE YOUNG
prince and there were the usual rumors of poison,
this time the story being that Valdemar had mixed
a potion which was to take off Magnus, Blanche, and Haakon, all three, leaving his daughter Queen of Sweden and
Norway; that Blanche drank her dose, but before the others
could sip, Kristoffer entered the room and unwittingly took
the remainder of the draught. Actually, it began at the siege
of Helsingborg, where the prince had been struck by a can-
non-stone, which broke his helmet and either fractured his
skull or gave him a concussion that resulted in a clot. His
health became steadily worse until his passing.

So the great line ends; the Volsungs are all dead. No Skjoldung more to be lifted on the shield of Viborg while a sword
is swung defiant to the four points of the world. Of males
who bear the blood of that kingly stem, there remain only
the sons of Gerhard, now in mercenary service under the new
King of Sweden, and Valdemar the Blockhead of Slesvig,
already rejected, with one sickly son of his own. Would any
Thing choose such as these? No: *Geme, plange, moesto more,
dolorosia Dania,* whose crown now falls from her own head to
scheming Mecklenburg or the degenerate house of Magnus
the Caresser.

A black prospect. Black as the hour in Valdemar the Victor's time, when men brought home from a hunt the dead body of the young third Valdemar, the hope of Denmark, whose own bride had died three months before with her unborn child, so ending the line of the lovely and beloved Queen Dagmar. There were left three sons of the ugly Beengjerd, the princess from Portugal. Their names were Erik, Abel, and Kristoffer; of the last two, men said that these were names never heard in Denmark before and no good would come of them. As to their upbringing, all three were quarrelsome and ill-disposed toward one another; Queen Beengjerd seldom made them less so.

After the death of Valdemar the Younger, the old King went to Skaane. At this time there lived in the great forest of Vastergotland a certain knight who had been a pilgrim and was now a hermit; it was said that he could see more deeply into the future than most men. King Valdemar sent a messenger to ask his advice, saying he was troubled lest his several sons should never be at one with each other. The reply of the wise knight was that the three sons would agree just as evilly as was possible, but that all three would be kings after him. King Valdemar was not a notably word-sparing man, but when this word was brought to him, he dismounted and stood a long time in silence beside his horse. It was at this time he let men search out the old laws of the realm to have them written down.

After King Valdemar died, Erik was chosen King. He had given no good promise in his youth, but when he became King, the begging friars came to Denmark and converted him to a better way of life. King Erik said that he wished to finish his own days as one of the grey brothers and to be buried in Roskilde cathedral. He told everyone he was going on a crusade to Esthonia, and to pay for this he laid a new tax on every plow in the kingdom, even those belonging to priests and hærmænd, which were exempt from taxation; therefore he was called Erik Plowpenny.

When this tax was announced at the Skaane Thing, the men of that province burst into rioting and drove the King from their land. They said that the tax was unlawful and that Erik did not wish to use the money for a crusade, but to make war against his brother, Abel, who was now Duke of Slesvig. The two brothers had been much in conflict, with many man-slayings and battles between their followers, but it was always Danes against Danes. All equally plundered the poor folk and the monkish cloisters as is told by the chronicler of Øm: "From this time on were the Danes a matter of laughter to the neighboring peoples and the lands they had conquered, because of their inner wars and destructions."

King Erik made peace with his brother and went to visit him, but Abel let the King be taken prisoner. There was a man named Tyge Bost; Abel gave the captured King to him and said Tyge should do whatever he liked. Tyge placed King Erik in a boat and rowed him out to a little island in the western sea, where there was a man named Lave Gudmundssen, who cut off the King's head with two strokes of a sword.

After this Abel was King, since Erik's children were all daughters; from him are descended the Dukes of Slesvig. Many of the Danes would not consent to his rule. The great men of the realm held a Thing, at which sentence was given that Abel should be banished for his brother's murder, and though the men of the Thing were not strong enough to get rid of him altogether, there was much unrest in the land. The chronicler of Øm says: "After King Erik's death, not Abel but Babel was seated on the throne and quickly showed his anger against God's church and the holy cloisters."

King Abel always had fighting men about him; with some of them he made a campaign against the marshbonders. They beat him in a battle; it is said that he was drowned among the marshes during his flight, but certainly no one ever saw him again, so that Kristoffer was chosen King and the prophecy of the wise knight was fulfilled in this manner.

II

King Valdemar entombed his only son in Roskilde cathedral under a magnificent statue of purest alabaster, but that did not help much. There is a note of authentic personal anguish in the fact that as soon as the services for the dead were done, the King left the country for a long voyage through Poland, Bohemia, Germany, Flanders, and France, though the vital peace conference with the Hansa was only a couple of weeks away.

Of course, Valdemar hardly undertook this trip to escape from his thoughts alone; it is only his haste in leaving that bears such an interpretation. He seldom did things singly, and at this time he assuredly did not wish to become involved in the inevitable and hopeless struggle of Magnus and Haakon to recover their throne at a time while the Hanseatic matter was still unsettled. The Marshal he left in charge of the realm was Anders Frost, less than a year in office. As such, he could reply to Magnus' importunities that he lacked experience and authority to order out the Danish forces in support of the two Folkungs.

We know also from Valdemar's itinerary that he was anxious to see Kaiser Karl again, and to persuade that glittering but somewhat insubstantial majesty to exert whatever pressure he could on the cities in the interests of peace. (Karl was willing enough, and his persuasion may have had some effect, but just how much is not clear.) In Flanders, Valdemar was busy on details of his agreement with the Dutch cities, and tried to use his skill as a mediator to obtain the release of the captive King of France. Edward of England sent a safe-conduct for a visit to that country, but King Jean died in captivity before it could be used. It is significant that after this personal contact with Edward, Valdemar never again touched the invasion project. In fact, the *Wanderjahre* exhibit him throughout in his coldest and most empirical phase, farthest removed from dream, as though the dream had died with the last of the Skjoldung line.

The final act of the grand tour was a trip down through Alsace to Avignon, where the pupil of Marsilio of Padua knelt in abject humility before Pope Urban V—after which the two men sat down to talk business. His Holiness was a sincere and pious man of reforming tendencies, a good deal like one of the popes of the Counter Reformation three hundred years later; and the tradition that had grown up around his Curia in the last quarter-century was one of friendliness to this King who made pilgrimages to the Holy Sepulchre.

This dated all the way back to the coronation, when so many bishops were present—not only as Danes, but also because of Graf Gerhard's social policy, which brought him into competition with the Church for revenues and led to a good deal of plundering of ecclesiastical property, usually under some guise of taxation. The Gerhardssons had slipped naturally into an attitude of hostility toward a Church which produced a Bishop Sveyn of Aarhus and placed a ban on Holsteiners after the Helsinge massacre. Valdemar had thus become, in some sense, the arm of the Cross in the north; and in the past he had not hesitated to use this position by a long series of embassies to Avignon, asking in the humblest terms for permission to handle some detail of Danish ecclesiastical organization without further reference to the Curia.

Thus Odensee falls vacant. Two German clerks complain that they have not been allowed to participate in the election of the new bishop, but Valdemar explains easily that they are peregrines, not regular members of the chapter—and establishes a precedent for keeping foreign priests out of Danish church elections. Thus there are two canonries vacant in Lund; Valdemar asks permission to appoint to them at the precise moment when Sweden (in whose territories Lund still lies at this time) is laying violent hands on the Peter's penny, while the King of Denmark is paying to the groat and giving so distinguished a reception to the Papal legate that the Holy

Father sends a special letter of thanks, accompanied by the desired document with regard to the canonries.

There had been a long range of minor incidents of similar character. The sum of them was that under the benignant smile of the papacy itself, all the necessary precedents had been established for making the Church of Denmark something unique in the Middle Ages—a national, self-contained organization. It is not clear whether Urban realized this, or, if he did realize it, whether he cared. The policy of Rome was so widespread in space and time as to make such a minor aberration unimportant beside the solid gains that would accrue through demonstrating to Valdemar's neighbors what they could obtain through fidelity to the Holy See. But the tenor of Valdemar's requests at Avignon shows that he knew perfectly well what he was doing. He was determined to freeze his temporary advantage into permanence—just as Valdemar the Victorious had sought to freeze into permanence his gains over the forces of anarchy through the promulgation of the codes of law.

Those requests included a number of purely religious significance, which were probably intended to, and actually did, emphasize the King's exemplary piety. Permission to build a chapel at Gurre and absolution for those who visited it on feast days; a commission composed of the bishops of Lund, Roskilde, and Odensee to inquire who were the holy men of Denmark, at whose graves miracles had occurred; church positions for ten of the King's private clerks and chaplains. Mingled with these were desires of considerably greater ambit —permission for Valdemar to fill two of the spiritual offices of Denmark arbitrarily; an undertaking that no Dane might be tried in the ecclesiastical courts of any country but his own; finally, that the Archbishop of Lund should have authority to ban, without appeal, "anyone who did wrong to the Danish King or kingdom," the ban not to be removed until the civil state decided that full reparation had been made. There was special mention of traitors in this connection.

All but the last request, His Holiness granted in the most impressive manner, adding the Order of the Golden Rose, a splinter of the True Cross, a lock of hair from the Virgin Mary's head, and an absolution to the King and his suite for seven years and seven and forty days. On that final item the form was slightly changed, but the substance was there and when Valdemar departed he was satisfied.

He might well be; for he had completed a process which began when the great Absalon wrote a separate Danish canon law. The power of nomination to Church offices was now established as a prescriptive right of the crown in some cases and it would not be hard to extend their number. An illustration was furnished in this very year, when Ribe bishopric fell vacant. The chapter elected a candidate, but Valdemar set him aside on the ground of doubtful loyalty, and transferred to the see a great friend of his, Bishop Mogens of Borglum. The Pope approved and the chapter had to accept.

With nomination went an implied power of removal which the King exercised almost at once by requesting Lund to eject a couple of Jutland churchmen for treason during the late rebellion, once more receiving what he wanted. That is, the interests of the Church had been indissolubly linked with those of the realm through these powers. Treason, in a certain sense Valdemar's own discovery, had been made a sin as well as a crime.

We tend to forget that the basic reason for the separation of Church and state was the preservation of freedom of conscience to the individual. In Denmark that freedom was never seriously challenged after Valdemar Atterdag's time, because the Danish church could not become the servant of an alien power or even of an alien ideology.

"And Those Who Fall Will Die for Naught"

In the meanwhile, the peace conference was sitting, Marshal Anders Frost being present for Denmark, with one Fikke Moltke, met here for the first time, one of the two sons of a Mecklenburg knight who came to Valdemar in von Lochen's train during the War of the Gerhardssons. He had the defense of Vordingborg against the Hansa raid during the last war and did well with it. The terms these two offered in Valdemar's name are the guarantee of his desire to have a peace without regrets. If the cities "will behave with him as their forefathers did with his forefathers," they shall have all the privileges they had before King Kristoffer II's time, with exemption from Sound tolls and the abolition of strand-right. (Pope Urban had been making a drive against this custom as unchristian; it was part of Valdemar's friendship to Avignon that he should give relief from it unasked.)

But by this time the cities had somewhat recovered, and as usual with Germans who are not on their knees, took the attitude that they were being cheated out of something that rightfully belonged to them. Valdemar's terms they utterly rejected; they wanted an indemnity for the losses suffered during the fighting and the abolition of all tariffs on goods taken to the Skaane market. When the Danish negotiators refused these demands, Lübeck's tertial laid a special tax on all Hanseatic goods and sent ambassadors to draw the Dutch and Prussian groups into a renewal of the war. A three-headed executive was appointed; letters of marque were offered to all who wished to raid Danish shipping and troops began to gather.

This looked very ominous with Valdemar afar, but the Lübeckers speedily found that the King had anticipated them. The Prussian tertial replied that their overlord, the Grand Master of the Teutonic Order (whom Valdemar had visited), refused to let them engage in exterior wars because of an incursion of heathen Lithuanians. The Dutch cities (which Valdemar had also visited) reported that they were not interested in fighting for something that had been given them without a contest. Of the princelings who might be helpful, Albrecht of Mecklenburg and the Gerhardssons were busy with Magnus and Haakon; Adolf, the heir of Johann the Mild, had been bought out by the Danish King, who gave him feudal rights over Femern island; and the only one left was the Blockhead Valdemar.

There were few takers for the letters of marque, and spring brought with it the news that a great Danish fleet had met in Øresund under Peder Ironbeard, with three thousand soldiers aboard, probably for an attack on either Rostock or Stralsund. Remembering what happened at Visby, the Hanseatics suddenly turned reasonable, arranging through Duke Barnim of Stettin an extension of the armistice to Candlemas Day four years hence, no terms attached save that the men of the cities should be allowed to take fish and salt them in Skaane. The embargo on commerce with Denmark remained.

Valdemar's old friend and enemy, the Duke of Slesvig, was in this armistice (he died soon after) but the Gerhardssons not. They were watching the frontiers for Magnus, who managed to assemble an army in Norway and with a few Danish adventurers, make one more try to regain the crowns he had lost. He failed in a battle; Magnus was taken prisoner and shut up in Stockholm castle. His fall dissolved the last impediment to Valdemar's return; he hurried home, for the stars were now in conjunction for peace and, that summer, the one after the extension of the armistice, it was made all round the circle.

Under it, Denmark received not only the last of Fyn, with Hindsgavl and Ørkel, but also Varberg castle and the province of North Halland, hypothecated to Norway during King Kristoffer's early years, taken by Iron Heinrich from Haakon, and now by him returned to Valdemar. Lübeck and her tertial reluctantly made a peace that gave the cities freedom from strand-right, allowed them extraterritoriality in Skaane in cases not involving wounds or death, permitted them to re-export unsold goods without paying duty and gave each city a clubhouse at the shore. They could sell goods at retail, but would have to pay a tax for the privilege. Valdemar rejected two other requests—that Denmark use Hanseatic weights and measures, and that the abolition of strand-right should be carried so far that jetsam goods were to be collected and placed under royal guard until called for.

The King's hands were now free to clear up relations with Sweden, where there was still some frontier bickering, since Haakon of Norway had not abandoned his father's cause. Medieval ideals required Valdemar to support his daughter's husband; he sent an army into Skaane under Erich of Saxe-Lauenburg, who did a little fighting and won a couple of castles before Duke Albrecht of Mecklenburg intervened, asking Valdemar for an interview. The two clever men met at Aalholm and spent several weeks trying to outwit each other, without either gaining anything he did not already hold. The result was a family peace, in which Valdemar was confirmed in his possession of Gotland and Albrecht the Younger in his Swedish crown. Haakon would not come into the peace without the release of his father and the Swedes would not let Magnus out, so Norway remained technically at war, but actually the fighting was all over.

22
Revenge (1368-1370)

T HE HERITAGE WAS NOW ALL RECOVERED SAVE SLESVIG alone, which had fallen away from the crown long back, when Kristoffer I succeeded King Abel, leaving the dukedom in the latter's family. Around the circle of the realm stood the royal castles, now more than forty in number. They were of all sizes, from little Ørum in Jutland, which had only a ditch and palisade wall, with six engines of various types, up to mighty Helsingborg and lordly Vordingborg of the seven towers. But even on the smallest the work of strengthening went forward constantly, for Valdemar attached to his castles an importance only shared by his fleet.

The map explains; not only are nearly all the structures on the sea or an arm of it, so that castles and navy form part of a single strategic complex, but they are so grouped that, whatever the direction of the wind, the fighting men accompanying the fleet will have a fortified sally port on each of the islands and on every important area of the mainland. Each of the larger castles is provided with a companion in such easy supporting distance that an attack on one risks being taken in the rear from the other. Thus even mighty Vordingborg is covered by the King's new foundation at Jungshoved, and the Middelfart crossing, key to Fyn and Jutland, has no less than five warders—Lærbeksholm, Hindsgavl, Koldinghus, with new castles at Middelfart itself and Hønborg, beside for a time the smaller building at Brobjærg, which seems to have been given up after Hindsgavl came to Valdemar.

Within each of these castles sat a royal foged, not only collecting taxes and administering justice, but also acting as commander of the garrison and superintendent of the local militia. The development in the position of these fogeds had been gradual, but by this time they were officers with broad powers. Nearly half of them were Germans, and there were complaints about this, especially from Jutland, where the obvious comparison with the days of Graf Gerhard was freely drawn.

The complaints were unjustified, the comparison unreal. Valdemar's castle-fogeds drew their income from a percentage on legal fees and from the royal treasury, not directly from taxes. They were required to conduct their government in accordance with Danish law, and the King on his ceaseless travels saw to it that nobody slipped. In the year of the long trip to Avignon, for instance, a certain Lyder Kale, foged in North Jutland, is fined everything he owns for preferring his own will to the law of the land.

A good many of the Germans found this accountability uncomfortable; names disappear from the lists and their proportion to Danes tends to decline. For close superintendence was not the only reminder that they were servants instead of independent vassals; there was also no permanence in office. From the beginning of the reign, the King had rotated men in such high offices as Marshal and Drost, to keep them from building up a vested interest, as not infrequently happened with Lord High Marshals or Constables in other countries. He kept men in these posts only about two years; after the castle system became thoroughly established, the fogedships were shifted quite as rapidly as the higher offices, and perhaps even more so. Thus Fikke Moltke was rewarded for his defense of Vordingborg against the Hansa, but Peder Nielssen Ironbeard was immediately brought down from Helsingborg to take over the castle, while Moltke moved over to Kallø. The following year Moltke has Randers in addition to Kallø, but the year after that he is commanding Koldinghus, while Peder Nielssen is next met with as captain of Lindholm.

These castle-fogeds were also the backbone of the King's Council, which at this time acquired a formal existence, and was significantly called *Rigets Raad* instead of *Kongens Raad* —"nation's advisers" for "King's advisers." The bishops sat on it constantly, and though it had no legalized force, Valdemar seldom did anything without winning its approval. "No man can rule alone." It really took the place of the promised annual general Danehof, which had been found too clumsy an instrument of government for any but extraordinary occasions, and was laid away in preservatives to be the key of the future. Valdemar tried to get as wide a geographical representation on this Council as possible, but he does not seem to have been particularly lucky, except with Jutlanders. Perhaps the requisite training in leadership was lacking in districts that did not have Jutland's peculiar social organization to sustain individuals in positions of authority against the disruptive forces of the Time of Uproar.

In the period following the peace with the Hansa, the King was mainly busy in Skaane, bringing various small estates and land-parcels into the royal domain, and letting them out again on his favorite system of leasehold. Most of these holdings he bought for cash, since there could be little question of repossessions in that province. It had been too long in foreign hands for the bygone royal ownerships to have much meaning.

He was too busy to remark the gathering stormclouds.

II

The cities of the Prussian tertial were restive and angry. Valdemar had considered them participants in the late war against Denmark and confiscated some of their ships, and there had been no reparation. There was a complaint that

Denmark levied an inheritance tax on the goods of burghers who died on her soil. In spite of the formal abolition of strand-right, objects of value continued to disappear from ships driven ashore. The King's fogeds refused to take Hanseatic copper money in payment for duties at the Skaane fair except at a one to one ratio, and—the immemorial wail of the monopolist whose monopoly has been broken—the duties were too high.

The Germans are a people of combination. The Prussian tertial summoned a meeting at Elbing, with delegates from Lübeck and some of the Dutch cities present, and secretly agreed to fight against the kings of Denmark and Norway until "the utmost freedom of commerce in those countries" was achieved, by which they meant until all tariffs were taken off and all but Hanseatic traders ejected from the markets. The sense of the gathering was that nothing should be done until the fall herring-run was over.

At that time a general convention of all three tertials was held at Cologne, where a tight treaty of alliance was drawn up, with provision for expelling from the Hansa any city that did not follow the plan. The shipment of weapons, steel, unworked iron, and the materials for beer (!) to Denmark was embargoed. The five Wend towns, with Riga, Dorpat, Reval, and Pernau of the Livonian group, agreed to furnish twenty cogs each, with a hundred weaponed men, the other cities to equip armaments in proportion. Each of more than sixty towns would levy a "poundtoll" of one-half of one-third on the value of all wares sold, in order to finance this war. The fleet of the western cities would meet that from the Baltic off Marstrand on Palm Sunday, and proceed to the conquest of Denmark.

Ambassadors had been sent to all the princes who might have a grudge against Valdemar, and all these were represented at Cologne—Albrecht of Mecklenburg, his son the King of Sweden, the Swedish nobles, the Gerhardssons, young Henrik, Duke of Slesvig. They all signed their names to a circular letter to the kings of England and Poland, to twenty-seven German princes, to the Kaiser and Pope, complaining of how Valdemar had imposed upon the Hansa "with seizures, bonds and imprisonments, with bloodletting and manslaying, confiscations of wares and ships and other acts of masterfulness."

That letter is a good clue to what was really going on, for in fact Valdemar kept extremely good order in Skaane, and this was the only time that bloodletting or imprisonments had been mentioned, even in the *pro forma* diplomatic complaints which are intended as a basis for bargaining. In fact, no real moral purpose was alleged or considered for this assembly of the general alliance against Denmark. It was simply a downright raid for plunder, a war of conquest to share up the wealth of the Denmark Valdemar had raised from poverty, and to destroy her as a nation. The allies agreed that the King was to be deposed or killed. With the Skjoldung line extinct, the Skaane provinces should go to Sweden; Sjælland, Falster and Møn to Mecklenburg; Jutland and Fyn to the Gerhardssons; Langeland to Duke Henrik. (Laaland was rather inexplicably forgotten.) All ransoms were to be shared.

The diplomatic preparations were handled with an eye to avoiding the mismanagement that had allowed Valdemar to defeat his enemies in detail in the war surrounding the second Jutland revolt. In a military sense the technique was to surprise the King by speed and secrecy, then crush him under overwhelming force. All the declarations of war were to be assembled at Lübeck in March for simultaneous delivery, while Hanseatic inspectors saw that the princes were ready. In the meantime no one was to cross the frontier from Mecklenburg, Holstein or Sweden without a pass from the Council of the Hansa.

Valdemar, nevertheless, got some hint of what was going on, and sent Bishop Henrik of Roskilde down to Cologne with letters of safe-conduct, to bring delegates from the cities back to Copenhagen, asking them to talk things out like reasonable men. The Hansa replied that the safe-conduct had been written on paper instead of parchment, and that only squires instead of knights had been provided for the ambassadorial escort; they would not come until these matters were corrected.

In February, Valdemar tried once more for an agreement, sending Baron Hummersbüttel (who once held Hohenstegen against Iron Heinrich) down to Lübeck to ask for a conference and arbitration of differences. The cities replied they might consider a conference if Valdemar would pay for "the damage done to their commerce" an indemnity of one hundred and fifty thousand marks—more than he had spent in the redemption of the entire kingdom, more than Denmark's whole income for a decade.

There was, then, nothing to do but fight. Valdemar provisioned and garrisoned his castles, made preparations to mobilize his fleet at the turn of spring, and awaited the coming storm.

It was heavier and darker than he had imagined. When the alliance sent in its declarations of war, all the lords of Jutland with the exception of the sons of Niels Bugge went over to the enemy and attacked the royal castles, Stig Anderssen and Klaus Limbek at their head.

III

The King had certainly fallen into one of the errors to which he was liable when personal observation was lacking —this time, that of underestimating the vindictiveness and the cohesion of the cities. But the previous war had demonstrated that with a united Denmark behind him, even the fleets of the united Hansa could be faced down.

The size of those fleets, to be sure, made the position difficult, and threatened the basis of Valdemar's navy-and-castle strategy. But in the earlier Hansa war, he had shown that he could overcome such an obstacle. The presence of the two Albrechts, Henrik of Slesvig and the Gerhardssons with the opposition was certainly very bad. But the Swedes were disorganized and incompetently led, young Henrik was as great a booby as his father, Albrecht of Mecklenburg was so unready that he had to borrow ships, provisions, and weapons from Lübeck, and the Gerhardssons had demonstrated that they were not fit to stay on the same battlefield as Valdemar Atterdag.

It was the defection of Jutland that made the weight too outrageous to be borne—removing something like a quarter of Denmark's fighting strength from the King's hand and adding it to those of his enemies. Not only in this defection but in its accompaniments, in the fact that Valdemar's service of information failed him, we may trace Klaus Limbek, performing his greatest act of treason to the man who had been his friend. (It was also Limbek's last treason; during the war he fell in a combat so obscure that it has no name, and his body was eaten by wolves.) The King had taken him down to Avignon, and when they returned, placed Limbek on the Rigets Raad, making him Drost and using him much. Given the way a medieval court was organized, it would have been easy for so intimate a councillor to conceal or distort the evidence to make some things seem other than they were—as he clearly distorted the evidence from Jutland, where he was the moving force of the whole combination. Valdemar had every reason to believe he had succeeded in that province. The countryside was quiet and even contented, the dam, road, and gristmill program had been in operation long enough to be producing results, and, after the recovery of Skaane, the extraordinary taxes of the first years of the reign had been taken off. But Klaus Limbek must have rule or ruin; he turned traitor and made the second war of the Hansa from its beginning a lost war for Denmark.

That much was evident as soon as the heralds delivered

their messages. The only question was whether the recently integrated realm could bear such a blow without another descent into the Time of Uproar. When the news of the Jutland rising came, Valdemar named Henning Podbusk commander of the forces, appointed Erich of Saxe-Lauenburg captain of Kallundborg and regent of the kingdom in the event of his own death, and disappeared into central Germany.

The idea that this was desertion in the face of difficulties was never advanced at the time, even by the King's worst enemies. In fact, they saw in Valdemar's journey only an attempt to soften the force of their blow by turning the struggle against the hated King into a war on innocent Denmark, and an effort to obtain military help from the belt of princely states that looked out on the Baltic. Certainly, Valdemar did seek alliances among those courts. But this was assuredly not the only reason why he went. His abdication of command removed from the field the only person who could give the struggle any character but that of passive defense, a dangerous method of war, which Valdemar never adopted at any other time or place. The chance of obtaining allies was hardly worth this much; we must seek another reason.

Particularly in view of the fact that Valdemar Atterdag was one of the more complex characters of history, who seldom did anything for a single or simple reason. He was an old man now, as his period counted ages, and without heirs male of the body. The crown was certain to fall to a foreign line; to that of Duke Erich, he seems rather to have hoped. That is, Valdemar could not even have the vicarious personal immortality of leaving what he had to his family. The only thing that remained was the work, and that work was Denmark.

By leaving the country in the face of the grand alliance, the King put to the ordeal of battle the question of how well he had builded, and gave Denmark herself the chance to become his heir—if she were strong enough.

The fleet from the Dutch cities burned out Marstrand in Norway and pushed on to meet the Baltic ships before Copenhagen. The real animus of the war appears in the cities' orders to their commanders that ships were to be the first objects of capture, and in their next proceedings. They attacked the town whose prosperity had become a danger to their interests. In May the city fell; the Hanseatics plundered it out, burning all the important buildings, including the churches, whose bells were carried off to Lübeck. Ships filled with stone were sunk in the harbor to keep the place from recovering, and it was ordered that as soon as Albrecht of Mecklenburg had brought Sjælland under his rule, the castle should be pulled down.

To insure communications between the two wings of the Hansa, Helsingør, Gurre, Søborg, and Kallundborg were now simultaneously besieged. The first place made a weak defense and fell some time in June. Leaving the men of the western Hansa to complete their work at the others, the Lübeckers and Prussians now sailed to the fishing districts, where they speedily captured Malmø with the smaller castles at Skanør and Falsterbo. It was announced that the market would be open that year. Danes might come but only unweaponed and to buy or to fish for wage under direction of the Hanseatic merchants. The embargo against selling iron to Danes was retained; they could not have beer either.

In the meanwhile Albrecht the Younger had arrived from Sweden with a considerable army, which took Lund and open country roundabout, proclaimed Albrecht King in Skaane, and laid simultaneous siege to Helsingborg and Varberg. The elder Albrecht entered the southern isles with Hansa help. Stege on Møn he took easily, but when the old Duke tried to storm Nykøbing of Falster, he was badly wounded and had to turn over his command to one of the leaders from the cities.

(They managed to get a surrender on conditions after a hard siege.) In Jutland the Gerhardssons and rebels between them took Riberhus, and one Erlend Kalv, who commanded at Aalborg, went over to them. Small castles at Aggersborg and Ørum were taken and destroyed. The Holsteiners now controlled most of the countryside and ruled it as acknowledged owners, granting feudal charters to all the royal estates and a parchment of privilege which gave "all the dear burghers in our kingdom" freedom to use the Skaane market.

Iron Heinrich now found things so favorable in Jutland that he committed operations there to his brother Nicholas, while he took his own forces to Laaland for a try at Ravnsborg and Aalholm. He was not quite strong enough to win either place, but the commanders of both (one our old friend, Baron Hummersbüttel) made armistices on the condition that they would stay out of the fighting unless attacked again.

Thus far the allies were winners, but as tidings of their behavior began to spread, there was a typical Danish rally. Helsingborg beat off Albrecht the Young and his people had no luck at Varberg either. The bonders of Skaane were all for Valdemar, though he had had them for only five years, neither paying nor giving to the Swedes. After an unpleasant summer King Albrecht lost interest and went back to Stockholm for the remainder of the war. Over in Jutland, a foged named Peder Axelssen made a surprise counterattack on Stig Anderssen's home castle, carried it by storm and slew that great man of war in his own hall. Skodborg made good its defense against the rebels; Skanderborg broke up the force attacking it; the revolters failed at Klaus Limbek's old house of Kallø and could not assemble strength enough for a serious effort against the complex of castles around the Middelfart crossing.

The defense of Sjælland was best of all. Erich of Saxe-Lauenburg commanded Kallundborg heroically, inflicting severe loss on the besiegers; Søborg held out and so did little Gurre. In the southern part of the island Hanseatic and Mecklenburg forces were led against Vordingborg, where a

foged unknown save for this struggle commanded, Hans Tyrbagh. He sallied on the attackers when they tried a storm,
giving them a crushing defeat, with so many prisoners taken
that the local leader for the allies agreed not to touch Vordingborg again in exchange for their release. The Hanseatic
high command repudiated the armistice on the ground that
no agreement with Danes was binding save an agreement on
their part to submit, and came back to the castle with more
ships and a stronger force of men. Tyrbagh had sworn to pay
out their deceit in a manner they would not forget. When
the armament reached Vordingborg, he came out under sig-
nals of peace, and with the appearance of a man much fright-
ened, delivered the keys of the castle up, and invited half a
dozen burgomasters, including he of Lübeck in to discuss
terms of surrender. They came; while they discussed, Tyrbagh's men changed all the locks and he ended the discussion
by throwing the burgomasters into a dungeon in chains. The
job was completed by a storm which wrecked many of their
ships, on the heels of which Tyrbagh made another sally and
crippled their landing force.

The losses from these defeats, with a bad failure at Jungshoved in the fall, and the inevitable tendency of victors to
wrangle over spoils, brought a certain amount of dissension
into allied councils during the winter, with a slackening of
effort and payments. The Lübeck tertial asked the Count of
Flanders to forbid his subjects to take part in Danish commerce, whereupon the Dutch cities announced that in view of
the astonishingly powerful and costly defense they were meeting, they had had enough of fighting for nothing. (They seem
to have taken the pounding administered by Erich at Kallundborg.) The Wend towns swore they would go on until Denmark was conquered, increased their own taxes and persuaded
Duke Albrecht to join them in a grand effort at Helsingborg,
which would give them control of both ends of the Sound,
a prospect which was so agreeable to the Dutch that they

came along for another year, though with somewhat less strength than before.

Both eastern and western fleets met at Helsingborg in the spring. The siege was even hotter than that in the first war, lasting nearly all summer, with heavy fighting. Toward the end of July, some of the outer defenses were taken. Fikke Moltke, who was in command, beat a parley and agreed to march out with his men on September 8 if the place were not relieved by that date. This could have ended the war in the real subjugation of Denmark, for about the same time Koldinghus fell to the combined efforts of the Jutlanders and Iron Heinrich, and the chronicles speak (without revelatory details, as usual) of a wave of misery, the Danes losing courage and hope. But there was no authority which would or could give the allies the universal surrender they demanded, and when they tried to exact it by force, they ran into a couple of tough-minded castle fogeds who turned everything upside down.

One was Peder Iverssen of Hindsgavl, which Iron Heinrich attacked simultaneously with Hønborg, in an effort to break up the Middelfart complex on the heels of his victory at Koldinghus. He failed expensively, was counter-besieged in his camp, and to get his men out, had to sign an armistice which bound him not to enter Fyn again during the war.

Beyond the Belts, Bruno Warrendorp, burgomaster of Lübeck in place of the one held at Vordingborg, sent Duke Albrecht's son Heinrich into Sjælland while he himself led the Hanseatic forces against Lindholm, which was needed to make the fisheries secure. The foged there was the redoubtable Peder Nielssen of the iron beard. He sat quietly till the men of the cities were round the place, then put on so thundering a counterattack that Warrendorp was killed and his army completely broken up. Duke Heinrich in Sjælland suffered a good deal from Danish small-war, and had to be recalled before the campaigning season was out, because

Valdemar had stirred the Duke of Brunswick up to invade Mecklenburg home territories.

That attack was the only result of the King's search for aid among the German princelings. His first visit had been to Brandenburg, but his friend, the dull dog Markgraf Ludwig, was dead, and had been succeeded by his brother Otto, an even duller dog, who had pawned away so much of his inheritance that he was negotiating to sell the rest. After a trip to Poland, Valdemar went on to Brunswick, where a Duke named Magnus had just succeeded. He was young, full of ambition, and a hard hater of the Hansa. While Valdemar was at his court, word came down from Kallundborg that Duke Erich of Saxe-Lauenburg had just died. The loss of the last friend of his youth was a heavy blow for the King in this time of dolor, but it lightened his diplomatic task. Erich left a young son, naming Valdemar as the boy's guardian. This guardianship the King now transferred to Brunswick, at the same time confirming to the Saxe-Lauenburg line the regency of Denmark in the case of his own fall. This seemed adequate payment to Duke Magnus, who promptly marched into Mecklenburg with fire and sword.

He was badly beaten, but the effect was to take much of the pressure off Denmark. The situation that confronted the cities during the second winter of the war was that they had already gained the Sound fisheries, but would now have to carry the burden of conquering the rest of Denmark for a group of thoroughly unreliable princes. Albrecht the Younger of Sweden was in trouble with his nobles and could do no more. The Gerhardssons had been driven from Fyn and nobody wanted them in the other islands. Albrecht of Mecklenburg would need a big loan to keep up hostilities and had demonstrated that he was incapable of dealing with the Danish castles. For that matter, so had the Hansa, if the war were viewed in their habitual economic terms of reference. After the first rush, they had taken only Helsingborg in a siege so costly that it wiped out an entire year's profit on the fisheries, and there was a good chance they might run into another Vordingborg or Lindholm, all cost and nothing taken.

In Lübeck itself rancor had not died. Before the annual convention that city voted to press the conquest to the utter destruction of Denmark, and organized a special "Strafcorps" to march through the countryside, plundering and burning everything in sight, after the charming manner of Graf Gerhard. The idea did not meet with universal approval from the other members of the partnership, particularly as there was a good deal of pressure for peace from churchmen all over the north as the result of an appeal from the Danish bishops. In addition, some of the cities were quite justifiably nervous about what Valdemar's diplomacy could do. He had persuaded the Dukes of Pommern to growl; now he reached the Grand Master of the Teutonic Knights, who spoke to his vassals among the Prussian cities, and one of them offered Henning Podbusk a safe-conduct to the convention. He came, offering terms; the vote went against continuing the war, and in the following May at Stralsund a peace was signed which permitted Valdemar to return to his kingdom and begin once more the task of lifting it from the ground.

23
Home from the Hill
(1371-1375; 1223-1227)

IT WAS A HARD, BAD PEACE. THE CITIES WERE TO HAVE EVERY right at the fisheries on which there had hitherto been any question; to be allowed to bring their own people to take the fish, and these people to live in Skaane under the fullest extraterritorial law, not being brought into Danish courts on any pretext, even as witnesses. At every market town six inns for the sale of beer might be set up, tax-free; imports of wine never to bear any duty, and no export tax to be levied on fish; Lübeck money to circulate in Skaane at a permanent rate of two to one against the King's new coinage. Sum it up that Denmark's richest resource was made over to the Hansa for downright exploitation.

As protection against any effort to change this peace by arms, the cities demanded possession of Skanør, Falsterbo, Malmø and Helsingborg castles for fifteen years, with the taxes from the appertaining districts to pay them for their trouble. As a protection against Valdemar's ingenuity, which they feared even more than his weapons, the cities wrote it that "if our Lord and King Valdemar should wish to yield his kingdom to another, he shall not do so without the express permission of the cities, and unless he shall give guarantees that the cities shall be maintained in all their rights and freedoms."

The provisions about the fisheries are about what might

have been expected, and that with regard to the castles was in line with the right of conquest, universally regarded as sound law in the Middle Ages. But there was one feature about the Peace of Stralsund which set it apart from every similar document of its time and made it a landmark. It was not signed by the King at all, nor even sealed by him until a full year after it had been placed in execution. The signatories and guarantors were the bishops of Lund and Odensee, Sir Valdemar Sappe, a Conrad Moltke who was a kinsman of Fikke Moltke the castle-foged, Peder Nielssen—in short the Rigsraad, which so describes itself in the subscription of the parchment. From this time forth that Council became the moving force in the realm, as though King Valdemar, satisfied with the manner in which the nation had carried its charge, were confirming in permanence the temporary grant of powers implied in his journey during the war.

The elevation of the Council to an active executive position was the last step in the process leading up from the Nyborg Danehof at the close of the first Jutland rising and through the great Kallundborg Danehof at the close of the second. It provided at last the needed implementation for the partnership of King and people outlined in King Valdemar's Haandfæstning, an implementation which could not be obtained through the annual Danehofs, chiefly because the means of communication were too slow and irregular.

The effect of the advance of the Council was to make Denmark into what later ages would call a constitutional monarchy, to modernize the whole state by giving the fogeds general as well as local administrative experience and responsibility. Nor is it insignificant that the majority of the fogeds whom we now find sitting on the Council were new and rather obscure men. Baron Hummersbüttel and Peder Nielssen bear almost the only familiar names encountered during the Second Hanseatic War; and the machinery had been set going. Though there were many checks and several periods in which it seemed likely to change direction, not even the fact that the Council was an administrative rather than a legislative body should conceal the other fact that the overall tendency was from this time on steadily in the direction of the almost model democracy that Denmark has become.

It is not worth while attributing to Valdemar a high degree of either generosity or prescience for doing this, though in the complex of governmental arrangements he achieved—a complex made up of the decisions at the Nyborg and Kallundborg Danehofs, the installation of fogeds in the castles, and the Council—there is more than a hint of the ideal state of Marsilio of Padua. His motives and compulsions are perfectly clear. The final and most thorough defection of Jutland had deprived him of his best group of trained administrators and those best qualified (according to Danish ideas) by membership in the lordly families. If he wanted fogeds at all, he was simply forced to reach down among less exalted stems.

The Council was also an extremely convenient arrangement physically for getting business done. No matter where his ceaseless movements took the King, he could always count on having a couple of fogeds and a bishop or two at hand to reach decisions in the kingdom's name. These decisions would be accepted beyond the borders, where it was not concealed from those with whom Denmark dealt that the aging King would be followed by some species of foreigner, who might repudiate any contract that lacked the adhesion of the chief men of Denmark—those who, in the persons of the castle-fogeds, could deploy her physical resources, and in the persons of the bishops, her spiritual. It may be doubted whether Valdemar thought in terms of training these men to work together, for that was hardly the type of concept which stirred a medieval mind. But assuredly he saw in this Council a method for accomplishing the one task of reintegration and unification that had so far eluded him—putting effective restraints upon the Jutland lords. Without the Council, it was the King's word against theirs; with it, it was theirs against Denmark's.

Finally, with the sickly Henrik of Slesvig the only surviving male Skjoldung, only the realm could care for the future of the realm. There must be in the land someone to rule when there was no King, lest there should come on Denmark a fate like that which befell in the days of Valdemar Sejr.

II

There was a man named Graf Heinrich of Schwerin. He was considered a notable lord, since he had been on a crusade to Egypt, where he bought from a Papal legate a casket containing a precious stone in which were shut up several drops of the blood of the True Redeemer; it worked miracles for the pilgrims who came to the church of Schwerin, in which it was placed. Graf Heinrich's dominions became much wider than those he had inherited, and he sought by every means to enlarge them still further.

This Heinrich was Graf in Schwerin together with his brother Gunzelin. Gunzelin's daughter was called Oda; she was given in marriage to Niels of Halland, who was a baseborn son of Valdemar the Victorious, though nobody thought any the worse of him for that. It fell out that while Graf Heinrich was fighting the infidels in Egypt, Graf Gunzelin died, as did both Niels of Halland and his wife Oda, leaving a very young son, also called Niels, as the only person in that branch of the family. King Valdemar now sent into Schwerin and took possession of Gunzelin's part of it as guardian for Niels the little. When Graf Heinrich returned, he was very wroth about this, but he said nothing at the time, only informed himself about the King's movements and his habit of going through the land with few men to guard him, since he was so much beloved.

Lyø is a little island off Fyn's southwest coast, only half a mile long. In those days it was covered with a thick forest, and it was considered that this wood held the best hunting in Denmark, but there was no lodge, so that when King Valdemar the Victorious went thither to hunt, tents were pitched at night. Graf Heinrich came to him there, but during the day he was careful not to make complaints or to show any sign of anger. Instead he offered gifts to the King. During the evening meal some good drinking was done and King Valdemar was seen to be somewhat unsteady when he retired to his tent. Graf Heinrich remained sober. In the depth of the night he and his men returned from the ship where they had been sleeping, cut down the watch and, casting into bonds the King and his young son, carried them off and shut them up in a castle in Graf Heinrich's own country.

Now it was seen that there was a grave defect in the ordering of Denmark, in that everything depended upon the King. He had never been a man to have about him close counsellors and deputies as Absalon had been with his father, but preferred to rule with the aid of his family. At this time there was no queen, since Queen Dagmar had died, but Valdemar was not yet married to Beengjerd of Portugal. The King's only son was taken prisoner with him. As for the Church, the Archbishop had laid down his office because of his age and sicknesses, and the choice of a successor was wanting. There was therefore no one to command in all Denmark, so that confusion and dismay fell on the country. The end of it was that the bishops and better men met together after a while and agreed to do whatever Graf Heinrich asked if he would release their King.

He said that they must pay fifty-two thousand marks of silver as ransom, beside delivering the keys and castles of two towns, with the release of all rights and suzerainties Valdemar held in Nordalbingia from the Elbe down to the Eider. This seemed so unreasonable to King Valdemar that he wrote letters to the Pope and Kaiser Friedrich. This Kaiser was a man who did not have to be asked twice to interfere in any difficulty. He came into the north with many men and gathered all the hosts of the north German princes about him before giving his decision in Valdemar's case with the help of a legate from Rome. The arbitration was no better for Denmark than Graf Heinrich's terms had been, for they said Valdemar must pay forty thousand marks in ransom, beside going on a crusade with a hundred ships, and giving over to the Kaiser and the princes the overlordship in Nordalbingia.

The Danes took this somewhat ill, believing that the Pope might have given more support to their King, who had stood so great a friend to the Church. After Kaiser Friedrich left the conference, there was some fighting against the princes in Holstein, but the Danes lacked leaders and were beaten, so there was nothing to do but for King Valdemar to release himself by an even higher ransom than had been asked before.

In the meantime the rule of various parts of Nordalbingia had slipped from Denmark's hands into those of the princes, and when the ransom was paid there was some shortage of money with which to equip fighting men. King Valdemar did not hesitate for this after he was released, but gathered all the men he could to regain his possessions. The princes assembled a great army against him and a battle was fought at Bornhöved on St. Mary Magdalene's Day. It is said that there were portents in the skies before this fight, which was long and very bloody; but the men of Ditmarsch turned traitor to King Valdemar, in whose ranks they stood, and the Danes were beaten. Four thousand of them fell; after this Denmark lost all claim to lands below the Eider, and Lübeck and Hamburg became free cities.

III

This was the background of Valdemar Atterdag's Council and (looking backward) another fiercely operative reason behind his trip to the south during the Second Hanseatic War. The lesson of the past, which he studied so closely, was all too specific. He could not afford either to meet his enemies in the field, or to shut himself up in a castle and risk being captured with it, while there was no authority to leave in Denmark. Doubtless things might have been different if Erich of Saxe-Lauenburg had lived or Klaus Limbek had not turned traitor. But these two losses left no alternative to placing the Council on so broad a basis that the defection of no individual, even of no group, could destroy the work in the event of a royal captivity or death.

The work—that was all he had. It need surprise no one that when he returned to Denmark (where it was observed that the tide of events had greyed his hair and wrinkled his forehead), the King plunged into the settlement of the war and the reintegration of his country at an even more furious pace than before. Albrecht of Mecklenburg gave no trouble. The war had not been a paying proposition for him, and without the help of Hansa funds and ships, it was likely to become still less profitable. In exchange for a document naming his daughter-in-law and Valdemar's daughter Ingeborg as heiress of Denmark, he agreed to give up "all his conquests"—which in a practical sense consisted of Møn alone. The Swedes were doing their fighting at home and were anxious to get out of the Danish war. They even let Magnus Smek out of prison in exchange for a ransom and a renunciation, whereupon that worthy ended a misspent life by getting himself drowned in an overturned ferryboat.

This left the Jutlanders, the Gerhardssons, and Henrik of Slesvig. Against them Valdemar turned the full strength of the royal army, summoned from garrisoning castles. There are few details of that struggle, which lasted a year and a half, save an anecdote that points to the intense bitterness of the old King, his intense determination to bring this thing to an end. It fell at the storming of a castle named Hagenskov, where one Benedikt Alefeld held forth. The first attack was beaten off; Valdemar was ordering his men in again when one of the great men of his entourage asked why he persisted in a hopeless effort.

"I see very well that you lords will never go forward for the realm, so I use those who will," replied the King. "The mothers of these bonders are not all dead, and there will be more of them where these came from." The place was taken.

The details of the campaign are sparse, but it is clear that the allies steadily grew weaker. They could not afford to fight a battle, the countryside was mainly for the golden lions and Valdemar's attacks on castles all succeeded save one at Tørning, while even there he took the neighboring post of Gram to leave Tørning under long-range blockade. The campaign was carried down into the winter, Valdemar marching across the frozen marshes of Frisia to lay the whole country under; then turned against Flensborg, which the Gerhardssons regarded as the anchor of their power in Slesvig. The castle was taken by assault, an event which cut the Holsteiners' communications with Jutland and evidently broke their hearts, for shortly after, they are making a capitulation under the usual form of asking Albrecht of Mecklenburg to "mediate."

His award was that Heinrich and Nicholas should give up everything they held in North Jutland and renounce the allegiances sworn to them there. The estates they had partitioned out returned to the crown and the rebels had to make the best terms they could with the King. There were no executions, but he made his sentences stiff enough to carry the lesson that one gains little by treason. One Niels Erikssen had to rebuild Aggersborg at his own expense, for instance; a certain Magnus Maltessen was charged with a like task at Ørum, also with the additional penance of finding engines and provisions for the reconstructed fortress. All the rebels had to make humiliating public submissions, to the accompaniment of dry Danish ridicule, as in the case of Erlend Kalv, whom the Holsteiners had rewarded for his delivery of Aalborg by giving him Riberhus in addition.

"Atterdage!" said Valdemar, as the man rose from his knees. "This calf is a good cow. I put it out to stud with one house and it comes back to me with two."

IV

Considering the strength arrayed against Denmark in the Second Hanseatic War and the temper in which the allies undertook their task (so very like that of the alliance against Valdemar II), the country escaped surprisingly lightly. Nobody took anything away from her but the Hansa, and even the cities found their gains were illusory. It would be a generation before the increased income from Skaane balanced the cost of the operation. The guarantee-castles were expensive to maintain and yielded no return. Moreover Valdemar undercut them even in Skaane by that method which was usual with him, but which no one of his time seems to have understood—close attention to details so insignificant that they escaped the notice of others until they had been welded into a menacing whole. He found new taxes to lay on operations at the market; his fogeds were remarkably unhelpful when, under the new extraterritoriality, cases arose which brought into conflict the laws of two different cities.

But Valdemar's main effort during the peace was another in the direction of seeing to it that there should be no third Jutland rising, or if there were one, that it should lack exterior support. The drive was to isolate Jutland from Holstein physically, by bringing Slesvig back under the crown from which it had departed a century before. Duke Henrik was so sickly that he evidently would not last long, and though Valdemar was his nearest heir, the gain would be in rights of overlordship only, while the Gerhardssons were evidently preparing to move in underneath by means of physical possession. They still held Gottorp castle, in some sense the capital, with the cities of Slesvig and Eckernfjørde, under the old pawnhold from the days when Blockhead Valdemar exchanged his dukedom against North Jutland. Iron Heinrich set up a new castle at Nyhus near Flensborg, and had made Henrik pay for his part in the war by granting a number of pawnholds to Holstein knights.

Against this quasi-violence, the King employed the unremitting pressure of small acts. As soon as the Jutland lords had done their homage, he went down into Slesvig, traveling far and wide in search for owners or pledgeholders who were hard up. Thus he bought out the pawnholder of Skovby and a little later obtained Melvedsgaard on Als, which rendered that island entirely his own. One of Klaus Limbek's sons parted with a whole herd, two impecounious knights took the King's money for Magstrup and Ringsted in the Haderslev district; and Graf Adolf of Holstein-Stormarn, old Johann the Mild's son, turned over a pledge his father had held on Haderslev town and castle, from which Valdemar promptly ejected an underpledgeholder.

These were financial operations, but the King was also active on the diplomatic front. On St. Hans' Day in the year after the Jutland peace, a general Danehof was held at Nyborg, with immense good will on all sides and flowers strewn over the carpets. Duke Henrik came and so did the dowager Duchess Rixissa, Erich of Saxe-Lauenburg's sister, both very friendly to the King. The Duchess gave Valdemar a letter making him guardian of her property and heir of her dower right in the duchy; Duke Henrik ceded the King the right to pay off the pledge on Gottorp and take it into his possession.

An ambassador promptly went down to offer the Gerhardssons the full sum due on this key castle, but the Holsteiners refused and began looking for allies, evidently intending to try one more war against this King who so bewilderingly outmaneuvered them. Albrecht of Mecklenburg was willing to join a combination, only specifying that it be made strong, but before matters could go to the sword blades, Duke Henrik died, leaving Valdemar in possession of a little better than half the duchy, with strong footholds in the rest. Now the King's efforts redoubled. He bought Aabenraa and made Tønder a royal castle, but as he left this work to make a progress through North Jutland, a heavy infliction of gout came upon him. Soaking his feet in ice-cold water gave some relief, but also drove the gout upward; he became so "sick and unmighty" that he must go to Gurre, complaining bitterly about the interference with his travels.

There the illness increased. Valdemar began to put his affairs in order, by confessing everything that lay upon his conscience, including the methods by which he had repossessed certain of the crown lands, which he directed to be returned to their former holders. A physician was called in. He gave the sick man a draught which caused a profuse sweat, after which there was so much improvement that all left the bedroom, but when they returned in the morning, the great King was dead. The date had been Wednesday, October 24, 1375.

24

Postlude—Seven
Securities

WHEN THE NEWS SPREAD ABROAD, GRAF NICHOLAS, "praising God to be rid of so mighty a king and enemy," whistled out his merry men, and with the help of the Mecklenburgers, laid the whole of Slesvig under by force or treachery, without anyone being able to prevent him. So the story ends in a kind of defeat, but it was a defeat that contained a victory. The reason Mecklenburg's bull-banner marched with Holstein was that Henning Podbusk had called the Council together, and they voted to have no Mecklenburger in Denmark, not even the young son Ingeborg had borne before she died, a little earlier than her father. Margrete, the other daughter, was at Kallundborg with her six-month-old son Oluf; Henning Podbusk waited on her there, then called a Thing of the realm, which elected the little boy king and his mother Queen Regent.

She had to give a Haandfæstning in Oluf's name, which bound both to follow the advice of the Rigets Raad. This could easily have been a source of strain and dissension; but the men of this Raad were King Valdemar's, trained in his school. They did not try to overreach; left the central executive authority in Margrete's hands, and even made a law that the great aristocratic landholders could not acquire new parcels from bonders without the crown's permission.

Albrecht of Mecklenburg did his best to win Denmark

for his grandson and even invaded Sjælland, but was soundly beaten and did not long survive his defeat. Soon after this the shadowy King Haakon of Norway died. Now Margrete, his widow, began to come forward greatly; "all men were amazed by her immoderate cleverness," and she ruled Denmark gloriously for thirty-two years more. It was Margrete who laid down the law that every Dane from highest to lowest should have six securities, for any violation of which he could claim the help of the royal fogeds—church-security, wife-security, house-security, plow-security, the securities of his stead and his Thing.

When Margrete's son Oluf died before reaching his majority, all the Things of Denmark and Norway elected her Queen in her own right without any question. It was not long before she became Queen of Sweden as well, for Albrecht the Younger was both a weak ruler and a bad, who gave everything in the country away to his Germans. Some of the Swedes revolted against him and sought the help of Queen Margrete; on his side, Albrecht made alliance with a number of German princes by promising them various lands and favors. They came into Sweden with strong forces, which met the army of the Danes in a dreadful battle at Fallköping, the end of which was that Albrecht's army was destroyed and he and all the German princes taken prisoners. After this, Norway, Denmark, and Sweden were under one crown, and so remained for over a hundred years.

For not only was Valdemar, after all, not the last of the Skjoldung kings (with such a daughter), but also he had builded better than even he believed. The realm he had found divided and despoiled, about to break up, he left incomparably the most powerful of northern states and the most efficient nation in Europe. It had withstood the shock of a disastrous losing war; it made gains under a long minority and a female regency; and as Margrete's true ability developed, no power within range could stand against Denmark. The Hansa became astonishingly humble before her, addressing her in terms of entreaty after one little row over the return of the Skaane castles. On the due date they were surrounded by determined armies of Danes, while the cities' commerce began to suffer from the depredations of pirates, over whom (like Elizabeth of England with the Spaniards) the Queen protested she had no control.

As to how Valdemar accomplished his integration, the evidence has been given in the preceding pages. The general method may be described as an intense concentration on minor details, one of taking tiny steps which together added up to the stride of seven-league boots. He was able to take these steps in many directions at once because of that unflagging restlessness which, in the physical domain, found expression in his continual travels; no king was so peripatetic. He had the unusual ability to disregard vast, showy projects and accept his little gains with a murmur of "Attenday." The extraordinary feature, certainly for the period, is the fixity of purpose with which he pursued each of his objectives through accidents, setbacks, treacheries and hope long deferred. The other day came on all those who made themselves his enemies except the Hansa; a black day it was, and we may be sure it would have been one for the cities as well, if Valdemar had lived to bring it.

As to his underlying motivation, there has been some disagreement. His own age described him as proud and commanding, cold and contemptuous toward those who did not reach his own level; Erich of Saxe-Lauenburg and Henning Podbusk were the only people who enjoyed his full confidence. The hatred of the Jutland lords pursued him beyond the grave, and the bonders and merchants who held another opinion were so little articulate that their view survived only in the songs and sagas, which are peripheral to history and received little attention.

He thus remained Valdemar the Bad, charged with every fault and crime in the calendar, not only by Swedish and German historians, but also by those of his own country, until the eighteenth century. At that time a process of re-examination began and Holberg the poet wrote that if he had to name a saint among Denmark's kings, it would not be the official St. Knud, but Valdemar Atterdag. Holberg, even in his lifetime, was recognized as the greatest literary figure of Denmark, so the statement produced the desired shock, and some alteration of the general view. But the old picture has died so hard that only recently a classic general history of Denmark denies Valdemar the name of patriot.

This is surely nonsense (unless one defines patriotism in a very peculiar way), for it requires the explanation that after the death of Junker Kristoffer, the King kept moving as a sort of automaton, going through the process of consolidating personal and family power because he had the habit. Yet the years following the prince's death are some of the most productive of the reign; they include the Church settlement, the rearrangement of Skaane, the appointing of the castle-fogeds, and the institution of the great Council. The real fact is that Valdemar was a builder, a craftsman, one of those characters to whom the perfection of the work is more important than the view other people take of why it was done.

The few phrases we have from the King's lips, the scanty record of his dealings with others when political motives were not involved, give little data for saying anything about his personal character save that he was a complex individual, very different from the normal medieval king, who was a swashbuckling extrovert. We are told that he loved music, and played the lute himself; that he had a nasty wit, which could take the hide off. He could be grim as another—witness the mutilation of prisoners in the Werle campaign and the sack of Visby—but these have the appearance of barbarities for calculated local effect. Neither was repeated. It is fair to set against them, and to claim as more truly indicative, the long patience with Klaus Limbek, the quite un-medieval reasonableness of the peace terms again and again granted to the beaten Gerhardssons, and Valdemar's ability to find a line of agreement in the cases he so frequently arbitrated.

Un-medieval also was the intellectual curiosity which sent him to Germany, Jerusalem, Flanders, and Avignon. No public personage of his time was so interested in seeing with his own eyes, talking to people in person. Indeed, few leaders of any time approached Valdemar in this respect. But there was in it no element of the absolutist touch, none of the desire to hold all reins in his own hands. All through his life, the King delegated authority right and left—in the beginning to Klaus Limbek and Stig Anderssen, later to Duke Erich, Henning Podbusk, the Council, Peder of the iron beard. Valdemar also had considerable ability to absorb what was seen and heard. The constitutional alterations show this in one direction; in another is the fact that, beginning as a distinctly indifferent soldier, he became after Brobjœrg one of the most dreaded battle-captains of his time. It would be interesting to discover how he managed his tactics (there must have been something original there) but we cannot. What we can say is that he developed an original strategy, adapted to his own means and those of the nation.

Yet over all this broods the shadow of the huntsman of Gurre wood, the romantic Valdemar. In the end we must judge him by the work.

II

What was that work?

In essence, this: he made Denmark into the first modern state, fixed upon her a form of organization whose efficiency forced or persuaded surrounding groups to imitation.

The matter of church organization, for instance. Valdemar's relations with Avignon remained in the honeymoon stage to the very end; yet the Danish church was the only one in Europe that did not contain a single foreigner, and the King's dominance was so complete that some anonymous complainant writes to the Curia that Valdemar was controlling the whole institution and using the seals of Lund as though they were his own. Late in the reign, the King himself wrote to the Pope: "Our nature we have from God, the rule from our people, our abilities from our forefathers, and our throne from our foregoers—from you we have nothing and to you will give nothing."

There is some Marsilio here, but essentially these are the accents of Henry VIII; and in fact, Valdemar's wholly friendly handling of the Church question was so effective that the Reformation was both unnecessary and unpopular in Denmark. In spite of a good deal of imitation-pressure and some vigorous advocates, it had to be imposed by the crown and with an accompaniment of physical struggle. Of course it would be difficult to establish any direct connection between Valdemar's Church of Denmark and Cranmer's Church of England; but ideas of this order do penetrate and rouse up armies far from home. At least two of Martin Luther's Ninety-Five Theses of Wittenburg are quoted directly from Marsilio.

There were other ideas that penetrated also. A certain note of economic determinism is in the reasons why Denmark, for which Valdemar did the work, failed to draw the fullest benefit from it. A few years after Queen Margrete's time, the herring that were the wealth and resource of the land began to leave the Sound and take their business to the North Sea, where in the next age they formed the foundation of the maritime supremacy of England and Holland. But there were other and more strictly political reasons as well. Queen Margrete was an extremely able ruler, but she lacked her father's close eye for the detail of internal affairs, and was nowhere near his equal as an employer of experts. When she died, the strength of the realm became the strength of the system alone, not that of the people who were in it, whereas any system requires able men to operate it, to make it alter and grow. The lack of Councils as good as Valdemar's own might have been supported by itself, but with the extinction of the dynasty, the Danes began shopping around among various German stems for a king and made a series of unfortunate elections. None of the new monarchs really understood Denmark; two of them had to be deposed, and another involved the country in a horribly costly civil struggle.

The ideas sift down through. The specific organization of Valdemar's Denmark, the peculiar combination of an aristocracy whose members obtained their administrative positions partly through the elective choice of an underlying democracy, partly by the personal choice of a monarch who was himself elective—this system found no imitators. It required a head profoundly imbued with Danish tradition; the Germans who followed Margrete did not know how to make it work. More; they did nothing to control the great families, and they closed off access to that group—something Valdemar had carefully avoided, witness the promotion of Peder Dene the fisherman. The result was that Danish society split apart for a considerable period, only re-integrating on quite a new basis.

The tale of that decline and the recovery from it does not belong here. But it is important to note that it was the peculiar political form that declined, not the heart. The essential lies in the six securities that Valdemar effectively guaranteed at the Nyborg Danehof and that his daughter put into words.

These were never really lost, and the decline was less a decline than the rise of the surrounding states to the position where Valdemar left Denmark. It was under the Danish administrative system, indeed under the Danish political system, that the torrential and terrible Vasa stepped forth in Sweden; and under it Gustavus Adolphus went on to conquer Europe for the seventh and greatest security—security of thought. When the medieval world rolled back from the smoking plain of Lützen it retreated, in a sense, before Valdemar Atterdag.

We are accustomed to think of the seven securities, the

four freedoms, as almost exclusively Anglo-Saxon possessions. We are myopic. Those ideals have been set forth before and challenged many times—by the Armada, in the Dutch republic, on the hillcrest of Valmy and the beaches of Dunkirk— but when they met their most serious challenge, England was an out-island of the world, as far away as Portugal, and she might have remained so but for the rescue from the north.

The Inscription
on Valdemar's Tomb

Valdemarus, cognomine quartus, Danorum rex, pater Margaretae, moritur Gurrae, anno Christi milesimo trecentesimo septuagesimo quinto et primum Varingborgae; deine, hoc translatus a filia Margareta tumulatur Sorae.

Valdemar, who took not the least place among Danish kings and whose remains lie in this marble tomb, fled from his land, but came back with great valor, drove the mighty Holstein enemies out over the borders of the kingdom and again won back his fathers' land and cities that had been pledged for a dear rental. Beaten on sea and land, the neighboring peoples and the cities of the Wends, so proud in their strength, felt the weight of the ever-unconquered king's weapons. Tired with life's business, he eventually came home to Gurre to die. His bones were then borne here to Sorø to lie in this grave; but his spirit went to high heaven and only his fame remains behind to be honored by his successors.

Index

Aabenraa, 294

Aalborg, 79, 99; *map*, 31, 178-79

Aale, 44

Aalholm, 74, 145, 279; *map*, 178-79

Aarhus, 193; *map*, 31, 178-79

Aarhus, Bishop of, *see* Sveyn, Bishop of Aarhus

Abel, King of Denmark, 17, 261-62

Absalon, Bishop of Roskilde and Archbishop of Denmark, 16, 50, 80-82, 108-10, 127, 130-31, 288

Adolf, Graf Holstein-Stormarn, 268, 293

Adolf, Graf Mecklenburg, 182-84

Acrø, 44, 136, 196, 198, 229; *map*, 31

afgifter (taxes), 164-65

Aggersborg, 279, 291; *map*, 178-79

Agriculture, transformation of, under Valdemar, 206-207

Albert, Bishop of Riga, 150-51

Albrecht, Duke of Mecklenburg, 17, 94, 115, 177, 180-81, 194, 205, 216, 253-58, 269, 290 ff.; in the Brandenburg campaign, 185-88; alliance with Valdemar, 188; projected attack on Sjælland, 218-19; alliance with King Magnus, 231-32, 240; joins the grand alliance against Valdemar, 273 ff.

Albrecht, Duke of Saxe-Lauenburg, 80

Albrecht the Younger, Duke of Mecklenburg and King of Sweden, 259, 273, 278-79, 282, 296

Albrekt of Osten, 143

Albrektsen, Ludvig von Eberstein, 44-45, 58, 60, 74, 88, 129

Alefeld, Benedikt, 235, 290

Algotta, Lady, 153, 202

Als, 136, 229; *map*, 31

Amager Isle, 82; *map*, 31, 239

Anderssen, Stig, 16, 95, 118, 120, 135, 142, 181, 196-97, 215-16, 225, 232, 235; joins alliance against Valdemar, 275; death, 279

Anholt, *map*, 31

architecture, military, *see* castles

Arcona, *map*, 49

army, *see* military organization

Arnholm, 195, 198; *map*, 178-79

Axelssen, Peder, 279

Barnim, Duke of Stettin, 229-30, 268

Bautzen, conference at, 187, 233

Beengjerd, Queen of Denmark, 261

Bengt Algottsson, 202-203, 240-41

Berengaria, *see* Beengjerd

Index

Bildebro, battle of the, 118

Black Death, 167 ff.

Blanche of Namur, Queen of Sweden, 16, 154-57, 177, 260

Blekinge, 43, 86, 231; *map*, 31

Bogø, 177, 180, 185

Bohus, 253

bonders, 21 ff.; 124-25, 130, 209

Borenburg, 221

Borgholm, 250

Bornholm, 22, 47-48; *map*, 31

Bornhöved, battle of, 289

Borningholm, 107

Brandenburg campaign, 185-88; *map*, 49

Bost, Tyge, 262

Breide, Marchwarden, governor of Esthonia, 141

Bremen, 46; *map*, 49

Brobjærg, 217, 270; *map*, 178-79

Brockdorf, Hein, 90, 94

Bugge, Niels, Lord of Hald, 17, 160-61, 193, 196-97, 207, 216, 223-24

"Bugge-penny," 225

Burnt Njals Saga, 14

castle fogeds, *see* fogeds

castles, 104 ff.; military architecture and construction, 105-107; vulnerability to blockade, 108, 113; strategic use of, 214-17, 270; administrative function of, 271-72

cavalry, *see* knights, armored

Church, 50-51, 73, 120, 149-51; special position under Valdemar, 264-66

Clement VI, Pope, 147, 202

coinage, *see* money

Cologne, assembly of grand alliance against Valdemar at, 273-74

Copenhagen, 44, 82, 85, 87, 115, 254; siege of, by Valdemar, 117-18; capture and sack of, by

Hanseatics, 278; *map*, 31, 178-79, 239

Council of the Realm, 272, 295; rise in importance as an administrative body, 285-87

dams, 206-207

Danehof, at Nyborg, 199-200; at Kallundborg, 216, 235; at the end of Second Hanseatic War, 293

Dannebrog, 43

Democracy, Valdemar's concept of, 92-94; development after the Second Hanseatic War, 285-86

Dene, Peder, "Ironbeard," 194, 196, 218, 221, 254-55, 268, 271, 281, 285

Ditmarschers, revolt of, 117, 127

Drost, 58

Dysiaa River, battle at, 131

Ebbessen, Niels, 15, 36-37, 83, 86-87, 129; assassinates Graf Gerhard, 77; death, 88

Eckernfjørde, 292

Edda, description of old Nordic society in, 129

Edward, the Black Prince, 78, 214, 226

Edward III, King of England, 214-15, 226-27, 263

Elizabeth of Holstein, betrothal to King Haakon of Norway, 247; proxy marriage to King Haakon, 257-58

Elsinore, *see* Helsingør

embedsmand, 68-69

Erich, Duke of Saxe-Lauenburg, 16, 80 ff., 186, 194-95, 219, 238, 240, 250, 252, 269; accompanies Valdemar to the Holy Land, 146-47; appointed regent of the kingdom in the event of Valdemar's death, 277;

defence of Kallundborg, 279-80; death, 282, 290

Erik, Duke of Slesvig, 54, 57, 59

Erik, Prince, son of King Kristoffer II, 60, 63, 88

Erik, son of King Magnus of Sweden, 156, 216, 218, 231; co-king of Sweden, 201-203

Erik VI, "Plowpenny," King of Denmark, 17, 261; death, 262

Erik VIII Menved, King of Denmark, 56, 141

Esbern the Quick, 53, 130

Esgers Juel, Bishop, 47-48, 56, 59, 88

Esthonia, 42; bonders' revolt, 136; history, 140 ff.; *map*, 49

Falk, Bo, 16, 96, 104, 120, 150, 197, 235

Fullköping, battle of, 296

Falster, 44, 61-62, 116, 122, 136, 177; *map*, 31

Falsterbo, 253, 278, 284; *map*, 178-79, 239

Femern, 44, 62, 116, 136, 197, 220, 229-30; *map*, 31

feudal system, 20-21, 27; its special form in Denmark, 30, 66, 71-73, 124, 148-50, 236; in Sweden, 203-204

financial system of Valdemar, 163-66

fisheries of Skaane, 30, 47, 115, 117, 238 ff.; rights of the Hansa in, 243; Hansa gains under the Peace of Stralsund, 284; *map*, 239

Fistup, 44; *map*, 178-79

Fjälemyra, battle of, 250-51

Flensborg, 221, 291; *map*, 31, 178-79

Flodsaa Mill, battle of, 120

fogeds, 199, 271, 286

Folkvard Lavmandsson, 189-90

Friedrich II, Kaiser of Germany, 227, 288-89

Friedrich von Lochen, 15, 36-37, 40, 116-17, 120

Frisland, 126

Frost, Anders, 263, 267

Fyn, 44, 68, 74, 86-87, 157, 162, 185, 193, 195-96, 219, 268

Gerhard the Great, Graf Holstein Rendsborg, 15, 44-45, 54, 74, 88, 132, 264; his social policy, 58, 62; defeat of King Kristoffer II, 59-60; "Protector of Denmark," 60-64; invasion of North Jutland, 76-77; assassination at Randers, 77

Gerhard of Hoya, 194

Gerhardssons, *see* Heinrich, Graf Holstein-Rendsborg, *and* Nicholas, Graf Holstein-Rendsborg

Germans, Danish detestation of, 65-66

Glambek, 221; *map*, 178-79

Gotland, 204; attack on, 250-51

Gottorp, 63, 292-93; *map*, 178-79

Gram, 291; *map*, 178-79

Greifswald, 46; *map*, 31

gristmills, 206-207

Gunderslevholm, 107, 135-36; map, 178-79

Günther of Schwarzburg, 182, 187

Gunzelin, Graf Schwerin, 287

Gurre, 137, 145, 189-91, 278-79, 294; *map*, 178-79

Haakon, King of Norway, 201, 230, 240, 247, 257, 269; becomes co-king of Sweden, 253; marriage to Margrete, 258; death, 296

Haandfæstning, of King Kristoffer II, 55-58; of Valdemar, 74, 84, 236, 285

Hadersleben, 60, 63, 293; *map*, 178-79

hærmænd, 71-72, 209

Hagenskov, 290

Hald, 196, 206; *map*, 178-79

Halland, 43, 268; *map*, 31

Hamburg, 45, 182, 184-85, 289; *map*, 49

Hammershus, 48, 95, 106; *map*, 178-79

Hansa, 24, 44-48, 57, 78-79, 85, 94, 114-16, 197, 203-204, 216, 230-31, 240 ff.; rivalry with Valdemar's sea power, 221-23; division of the League into "tertials," 241-42; interest in Skaane fisheries, 243-47; coalition with Sweden against Valdemar, 252-57; treaty of Rostock with Valdemar, 257; peace conference with Valdemar, 267-69; grand alliance against Valdemar, 273-83; gains under the Peace of Stralsund, 284; relations with Queen Margrete, 296-97

Heinrich, Duke of Mecklenburg, 188, 255, 281

Heinrich, Graf Holstein-Rendsborg, "Iron-hard," 16, 78-79, 84, 86-87, 97, 161, 192 ff., 230, 252-54; war against Valdemar, 114 ff.; in the last Jutland revolt, 215 ff.; in the grand alliance against Valdemar, 273 ff.

Heinrich, Graf Schwerin, 17, 287-89

Heinrich Tusmer, Grand Master of the Teutonic Order, 143

Helsingborg, 60, 130, 188, 205, 230-31, 238, 240, 253-56, 270, 278-81, 284; *map*, 31, 49, 178-79

Helsinge massacre, 119, 121

Helsingør, 84-85, 188, 278; *map*, 178-79

Helvig of Slesvig, Queen of Denmark, 16, 79, 139, 189-90

Henrik, Duke of Slesvig, 273, 276, 287, 292-93

herred, 24

herregaarde, 209

herremænd, 72, 209; see also *hærmænd*

herring fisheries, see fisheries of Skaane

Hindsgavl, 74, 162, 192, 197, 209, 219, 268, 270, 281; *map*, 178-79

Hohenstegen, 161-62

Holberg, Ludvig, 298

Holstein, *map*, 49

Hønborg, 270, 281; *map*, 178-79

Horsens, 79

Hummersbüttel, Baron, 161-62, 275, 279, 285

Ingeborg, daughter of Valdemar, 188, 290; marriage to Duke Heinrich of Mecklenburg, 255

Ingeborg, Queen of Sweden, 152

Innocent III, Pope, 42, 151, 185, 227

Itzehoe, 182, 184; *map*, 178-79

Iverssen, Peder, 281

Jellinge, 43

Johann, Bishop of Roskilde, 83, 86

Johann the Mild, Graf Holstein-Stormarn, 15, 44-45, 54, 62-63, 78, 85, 90, 94, 116-17, 121-22, 144, 193, 195, 197, 216, 220, 230, 232

Johann Wittenburg, Burgomaster of Lübeck, 253, 255; defeat of, by Valdemar, 256

Jonsen, Palle, 216, 235

Jonssen, Laurids, Lord (Drost), 44, 58, 60, 74, 88, 129

Jungshoved, 270, 280; *map*, 178-79

Index

Junker Kristoffer, 16, 139, 212-13, 223, 225, 235, 238, 250, 256, 259

jury, see Nævninger, and Sandemænd

Jutland, 44, 75-79, 83; first revolution, 114 ff.; freed from Holsteiners, 145; second revolution, 192 ff.; the last revolt, 215 ff.; map, 31

jydske Lov, Den, 66

Kallø, 75, 79, 132, 198, 206, 279; map, 178-79

Kallundborg, 85, 90, 96-97, 106, 120, 278-79; capture by Valdemar, 122; Danehofs at, 216, 235; map, 178-79

Kalmar, 252

Kalv, Erlend, 235, 279, 291

Kalvsholm, 232

Karl IV, Kaiser of Bohemia, 151, 181-82, 185, 187, 263

Kasimir, Wendish leader, 109-10

Kattebjærg, 232; map, 178-79

Kattegat, 195; map, 49

King's Council, see Council of the Realm

Kjøge, 123, 144

Klaus, Graf Holstein-Rendsborg, see Nicholas, Graf Holstein-Rendsborg

Kleitrup, 106; map, 178-79

knights, armored, 70-71, 101-105, 110-11

Knud V Lavard, 16, 51-52, 54

Knud VI, 70-71, 183

Knud Porse, 56, 60, 88, 90, 129

Kolding, 43, 79, 197; map, 31, 49

Koldinghus, 56, 74, 197-98, 206, 270, 281; map, 178-79

Kongens Raad, 272; see also Council of the Realm

Kristoffer I, 261-62, 270

Kristoffer II, King of Denmark, 15, 48, 54, 61-63, 88, 141;

Haandfæstning of, 55-58; defeat by Graf Gerhard, 59-60; death, 63

Laaland, 44, 62, 136, 144-45; map, 31

Lærbeksholm, 270; map, 178-79

Læsø, map, 31

land tenure system, 21, 71-73, 163-66, 233-35; see also pawn-loan system

landgifter (ground rents), 164-65

Langeland, 44, 60, 136, 195-96, 198, 229; map, 31

Langsundoft, 127

Lauenburg, 183

Lave Gudmundssen, 262

Law of the Jutland Men, see jydske Lov, Den

laws, 65 ff.; conflict between Danish and German concepts, 65; the three codes, 66; democratic aspects of, 67 ff.; Queen Margrete's "six securities," 296

Libau, map, 49

Limbek, Klaus, 16, 128, 132 ff., 143-44, 150, 157-58, 160, 192 ff., 207, 215-16, 232, 235, 238; governor of Sjælland, 134; desertion of Valdemar, 193; restored to office as Drost, 197; final treason against Valdemar, 275-76

Lindholm, 238, 281; map, 178-79

Livonia, 151

loan nobility, see hærmænd

Lohede, battle of, 63, 132

Louis XI, King of France, 205

Lübeck, 46, 115-16, 182, 184, 221-22, 229-30, 283, 289; agreement, 78 ff.; meeting of princes at, 205; in the coalition against Valdemar, 253 ff.

Ludwig, Markgraf of Brandenburg, 15, 114, 141, 186-87, 282

Index

Ludwig of Bavaria, 40-41, 114, 151, 181
Ludwig the Roman, 186
Lund, 278
Lyndanise Rock, battle of, 42, 46, 151
Lyø, 287

Magnus, Duke of Brunswick, 282
Magnus, son of King Niels, 51-52
Magnus Smek, King of Sweden, 16, 45, 84, 86, 90-91, 105, 115, 118-19, 177, 201-205, 229, 245-48, 263; character, 152 ff.; alliance with Duke Albrecht of Mecklenburg, 231-32; in grand alliance against Valdemar, 252-56; unsuccessful attempt to regain crown, 268-69; death, 290
Malmø, 238, 278, 284; map, 31, 178-79, 239
Malvø Vig, 54
Margrete, Queen of Denmark, Norway and Sweden, 17, 230, 247; marriage to King Haakon of Norway, 258; becomes Queen Regent, 295-96; her law of the "six securities," 296; union of Denmark, Norway and Sweden, 296
Marienburg, map, 49
mark lubs, 208
marshbonders, 126-28
Marsilio of Padua, his doctrine of the State, 92, 147, 286, 300
Marstrand, 253
Mecklenburg, 186
Melvedsgaard, 293; map, 178-79
Middelfart, 209, 224-25, 270, 279; map, 31, 178-79
military organization, see castles; knights, armored; and warfare, medieval
Mols, 194, 196
Moltke, Fikke, 267, 271, 281, 285
Møn, 87, 105, 116, 136; map, 31

money, 10, 69-70, 207-208
"mustering penny," 209

Næstved, 85, 135; map, 178-79
Nævninger, 68
navy, founding of, 113; role in second revolution, 192 ff.; use in blockade, 196-97; Valdemar's program for developing, 210; in last Jutland revolt, 217-20
Nicholas, Graf Holstein-Rendsborg, 16, 78-79, 86, 161, 215-17, 230, 273, 279, 291; overruns Slesvig, 295
Niels, King, 51, 54
Niels Eriksen of Linde, 193, 235
Niels Goldsmith, 248
Niels of Halland, 287
Nielsen, Erik, Gyldenstjerna, 95, 193
Nielsen, Peder, see Dene, Peder
Nødefald, 128, 232; map, 178-79
Nordalbingia, 182, 184, 227, 288-89; map, 49
Nordborg, 219; map, 178-79
Nordic civilization, autochthonous character of, 29-30
Nyborg, 63, 162; first Danehof, 199-200, 235-36; second Danehof, 293; map, 31, 178-79
Nyhus, 293; map, 178-79
Nykøbing, 121-22, 162, 278; map, 178-79

Oda, 287
Odensee, Bishop of, 36, 39, 87, 157, 285
Odersburg, battle of, 186
Öland, 250, 254
Oluf, King of Denmark, 295-96
opsynsmænd, 206
Order of the Sword, 43, 136, 141, 151
Ørkel, 162, 192, 197, 268; map, 178-79

Index

Ørum, 270, 279, 291; *map*, 178-79

Otto, Markgraf of Brandenburg, 282

Otto, Prince, 63, 78-79, 137, 143

Otto the Welfing, Kaiser, 17, 183-85

partition of Denmark, *map*, 49; *see* Time of Uproar

pawn-loan system, 44-45, 62, 73, 164-66

Peder, Bishop of Lund, 36-39, 83, 86-87

Peder, Bishop of Ribe, 193, 200

Pe-Ycw, 167-68

Philip Augustus, King of France, 42, 185

Philip of Maizières, his description of Skaane fisheries, 243-44

Philip of Swabia, 183-84

Podbusk, Henning, 16, 137-38, 160, 190, 235, 250, 277, 283, 295

Poel island, 185

Poictiers, battle of, 215

Pommern, 186; *map*, 49

public works program of Valdemar, 206-207

Randers, 39, 77-78, 84, 206, 216; *map*, 31, 178-79

Rastorf, Marchwarden, 87

Ravnsborg, 74, 145, 279; *map*, 178-79

Rendsborg, 59, 117, 161, 182; *map*, 178-79

Reval, 42, 45, 140-41; *map*, 49

Ribe, 43, 75, 79, 198; *map*, 31

Ribe, Bishop of, *see* Splitaf, Jakob, Bishop of Ribe, *and* Peder, Bishop of Ribe

Ribehus, 56, 198, 206, 279; *map*, 178-79

Riga, Bishop of, *see* Albert, Bishop of Riga

Rigets Raad, *see* Council of the Realm

Ringsted, 120, 135, 165; *map*, 31, 49

Ritterthing, 199

Rixa, 78-79

Rixissa, 220, 293

roads, 207

Roskilde, 53, 73; conference at, 97, 206; bishopric of, 105; *map*, 31

Roskilde, Bishop of, *see* Absalon, Bishop of Roskilde, *and* Johann, Bishop of Roskilde

Rostock, 46, 177, 188, 218; treaty of, 257; *map*, 31, 49

Rügen, 44, 82, 87, 105, 108, 136-37, 180, 185, 188; *map*, 31

St. Birgitte of Sweden, 16, 154 ff., 177, 201

Saltholm, *map*, 239

Samsø, *map*, 31

Sandemænd, 68

Saxo Grammaticus, 113

Schwerin, *map*, 49

sea power, *see* navy

Segeberg, 116-17, 182; *map*, 178-79

sheriff, *see* embedsmand

Silkeborg, 44, 106, 206; *map*, 178-79

Sjælland, 44, 84-85, 105, 116-17, 119, 194, 233; liberation from the Holsteiners, 145; *map*, 31, 239

Skaane, 43, 54, 79, 82, 86, 152, 192; fisheries, 30, 47, 115, 117, 238 ff.; under Kristoffer II, 57-60; rebellion against Valdemar I, 130-31; Valdemar Atterdag's project for the redemption of, 201 ff.; deeded by Magnus to Denmark, 258; after peace with the Hansa, 272; supports Valdemar against grand alli-

· 311 ·

Index

Skaane (*Continued*)
 ance, 279; Hansa rights under
 the Peace of Stralsund, 284;
 map, 31, 239
Skanderborg, 44, 74, 106, 206,
 279; Niels Ebbessen's attack
 on, 87; *map*, 178-79
Skanør, 117, 183, 253, 278, 284;
 map, 178-79, 239
Skjoldnæs, 145
Skodborg, 279
Skovby, 293
Slagelse, 223-24
Slesvig, 270; Valdemar's last cam-
 paign, 291-92; overrun by Graf
 Nicholas, 295
Slesvig, Bishop of, *see* Valdemar
 Magnusson, Bishop of Slesvig
Smaland, 256
Søborg, 122, 278-79; *map*, 178-79
Sølvesborg, 231; *map*, 178-79
Sønderborg, 219; *map*, 178-79
Spandau agreement, 74, 77-79,
 84, 141
Splitaf, Jakob, Bishop of Ribe, 75,
 83, 127
Stege, 162, 278; *map*, 178-79
Stettin, *map*, 49
Stjernaa, 83
Stockholm, *map*, 49
Stormarn, 195
Stove, Marchwarden, 91, 118,
 134, 142-44
Stralsund, 46; Peace of, 283-85;
 map, 31
strand-right, 269-273
Sune, brother of Absalon, 130
Sveyn, Bishop of Aarhus, 36-37,
 40, 74, 83, 96, 120
Sveyn Grade, *see* Sveyn IV Peder
Sveyn IV Peder, 16, 52-53, 64, 71
Sweden, 201 ff.

Taarnborg, 60, 85, 121, 136, 143;
 map, 178-79
taxation, 55 ff., 72, 127, 133, 163-
66, 210, 246-47; *see also afgifter
and landgifter*
Teutonic civilization, 25-30
Teutonic Order, 45, 141-43; *map*,
 49
Thing courts, 24, 59-60; 62, 68,
 124, 127, 199-200; Great Thing
 at Ringsted, 165; *see also*
 Danehof
Thingmannalid, 70-71
Time of Uproar, 19-21, 29, 31,
 36, 64
tithes, 82, 130-31
Tønderhus, 126, 216, 230, 232,
 294; *map*, 178-79
To-Nwan-Timur, Prince, 167
Tørning, 132, 291; *map*, 178-79
Tove, 16, 137-39, 189-91
Tranekjær, 60, 195, 198, 219;
 map, 178-79
Travemünde, 182
Tyrbagh, Hans, 280

Uckermark of Brandenburg, 186
Ulf Gudmarsson, Jarl, 154
Upsala, 259
Urban V, Pope, 264
Usedom, 108; *map*, 31

Valdemar I, the Great, 15, 39,
 53, 80-82, 130-31; fight with
 Wends at Julin, 108-10
Valdemar II, the Victorious, 15,
 43, 45, 150, 158-59, 182-85,
 260-61; battle of Lyndanise
 Rock, 42, 46; laws of, 65 ff., 84,
 124, 200; feudalism under, 71-
 72; war with Tartars, 140-42;
 campaign in North Germany,
 227-28; abduction by Graf
 Heinrich of Schwerin, 288
Valdemar IV Atterdag, 15, 40, 42,
 78, 83; coronation, 35-38, 84;
 seal of, 74; royal residence, 89-
 90; his concept of democracy,
 92-93; efforts to restrain Jutland lords, 110-13; founds navy,

113; war with the Gerhardssons, 114 ff.; peace treaty with
Johann the Mild, 122; social
policy after first Jutland revolt,
123-25; interlude on Rügen,
136-39; cedes Esthonia to
Prince Otto, 143; pilgrimage to
the Holy Land, 146 ff.; Knight
of the Holy Sepulchre, 147; arbitrator of disputes, 148; financial system, 163-66; land tenure
system, 163-66, 233-35; as
moneylender, 164; Brandenburg campaign, 185-88; use of
navy in second revolution, 192
ff.; re-establishes Danehof, 199-
200; legal reforms in Jutland,
200; projected recovery of
Skaane, 201 ff., 229-31; public
works program in Jutland, 206-
207; transforms agricultural
economy, 207; currency reform,
208; military and naval program, 209-10; in last Jutland
revolt, 215 ff.; negotiations with
Jutland rebels at Slagelse, 223-
24; projected attack on England, 228; his "Haandfæstning,"
236-37, 285; Skaane campaign,
238 ff.; war with Magnus and
Hansa, 252-56; Treaty of Rostock, 257; acquires Skaane from
Magnus, 258; European journey, 263; position of Church
under, 264-66; peace conference
with Hansa, 267-69; grand alliance against, 273-83; last Jutland campaign, 290-91; death
at Gurre, 294; estimate of character and achievements, 297-
302

Valdemar Dosmer, Duke of Slesvig, 15, 36-37, 43-44, 57-59, 75-
76, 78-79, 90, 96, 136, 193,
216, 229, 235

Valdemar Magnusson, Bishop of
Slesvig, 17, 158-59
Valdemar Sappe, 232, 235, 250,
256, 285
Varberg, 253, 268, 278-79; *map*,
178-79
Vastergotland, 52
Ve-bjærg, *see* Viborg Hill
Vendelbo, Peder, 95, 135, 198
Viborg, 111
Viborg Hill, 35-36, 39
Vidaa River, 126
village culture, recovery under
Valdemar, 123-25, 128
Vindinge Aa, Treaty of, 197-98
Visby, 15-16, 115, 232, 248; im-
portance as a Hansa city, 204;
capture and sack of, by Valde-
mar, 250-51; *map*, 49
Vissing, 44
Vordingborg, 60, 81, 85, 90, 106,
176, 180, 211-12, 254-55, 267,
270, 279-80; King Kristoffer's
assault on, 61; falls to Valde-
mar, 144-45; description, 145-
46; *map*, 31, 49, 178-79

Waldemar, pretender to the
throne of Brandenburg, 181,
187
warfare, medieval, 70-72, 99 ff.,
209-11; armored knights, 70-71,
101-105, 110-11; *hærmænd*, 71-
72, 209; infantry, 100; Viking
axemen, 102; role of castles,
104 ff., 214-17, 270; first use
of cannon, 254
Warrendorp, Bruno, 281
Wend towns, 46, 115, 253, 273,
280; *see also* Hansa
Wends, 81-82, 108-10
Werle, Princes of, 193, 195
Westensee, Marchwarden, 161
Wismar, 46, 221-22; *map*, 31
Wolgast, Dukes of, 186, 228
Wollin, 108; *map*, 31